DATE			

Landholding and Commercial Agriculture
in the Middle East

Landholding and Commercial Agriculture
in the Middle East

Edited by
Çağlar Keyder
and
Faruk Tabak

STATE UNIVERSITY OF NEW YORK PRESS

The cover illustration courtesy of *Mir'at*
(Şevval 1279, March 1862).

Production by Ruth East
Marketing by Dana E. Yanulavich

Published by
State University of New York Press, Albany

© 1991 State University of New York

Printed in the United States of America

For information, address State University of New York
Press, State University Plaza, Albany, N.Y. 12246

Library of Congress Cataloging-in-Publication Data

Landholding and commercial agriculture in the Middle East / edited by
    Çağlar Keyder and Faruk Tabak
        p. cm.
    Includes bibliographical references.
    ISBN 0–7914–0550–8 (alk. paper).—ISBN 0–7914–0551–6 (pbk.:
alk. paper)
        1. Agriculture—Economic aspects—Middle East—History. 2. Land
    tenure—Middle East—History. 3. Peasantry—Middle East—History.
    4.Turkey—History—Ottoman Empire, 1288–1918. I. Keyder, Çağlar.
    II. Tabak, Faruk.
    HD2056.5.L36   1991
    333.23'5'0956—dc20   90-35231
                                                                            CIP

10 9 8 7 6 5 4 3 2 1

Contents

Acknowledgments

"Large-Scale Commercial Agriculture in the Ottoman Empire" was the title of the Second Biennial Conference on the Ottoman Empire and the World-Economy, held in October 1986 at the State University of New York at Binghamton. The conference was organized by the Fernand Braudel Center for the Study of Economies, Historical Systems, and Civilizations, and the Southwest Asian and North African Studies (SWANA) Program of the State University of New York at Binghamton. Additional funding was provided by the Institute of Turkish Studies to prepare the papers for publication. We would like to thank the participants in the conference, staff of the Fernand Braudel Center and the SWANA Program, and the Institute of Turkish Studies for having made this volume possible. We would like to express special gratitude to Immanuel Wallerstein, director of the Fernand Braudel Center, whose interest and unfailing enthusiasm have made the Ottoman conferences and, in particular this volume, possible.

Introduction: Large-Scale Commercial Agriculture in the Ottoman Empire?*

Çağlar Keyder

The papers collected in this volume were prepared as contributions to a conference on the subject of "Large-Scale Commercial Agriculture in the Ottoman Empire." The object of the conference was to investigate the question of the *çiftlik*, a superimposition on the peasant economy whose protean nature and diversity of historical incarnations make it difficult to define or identify. We may provisionally define çiftlik as private control over landed property which tends to reduce the autonomy of the peasantry. Despite the problem of identification, most scholars in the field would agree that the implicit debate on the çiftlik raises the principal questions of Ottoman history. First of all the existence of çiftliks contradicts the self-understanding of the ruling class of the Empire. According to this conception, the legitimacy of political power is based on the perpetuation of an independent peasantry who enjoy unassailable usufructuary rights over state lands. They pay a customary tax to the designated representatives of the state and are thereby protected from expropriation. Revenue collection or appropriation of the agricultural surplus is a privilege granted by the central authority to those who render a service to the state or who farm the various taxes. In this regulated universe, extra impositions on the peasantry, such as arbitrary taxation or

* I would like to express my thanks to S. Faroqhi, I. Wallerstein, and M. Petrusewicz who kindly read and commented on this paper.

1

corvée, do not simply threaten the independence of the direct producers, they also violate the law of the realm. The question then is to
what extent was the idealized version of the Ottoman agrarian structure subverted by private usurpation of landed property. If such
transgressions occurred to a significant extent, then the Ottoman self-
definition is under risk of collapse, especially if it can be shown that
the çiftlik was common and indeed tolerated from the very beginning
of the Empire's existence. Independent peasant farming would then
be bracketed as one form of production among others. Under these
circumstances a redefinition of the Ottoman social formation would
be called for, perhaps assimilating it to a variant of feudalism.

A similar problem arises if it is maintained that the çiftlik gained
growing importance over time. Such an argument would suggest that
the initial model of a centralized empire with a tax collecting polity
gave way to locally controlled units based on the subjugation and
exploitation of the peasantry. According to this theory of çiftlik formation, the "strong central power–independent peasantry" equation
would reflect an unstable balance, and the Ottoman classical system
would be only a temporary exception to an otherwise all encompassing feudal universe.

In Part I of this volume İnalcık and Veinstein discuss the concept
and the practice of the çiftlik as these relate to interpretations of the
Ottoman system. Halil İnalcık sets the stage by reviewing the various
uses of the term çiftlik in Ottoman state practice. He identifies those
cases where private persons, in fact, appropriated state lands. Gilles
Veinstein discusses the diverging schools of thought concerning the
genesis of the çiftlik, concluding that its resemblence to the landlord-
managed estate is exaggerated. Despite İnalcık's greater willingness
to entertain the notion of çiftlik as an estate, the balance of these
contributions suggests that Ottoman exceptionalism is not yet to be
discarded. In other words, the Ottoman social formation seems to
have embodied a logic in which privatized large property was
marginal.

One way of transcending the insular model based on the interdependence of the central authority and the small peasantry is by
introducing the impact of the capitalist market on the Ottoman social
structure. The argument of external impact and commercial opportunity leading to a rupture with the classical model would seem to
solve the problem by safeguarding Ottoman exceptionalism. According to this project the dissolution of classical Ottoman balances results
from the various dynamics brought into the picture via the economic
integration with Europe. The çiftlik, once again, lies at the center of
the questions relating to the mode of incorporation of the Ottoman

Empire into the world capitalist system. It becomes the Ottoman version of the landed estate engaging in commercial agriculture, employing enserfed or dependent peasants. In this perspective, the çiftlik is supposed to belong in the same category as Prussian estates, Latin American and Italian latifundia, Asian plantations and the Egyptian *izba*. It is supposed to be a product of increasing trade with the core countries and the local seizing of commercial opportunity.[1]

This is the model of peripheral transformation that most of the papers in Part II of this volume question. İslamoğlu-İnan looks at an earlier period of commercial expansion and its impact on the peasant economy. She finds that politics and ideology prevented officials from increasing the scale of exploitation, despite growing trade opportunity. Suraiya Faroqhi brings a unique perspective on the subject through the study of a wealthy individual, a small *ayan*, his attempts at accumulating land, riches and power through controlling the peasant economy, and the political factors that constrained him. Elena Frangakis-Syrett describes the accommodation of the İzmir hinterland to the expanding trade in cloth, the monetary mechanisms which fueled it, and the channels that served in intermediation. The impact of market integration and commodification of the peasantry is also discussed by Reşat Kasaba who concentrates on the role of seasonal and permanent migration which served to counteract the perennial labor shortage in Anatolian agriculture. Tosun Arıcanlı in his overview argues that the absence of inviolable property rights in the Ottoman context rendered a lasting privatization of land an unlikely event. Since property was not recognized, estates could not be formed. Faruk Tabak, Dina Khoury, and Linda Schilcher in their respective papers on the Arab provinces of the Empire describe the modes of commercialization of the peasantry and the channels of intermediation between urban and rural economies that insured a market-oriented transformation of the agrarian structure. In these richly textured studies it becomes apparent that commodity production by small-owning peasantry represents an alternative mode of integration into the market, and that this path excluding large-scale commercial exploitation characterized most of the Ottoman lands. Together the papers provide a diversity of perspectives and a wealth of social historical data on the agrarian structure of the Middle East.

Instead of summarizing the various arguments elaborated in the individual contributions, it may be useful to trace the steps of the implicitly comparative perspective concerning the formation of large-scale commercial agriculture in the periphery and to discuss its applicability to the Ottoman case. This gloss will serve to introduce the principal themes debated in this volume.

The conventional wisdom that integration into trade networks brought about the formation of large-scale commercial agriculture derived its model from the experience of eastern Europe, the first region to be peripheralized.[2] Starting with an agrarian structure characterized by the feudal patterns of lordly landholding and servile labor, eastern Europe experienced an intensification of impositions on serfs and growing labor obligations precisely during the period when personal freedom and a commercialization based on yeomenry were being consolidated in western Europe. In the areas east of the Elbe, the nobility were able to arrest the dissolution of feudal relations and re-assert their traditional privileges. As they oriented their production to the international market, they also sought to manage their estates in order to maximize the extracted surplus. The transition had been from rent-collecting feudal ownership without management (*Grundherrschaft*) to large properties managed as commercial estates (*Gutsherrschaft*). The process of re-enserfment was accompanied by an increased rate of exploitation as landlords gradually imposed heavier labor services on the peasantry.

The generalized version of the eastern European model suggests that commercial opportunity would exercise a similar impact on all peripheral landlords who rely on customary rent and dues for their surplus. Confronted with lucrative markets and profit opportunity, they would attempt both to impose heavier obligations on the peasantry and to manage their properties as economically efficient enterprises or estates, rather than in the grundherrschaft mode. Obviously, the transition to managed estates would be ideal for purposes of rationalizing market integration and maximizing the extraction of surplus while reducing the peasantry to subsistence. If such radical restructuring were not possible, however, the landlord would still try to benefit indirectly from the increasing availability of markets by imposing higher rents on the peasantry or by raising additional revenue through monopolizing commercial channels. The direct producers, tax/rent paying peasants, may in turn switch out of their traditional patterns of production as a consequence of greater commercialization.

The question of large-scale commercial agriculture in the Ottoman Empire was initially posed within the East European model as an attempt to uncover instances of radical restructuring resulting in landlord-managed estates. Recent historical research seems to show, however, that such a transformation from small property dominated agriculture, where peasant households were only obligated to pay the tax/rent, to large-scale estates with increasing obligations imposed on the peasantry, was not a strong element of the Ottoman incorporation into capitalist markets. The papers collected in this volume argue that a transformation toward large landlord-managed estates was not prevalent; yet, they point to various ways in which local notables, merchants or tax collectors endeavored to benefit from changing conditions by attempting to capture a greater share of the peasants' surplus. In other words, increasing trade did not result in a change in the relations of production; but it did allow various well-placed officials to benefit from new opportunities in the circulation of products and money.

***

The obvious objection to searching for a model for Ottoman history in European experience is that the political and legal context of a strong state coupled with tax-paying peasantry in the case of the former, and parcellized sovereignty and serfdom in the latter, should not be expected to evolve in a parallel fashion. In considering eastern and western Europe, we are dealing with essentially comparable agrarian structures with a common genesis differentiated through historical contingency and dissimilar temporality. The pre-requisites for the application of the comparative method are indeed there. In the Ottoman case, however, the agrarian structure characterized by an independent peasantry without significant servile obligations, the absence of a propertied, hereditary noble class, and the apparent ease with which the monarch could eliminate and confiscate the wealth of private individuals make it difficult to justify a comparison with either version of the continental European experience. Nonetheless, the arguments usually found in the literature comparing eastern and western developments in Europe might serve to underline various dimensions of the Ottoman specificity.

The argument (as found in Max Weber, for example) proceeds on the basis of an elaboration of factors that were present in one case and absent in the other.[3] We may summarize these factors in three categories: those relating to the character of the settlements in terms of peasant traditions and population density; those pertaining to the degree of commercialization and monetization of the producers; and finally, the most important from the point of view of discussing the Ottoman case, those concerned with the relationships among the central authority, landlords, and the peasantry.

The arguments in the first group derive from the relatively late history of settlements in eastern Europe. Peasants had originally been attracted to the new settlements by relatively less oppressive conditions, but, because these were new settlements, they had never enjoyed the support of customary law and the solidarity of the village community. The balance of rights and obligations which was valid in the old lands and helped defend acquired rights, such as privileges on the village commons, had been lost with the move to newly reclaimed lands. In addition, the lord had been freed from the checks on his authority and he emerged as the sole purveyor of justice. In terms of the material topography of seigneurial property as well, the newly settled lands were compact in the sense that they did not permit the claiming of overlapping rights by rival landlords or suzerains, thus according no space to maneuver to the peasant. The lord's domain was usually an undivided, consolidated property, enclosed from inception. All these conditions conspired to render the serf defenseless against the lord who would impose on him yet more onerous obligations.

Colonization was possible because these lands were not densely populated; there were not many towns, hence not much local trade. In the West, the peasants had been able to realize their own surpluses in nearby markets, which was a precondition for the commutation of labor services to money rent; in the East it was the lords who controlled access to the markets and sold the surplus produced by the serfs. The dominant mode of commercialization was through exports. It is precisely at this juncture that the world-systems argument concerning the importance of the division of labor which characterized the peripheralized lands of second serfdom becomes important. Agrarian surpluses were marketed as exports, and the revenue served to support the noble life style and luxury of the lords. The economy of the grain-producing East was disarticulated, since the particular utilization of the surplus prevented the development of an expansive internal market and local accumulation of productive capital. Without such accumulation and the concomitant formation of an urban bourgeoisie as an estate independent of the aristocracy, eastern Europe became peripheralized. This peripheralization effectively guaranteed the longevity of the lords' economic and political power.

Finally, and most decisively, the lords in the East were able to protect their privileges and increase the servile obligations of the peasantry because during the period of the second serfdom the central authority (monarchy) was not strong enough to curb the nobilities' power and privileges. In an attempt to usurp political power from the aristocracy, absolute monarchies of the West (especially in France) had found it in their interest to pursue a policy which amounted to a protection of the peasantry. Monarchies imposed royal justice and intendants and defended the peasantry, whose tax payments had become the principal source of revenue for the royal fisc, from the lords' encroachments. Unable to subjugate the peasantry, the lords had evolved as a rent-collecting class, deriving their authority from their association with the monarchy. This difference led to the two confronting ideal types of political development: an implicit alliance of the monarchy and the peasantry which kept lordly reaction at bay and eventually allowed the evolution of a free peasantry, as in France and south and western Germany; and, in the East, a monarchy which did not succeed in becoming anything more than a representation of the collective identity of the seigneurial estate.[4]

Let us temporarily suspend the argument that eastern European estates emerged out of a background of feudalism that had no parallel in the Ottoman case. If the strong model predicting the creation and survival of estate agriculture were applicable in Ottoman history, we would expect that the eastern particularities sketched in the arguments above would have some parallels in Ottoman class structure and political and institutional balances. First, there is the colonization of new lands that contributed to giving the lands East of Elbe their unique character. In the Ottoman Empire, most land reclamation in the margin seems to have been undertaken by the peasantry themselves. The famous provision concerning the payment of taxes on previously empty state property for ten years which made the peasant into the recognized "owner" of the land seems to have been of general use. When such an opening-up was undertaken under state auspices, as in large-scale settlements of immigrant populations, the object was to create a peasant sector, and there was no question of establishing an ownership structure discordant with the preferred mode of production.

If nineteenth-century examples provide a model, such state-directed settlement of newly opened lands often resulted in a purer form of peasant agriculture, true to the model of village communities exhibiting little inequality in terms of landholding. There were, however, instances of colonization that resulted in a structure somewhat resembling eastern European estates. This is the case of the opening up (*şenlendirme*) of uncultivated or waste (*mevat*) lands, which İnalcık and Veinstein discuss. Here, colonization was the prelude to the setting up of a farm, called çiftlik in official registers, ordinarily larger than typical peasant holdings, but nowhere near the size of an east European estate or a new world plantation.[5] The principal factor restricting the size of exploitation in the çiftlik was the difficulty of finding labor. Faced with a central authority that would not cooperate, the colonizer landlord could not change the legal status of the peasant or his right of access to land. He rarely owned slaves, and since he could not control a servile labor force, he was dependent on peasantry from adjacent villages who otherwise cultivated their own land while also working on the newly established çiftlik as sharecroppers or on a seasonal basis. The çiftlik constituted on waste (mevat) land remained the legal property of the state, and the owner was liable to pay the ordinary taxes levied on all direct producers on the land. As such, his privileges were also liable to be revoked.

The second category of distinguishing factors concerns the degree of commercialization, the use of money, and the presence of local markets. In general, Ottoman towns remained important as did local markets and short-distance and regional trade. Empty lands distant from urban markets did not prove to be attractive sites to be exploited in large-scale agriculture. In such regions as the central Anatolian plateau, reclamation of land seems to have been a small-scale undertaking, resulting from population movements. The only instance of freshly settled, commercial agriculture oriented to distant markets could arguably be found in the Balkans. These settlements were distinguished not only by fertile soil, but also the easier access to long-distance markets. In fact, according to one of the first applications of the eastern European model to the Ottoman case, large estates based on the utilization of servile peasant labor appeared in the Balkans precisely because export markets seemed to play an important role in the local economy.[6] Yet, subsequent research has shown this conclusion to be misleading, because çiftliks in the Balkans were rarely if ever managed estates. Even when commercialization played an important role most landlords were unable to "enclose" and remained as collectors of taxes.[7] It was attempts to overtax rather than the enserfment of the peasantry which characterized the Balkan çiftlik.

Despite their proximity to European markets and the relative ease of transportation, the export trade from Ottoman lands never developed to any significant degree. Aside from the arguable case of the Balkans (and that of nineteenth-century Egypt, which is outside the purview of our discussion), there is no indication that Ottoman exports originated in rural units of production resembling estates. Exports were predominantly agricultural, but unlike what would be expected of estate-dominated regions, no single product ever accounted for more than a small fraction of the total export revenues. Even toward the end of the nineteenth century, when railways could be built and steamships regularly traversed the eastern Mediterranean, a mono-crop pattern did not evolve. The biggest item in exports accounted for around one-eighth of the total.[8] The absence of a mono-crop pattern reflects the absence of large-scale commercial exploitation. Exports originated predominantly in peasant production and derived from peasant surpluses, not from landlord-managed estates. Peasants were not quick to change their patterns of diversified production, hence the volume of exports increased slowly; the Ottoman lands exhibited a mediocre performance in terms of integration into world commodity networks.[9] This is significant both because it is indicative of the absence of the plantation model and because it determined that internal trade would not lose its importance. Commerce and monetization based on the domestic economy conducted along traditional networks continued to be primary.

The crucial argument concerning the dissimilarity of the Ottoman case with historical examples of the estate-agriculture model derives from the political balance developed among the overlords, peasants, and the central authority. In the case of Europe the model is bound up with understanding the genesis of the absolutist state, which grew increasingly autonomous from the landowning aristocracy. In the Ottoman case, however, the logic is necessarily the opposite: since the strongly central "absolutist" state is the pre-existing condition, the corresponding question would have to inquire first if a landholding class could develop, and secondly, if this class could wrest any autonomy out of the central authority. Without pretending to write a history of the Ottoman state, it is possible to assert that there were indeed periods when a group of powerful notables emerged, and, particularly during the eighteenth century, this group almost developed as a class, conscious of its interests and willing to defend and promote the same.[10] What characterized the members of this potential class was that they owed their status to the initially bureaucratic positions they occupied, which then became the vehicle for the usurpation of economic power. In other words these ayan had been provincial administrators and tax farmers whose ideally and previously revokable tenure or farm had gained permanence due to the incapacity of the central authority. The terminus of such a development could have been the birth of hereditary landownership with an aristocracy-like class sufficiently autonomous to withstand a summary re-appropriation of all power by the central authority. They would then have used their gained immunity to monopolize the land and to impose on the peasantry servile obligations or to reduce them to the status of landless workers. In other words, the strong model of estate agriculture would have become operative.

The possible scenario, however, remained hypothetical. The ayan were unable to transform their transgression of the patrimonial mandate into a more lasting autonomy. Thus, they were unable to break the ties of mutual defense between a strong state, which resisted the formation of an intermediary estate, and the tax-paying, independent peasantry. The ayan remained content to exploit the tax-collecting relationship, to consolidate and diversify their revenue bases, to use their influence in avoiding competition to obtain the tax farms, and perhaps to marginally increase the impositions on those direct producers with fiscal liability. In short, they never successfully challenged the authority of the central state. It was thus not surprising that they entirely and drastically lost the status they had usurped when the central authority took the initiative to reassert its prerogatives during the first half of the nineteenth century. Hence the single most noteworthy episode in Ottoman agrarian history that can be construed as the beginnings of a development along large-scale commercial exploitation remained a truncated version of the model because the essentially independent status of the peasantry did not suffer any change.

The state was, of course, the crucial element in the failure of the ayan. Ultimately, the identification of landlord interests with those of the central authority underwrote the power of the European seigneurs. In the Ottoman case the central bureaucracy maintained its self-avowed mission to uphold the status of an independent peasantry—both for reasons of fiscal expediency and because the alternative would have amounted to recognizing rival nodes of authority. Hence, the ideological contract stipulating the exchange of order and justice emanating from the state against revenue from the direct producers was upheld. The power won by the ayan remained interstitial and episodic and depended for its exercise entirely on the weakness of the state. When the state made the attempt to reestablish its authority the ayan quickly capitulated.

Perhaps the most revealing component of the systemic inertia conducing to the central state's ascendancy over centrifugal tendencies was coded in the legal context. Unlike its obvious precapitalist counterpart—feudalism in Europe—the Ottoman political and legal system never developed a category of alienable property rights. As early as the thirteenth century, jurists in France had begun to worry about the application of Roman concepts of absolute property rights to feudal practice.[11] The so-called conditional property of feudalism contained the concept of "private" property for the lord and soon evolved to recognize private property rights for the serfs as well. This was a smooth transition, via the revival of Roman Law, to capitalist property rights. Not so, however, in the Ottoman Empire, which arguably inherited a combination of eastern Roman and Islamic practice. Here, absolute property for the subjects was never recognized, and, in addition to the legal dictum of the sultan enjoying the

"ownership" of the entire realm, the actual practice suggested strongly that confiscation of subjects' possessions as the ultimate sanction
was never far away.

Although confiscation was justified by reference to law, its very
arbitrariness made it into a weapon that became a naked index of the
balance power. So, it was conceivable that at certain times (notably in
the eighteenth century) and in certain places, the balance of power
would obtain in such a way that would-be landlords enjoyed property rights which seemed almost absolute. The problem with balance of
power, however, is that it is, by definition, subject to change; and,
failing the qualitative transcendence into socially recognized and en-
forcable legal ratification of claims to property, it remains a flimsy
ground on which to build the kind of economic organization characteristic of lands with a feudal heritage. "Almost" is never good
enough when the ever-present threat of confiscation has to be reckoned with. Besides, the ideological compact between the state and the
reaya was such that even after the ambiguous declaration in 1858
which recognized titled and alienable property on land, the "social
recognition" of private property, in other words its subjective acceptance by the peasantry (reaya), was much later in arriving. On the
whole, in Islamic Law (*shari'a*), village communities had recourse to a
body of legal doctrine which could be interpreted by the *ulama* to
defend their customary rights to land.[12] As a result, except in Syrian
and Iraqi provinces, tax and rent collecting landlords were not able to
"enclose"—even after the Land Code of 1858.

***

Both agricultural capitalism and estate agriculture based on the
employment of unfree labor derived from a feudal past. Specifically,
seigneurial rights bolstered with the legal framework of absolute
property prepared for large-scale managed units. When the peasantry were not able to resist the imposition of greater obligations,
export-oriented, landlord-managed, large-scale agriculture came into
being. Compare, however, the Ottoman case. Since there was no
prior feudalism, the peasantry were not confronted with an immediate adversary whose economic logic conflicted with their own practices. There was no tradition of intervention in the immediate production process of the peasantry. The position that the feudal lord
occupied in the West had first to be invented. Hence, rather than
seeking similarities to feudal practices in Ottoman realms, the direction of inquiry in Part II of this volume points toward a related and
more fruitful question: when estate formation is not a ready option
what are the alternative modes of accumulation?

The contributors generally agree in denying importance to the strong (managed estate) model of the çiftlik. From Mosul (Khoury), through the Fertile Crescent (Tabak) and Syria (Schilcher), by way of central Anatolia (İslamoğlu-İnan), and finally in the fertile and export-oriented plains of the Aegean littoral (Faroqhi, Frangakis-Syrett, Kasaba), they find the "çiftlik owner" collecting taxes, organizing trade, extending loans, and attempting to squeeze the peasantry. One constant, however, was that the çiftlik owner left the organization and the independent status of the peasant alone: even the mighty Kara Osmanoğlu family of the Aydın province were marginally involved in production and derived most of their revenue from tax-farming and commerce. By mid-nineteenth century the Kara Osmanoğlu family had lost their pre-eminence; they were just another urban patrician dynasty. In fact, forming a conspicuous estate might have brought the mighty down even sooner because the threat of confiscation was real and, as Faroqhi notes, wealth could rarely, if ever, be transmitted to a second generation. It is certainly true that no landlord family of the eighteenth or early nineteenth century was able to survive into the modern age with its fortune intact.

An agriculture based on small peasant farms was no impediment, however, to the world-market-oriented structuring of production patterns. Small and middle peasants responded to market signals (Khoury), reflected, in their organization and behavior, fluctuations in demand and prices (Tabak), and successfully contributed to the expansion of the export trade (Frangakis-Syrett). In fact, the significant increase in exports from the Aegean littoral coincides not with ayan ascendancy but with the consolidation of an agrarian structure dominated by small production (Kasaba). The conclusion to be drawn from these investigations is that world market demand was an important element that contributed to shaping the rural economy. The new structures that evolved allowed various degrees of indirect control to be exercised by the ayan, the *mültezim*, the merchant, and the creditor, all acting as intermediaries over the direct producer—who himself was a family farmer. Expanding land ownership and the formation of estates accompanied by an enserfment of the peasantry, however, never became an option. The final arbiter in any bid to form an estate remained the ability of the state to exercise its prerogatives, specifically that of confiscation. The careers of high bureaucrats punctuated by short tenures, frequent dismissals, and sometimes beheadings;[13] the once mighty *derebeys* of Çukurova reduced to sinecured bureaucrats;[14] the rapid fall of the feared masters of Anatolia that were the ayan, all point to a drastically lopsided equation in favor of the strong state which exercised its prerogatives with impunity.

The çiftlik as an estate, in those rare occasions when it was formed, was a fleeting and easily reversible phenomenon. Otherwise, the word often referred to that practice where wealthy officials, tax farmers, or merchants diversified their businesses to engage in a disparate collection of revenue-bringing investments with no legal ratification. For this reason, this çiftlik expanded in an economically irrational manner; there was no logic to it, no economic theory to understand and explicate it.[15] Only the conjuncture and the weaknesses of the central authority could shed light on activities of the wealthy who tried to control the rural economy without incurring the state's wrath. As the papers in this volume demonstrate, they seized whatever opportunity arose interstitially within the restrictive context and practice laid out by the state. Hence the expansion of the çiftlik was unpredictable and most haphazard; in practice it became a collection of unlikely money-making practices that were in a particular moment possible. This is precisely the reason why "*çiftlik*" has remained so elusive and confusing a concept; it has been used to describe phenomena so diverse that it might be best to avoid the term altogether for purposes of clarity. The papers in Part II of this volume could have been written without using the word at all; they may, in fact, provide the groundwork necessary to retire the model built around the overworked concept.

Part I

1

The Emergence Of Big Farms, Çiftliks: State, Landlords, and Tenants*

Halil İnalcık

The legal framework for landholding of agricultural lands in the Ottoman Empire was provided by the Islamic Law (*shari'a*), and the state laws (*örfi kanun*) issued by the Sultan. While the Islamic Law protected free-hold rights of the individual on land in general, the *kanun* system was concerned with the maintenance of state control on agricultural lands. The history of landholding in the Ottoman Empire, or in Islamic countries in general, can be summarized as a constant struggle between the state and the individual for control of agricultural lands which constituted the principal source of wealth for capital formation or state finances. The state's concern to maintain its control of agricultural lands was primarily determined by its absolute dependence on agrarian production for its finances and for the maintenance of its mounted (*sipahi*) forces. The state was also concerned with the *çift-hane* system as the basis of the traditional system in agrarian production peculiar to the Middle East.

*Reprinted with minor changes from Jean-Louis Bacqué-Grammont and Paul Dumont, eds., 1983. *Contributions à l'histoire économique et sociale de l'Empire ottoman.* Louvain: Peeters, 105–26.

17

The *Çift-hane* System: Small Family Farm Units

The law guaranteed a tenant, normally a married man, and his heirs of male descendence, the right to enjoy, permanently and freely, possession and use of state-owned or *miri* land when this land was duly acquired and used under the specified conditions.[1] Permanent tenancy under a perpetual lease amounted to an actual possession of land by the farmer-*reaya*. In addition, the state saw to it through its agents on the land, sipahis and *kadıs*, that third persons did not alter the original status of the land.[2] The land and labor of the farmer-reaya were scrupulously protected by the state against third parties who might attempt to convert these lands into privately owned farms and reduce the peasants to laborers, sharecroppers, or serfs on these lands.

The çift-hane system consisted of an organization of agricultural production on the basis of peasant households, *hanes*, each of which was given a *çift* or *çiftlik*, i.e., a plot of land of sufficient size to sustain one peasant household and pay the "rent" to the landholder (the state). The size of the çiftlik varied with the fertility of the soil from 60 *dönüm* to 150.[3] This was the basic agricultural unit. If a çiftlik was found to be divided among several possessors, it was, as a rule, restored to its original form. Also, if the head of the household in possession of a çiftlik died leaving several sons, they were to possess it collectively. Household size varied according to the region.

The çift-hane system was an integral part of the *tımar* system, the basic military institution in the classical period. In the tımar system[4] control of agricultural production, and thence of the land, is shared actually by the state, the farmer, and the mounted soldier of the imperial army (sipahi) living in the villages. The sipahi was assigned a tımar which consisted of collecting the fixed amount of state revenue from the peasants in a defined area of land as his salary. The assignment of tımar gave him some rights of control over the land: he implemented the state regulations on the transference and use of land by the peasants.[5] Since the tımars were indivisible and unalterable units as recorded in the survey books, the çift-hane units too were held indivisible and unalterable in order to protect the fixed tımar income. The tımar system and the rigid, state-controlled system of the çift-hane was undoubtedly one of the main reasons why the organization of agricultural production in the Ottoman Empire remained static and resistant to change entailing other forms of landholding and production.

This system was prevalent in Anatolia and the Balkans and was closely monitored by the state. It was considered an ideal system best suited to the socio-political conditions of what we might call the Middle East empire tradition.[6] It was scrupulously maintained by a traditional bureaucracy as the basis of a unique imperial system of state and society. However, despite the efforts of the central bureaucracy to safeguard state control on state-owned lands, such lands came partly under control of private individuals, especially during the period of decline and decentralization beginning at the end of the sixteenth century.[7] The principal form of alteration of the miri lands came about as a result of the Sultan's granting certain rights of control to the individuals on such lands. While such rights were rarely granted during the period when centralization and the tımar system prevailed, they became widespread through administrative abuses during the sixteenth century. Influential figures from the palace or those close to palace circles obtained state lands in the form of appanages, or property grants, and subsequently turned them into trusts for pious endowments or *waqfs*. The change in the legal status of the land and labor on it did not in most cases involve a change in the organization of production. The çift-hane system continued and the relationship between the farmer-reaya and private individuals or waqfs was the same as under the tımar system. As before, the newcomers were simply collectors of the "rent" in the form of dues, and as a rule, did not attempt to reorganize the labor and production on these lands. In brief, plantation-like farms rarely emerged on the waqf or *mülk* lands from miri origin. It should be added that the state reverted, though not so extensively and energetically as in previous centuries, some of these lands to their original miri status.

Big Farms on the *Mevat* Lands

In the Ottoman Empire, plantation-like farms, that is, large agricultural lands organized as a production unit under a single ownership and management and usually producing for the market, came into being mostly on waste or abandoned (*mevat*) lands outside the areas under the çift-hane system. Prior to the eighteenth century, such big farms were usually developed by members of the ruling class on mevat lands, and labor on them was mostly supplied by slaves or sharecroppers.[8]

Reclamation, *şenlendirme* or *ihya* was accomplished under special provisions of Islamic Law, and encouraged by the state. The first prerequisite to it was the introduction of substantial improvements on waste land, such as the construction of water canals and preparation for cultivation. The second requirement was the Sultan's (İmam's) permission through a special document which recognized proprietary rights on the reclaimed land. The shari'a provided freehold (mülk) status, for the land reclaimed by individuals, including non-Muslim subjects, and the Sultan (İmam) readily authorized reclamation and ratified mülk character of duly reclaimed land. The state encouraged such reclamation projects for reasons such as extension of arable land, most of which eventually became converted into pious endowments for charitable purposes or public use. The formal procedure for issuing a document of ownership, *temlikname*, was that the promoter of the project submitted to the Porte his project, defining the land and specific reclamation method and objective, and asked the Sultan's permission. In the early period of Ottoman history we find examples of entrepreneurs first restoring the land and later obtaining the Sultan's temlikname. The Finance Department issued an imperial firman with the permission. The final temlikname was a diploma which granted freehold ownership and specified boundaries of the land. Usually a detailed document describing the land in detail (*sınırname*) after an on-the-spot inspection was drawn up.[9] At the same time, the new status of the land was recorded in the imperial land survey book, *mufassal defter*, which served as a basis and reference in all future decisions to be made by the central government. In the Sultan's temlikname, it is noted that the land in question was originally of the mevat category, and that when reclaimed, it would be cultivated by the reaya only if they agreed to work as paid hands and not as forced laborers. Also, their share of the produce was to be surrendered to them according to a proportion predetermined in the document. Since the state did not allow the change of status of the miri lands, most of the typical big farms owed their origin to the reclaimed lands.

Reclamation usually meant investment of considerable amounts of capital and thus "entrepreneurs" were almost always members of the higher echelons of the ruling elite, including the military and clerical. Cases of merchants or urban guild masters owning such lands were rarely found in the survey books before the eighteenth century. In the period when the central bureaucracy was powerful, it was a deliberate policy on the part of the state to favor the ruling elite while social and economic developments with decentralization would bring about considerable changes in the composition of the class of the "entrepreneurs" in the eighteenth and nineteenth centuries.[10]

Even in the early period, labor was sometimes supplied by reaya agreeing to do extra work outside timar lands or by runaway peasants or free reaya unregistered in the imperial survey books. Sharecropping was a common mode of labor of reaya origin. However, it became necessary for the "entrepreneurs" to look for labor on reclaimed lands outside the reaya since the state strictly adhered to the çift-hane system to protect its regular source of income. On farms of mevat origin, use of servile labor was a general practice from the earliest times, though under various conditions this kind of labor did not prove to be as effective as sharecroppers.[11]

In summary, through obtaining mülk lands from mevat, Islamic Law provided a legal framework to bring about large farms owned by individuals, and the Ottoman state, as a rule, encouraged the application of this legal device to expand the area of such lands.

A typical example of a project of this type in the mid-sixteenth century is a project for rice cultivation near the village of Yenice, submitted by Feridun Ahmed Bey and the Grand Vizier Sokullu Mehmed.[12] They proposed jointly to spend their own money to build a dam and canals to secure water from the Sakarya river. The total length of the canals was estimated at 17,000 *zira* or 12,876 meters. They proposed to grow rice by irrigating the land fallen into disuse near the village of Çaltı and others, and predicted to be able to sow 75 *mudd* of seed in the area (one rice mudd = 256.4 kg.). The maintenance of the dam and the canals was to be performed by the founders.

They therefore applied for a firman through the Department of Finance in order to grant the Sultan's permission for the project. The total amount to be sown was fixed at 50 mudd for Mehmed Pasha and 25 mudd for Ahmed Bey. The produce was to be shared equally between them and the reaya and others who chose to work for them. The tithe due to the tımar-holders was to be paid by the peasants out of their share. From their share, Mehmed Pasha and Ahmed Bey vowed to meet the expenses for burning three candles or candalebra at the mausoleum of Ak-Şemseddin, as well as to construct a caravanserai and five fountains in the town of Göynük. Mehmed Pasha promised to expend funds for the repair of the caravan highway ruined by the flooding of the Sakarya river, as well as for repairing a damaged dam in a nearby village (Nerdivanlu). Those farmers who would use the water supplied by them for their own cultivation of cotton and other staples would be required to surrender one half of their harvest. Where the land leased by Mehmed Pasha was worked by those in his employ, the whole produce belonged to him. The Sultan gave his approval by a decree through the Department of Finance on the condition that the tımar-holders and the reaya of the area consented, and that when reclaimed, the land would be cultivated by the reaya only when they agreed to work as paid hands and not as forced labor. Also, the peasants' share of the produce was to be surrendered to them according to a predetermined proportion.

The Spread of Big Farms: Muqata'a-Malikane System

Along with the expansion of plantation-like farms of mevat origin, there emerged processes leading to conversion of miri lands into big farms in some areas especially during the celali disturbances at the end of the sixteenth century.[13] According to a justice decree, dated 1609,[14] influential people among the military, including kapı-kulu in the provinces, appropriated for themselves lands abandoned by the villagers as a result of the Celali disorders. Settling in them slaves or hired men, they converted them into their own private estates. Because of the general shortages of labor, lands of this sort were usually fenced and turned over to livestock raising, thus becoming veritable ranches. Use and appropriation of peasants' lands abandoned in the periods of internal disorder had became normal procedure in converting the reaya-miri lands into estates of big landholders. (Incidentally, livestock raising, for the same reasons, constituted the prevalent economic activity on many big farms of mevat origin, as well).

Also, extensive lands of miri origin were converted to waqfs or privately owned farms mostly as a result of administrative inefficiency in the period of decline. Many indebted villagers lost their fields to local notables and military chiefs through a simple decision of the local court.[15] Thus, usurers, mostly town-based military or ulama, took over the possession rights of the reaya on miri lands, and over time, as a result of administrative inefficiency, such lands turned into privately owned properties. In a different process, the leasing of state-owned lands also led to conversion of miri lands into big farms. From the earliest times the practice was established that abandoned arable lands of miri status, commonly called mazra'a or hali çiftlik in the survey books, were rented by the state to individuals. These lands became part of private estates, owing to the inefficiency of government book-keeping or abuse of the muqata'a system in the decline period. In fact, the most important development came with the changes in the leasing-out or muqata'a system. During the period of decline after 1600, under financial constraints, the treasury leased out a growing number of miri lands to individuals for a life term, and later, on a hereditary basis which was called malikane, so that such holdings became virtually like property, leasers actual landlords, and peasants their tenants. In other words, a whole class of lease-holders (*eshab-ı muqata'a*), now intervened between the state and peasants. Çift-hane as a system continued to exist as the predominant organization of agricultural production on these lands, but the relationship between landholder and farmer underwent a profound change. Now leaseholders who substituted for the state were naturally inclined to maximize their share in production and squeeze the reaya labor to achieve their goals. Under a short lease, this resulted in the ruin of the area and degeneration of çift-hane units. To remedy this, the state introduced an extension of farming-out period or *iltizam*, primarily with the expectation that the leasers would be more concerned with the continuous prosperity of the area and the reaya under their control.

The leasing-out system became more widespread than ever during the decline period, practiced not only by the state treasury, but also by higher members of the ruling group, palace favorites, governors, and appanage holders, who were all a kind of absentee landlord. Most of the leaseholders in the provinces emerged as a new class of provincial notables, ayans who as on-the-spot operators, controlled a greater part of miri lands as muqata'a or malikane.

The *Ayans* and *Çiftliks*

Along with their control as leaseholder of the lands under the old çift-hane system, the ayans also emerged as a new type of "entrepreneur" in land reclamation and expansion of plantation-like farms. They were economically motivated to maximize their revenues under both the impact of an expanding external market, and under the pressure of pecuniary needs in order to sustain their position as tax farmers and heads of local mercenary forces.[16]

It is assumed that in the decline period the Ottoman economy and social structure were transformed from being based on an asiatic mode of production to a complete dependence on European capitalism which entailed fundamental changes in the conditions of agricultural production and peasant-landlord relations.[17] But this hypothesis can not be substantiated with the available documentary evidence. The process of conversion of the miri or waste lands into plantation-type çiftliks as a result of commercialization of agriculture and, subsequently, growing alienation of the peasants from the land and more intensive exploitation of cultivators by landholders, were developments which affected only certain regions which were particularly exposed to external conditions.[18]

The Ottoman land regime, despite these developments in certain areas, remained unchanged in its basic çift-hane structure as revealed by contemporary Ottoman documentary evidence. It appears that we are not justified in seeing in the Ottoman land regime a parallelism with what was happening in other eastern European countries under the impact of the European capitalist world economy.[19] Appanage-like land grants with large income, which were usually granted by the Sultan to the members of the court and of the ruling class from miri lands and even malikane leases, should be distinguished from the plantation-like çiftliks since appanages simply constituted a fiscal-administrative rearrangement in the possession of the lands, and did not necessarily bring about a change in the çift-hane system. As far as their economic organization was concerned, they were not different from the lands where production was based on the çift-hane. Thus, the large appanages can not be included in the category of big farms under study, unless their possessors reorganized these lands as plantation-like çiftliks. That would be a rare case since most of these appanage-holders were in a position of absenteeism, simply leaving the collection of their incomes to their agents (*kethüdas* or *voyvodas*), usually chosen from among influential local people. When the system of collection of income or state revenues through such local agents or tax-farmers became a widespread practice from the seventeenth century on, these agents emerged over time as ayans, provincial notables controlling sources of revenue and thence landholding and agriculture in the provinces. In the eighteenth century, the period 1760–1808 in particular, witnessed the rise of ayans which coincided with the growing European demand and higher prices for agricultural products of the Levant as a result of what is called the commercial revolution in the West. During the new period, the ayans brought under their control much of the miri lands under the çift-hane system as muqata'a or tax-farming leases,[20] but at the same time, under growing western demand, they began to open much abandoned or waste land to agriculture, and it was mostly on the latter category of lands that we find plantation-like farms.

The Plantation-like *Çiftliks* in the Eighteenth Century

Our notion of the plantation-like çiftliks in the Ottoman Empire comes mainly from Cvijić, Busch-Zantner, and Stoianovich.[21] Physical descriptions of çiftliks were made by travellers in the nineteenth century: a çiftlik was composed of a manor where the landlord or his agent resided, a number of huts for quartering laborers, a stone tower (a new indispensable element) for defense against rival ayans, the stalls for the animals, storehouses, a bakery, and a smithy. The plantation-like çiftlik consisted of a whole village, or one might say that the big farm was, as a rule, a çiftlik-village.

As far as socioeconomic features of the new çiftlik were concerned, the following definition is given. The çiftlik, Stoianovich says "marks the transition from a social and economic structure founded upon a system of moderate land rent and few labor services to one of excessive land rent and exaggerated service."[22] Stoianovich also adds that sharecropping with field, transportation, and other services supplement the rent given to the landlord labelling this development as an "internal colonialism." He also points out that the new plantation-like çiftlik spread in the regions with special geographical conditions such as coastal plains and interior basins along the arteries of communication, and it involved staple agriculture with irrigation. Furthermore, he draws attention to the fact that the expansion of the çiftlik system was interrelated with the growing demand of European markets for the agricultural products of the Ottoman Empire. For example, cotton was the main staple for export from the Serez plain in Macedonia, where some three hundred villages were divided among several ayans by the last decades of the eighteenth century. In the Balkans, Thessaly, Epirus, Macedonia, Thrace, the Maritsa Valley, Danubian Bulgaria, the Kossovo-Metohija basin, the coastal plains of Albania and parts of Bosnia are mentioned as areas where the çiftlik-village spread by the end of the eighteenth century. It should be added that such expansion coincided with the land reclamation and improvement activities in these areas.[23] In other parts of the Empire, in Egypt, Syria, and in the coastal plains of southern and western Anatolia, parallel developments took place in an earlier or later period.[24]

The use of Ottoman archival materials in the last three decades has shed new light on the question concerning the emergence of the çiftlik system in the Ottoman Empire. Now the questions of how and why changes in the social structure in the rural areas and in the internal reorganization of agricultural production occurred, have been examined in more detail and on a more solid basis. For instance, we are now able to scrutinize the extent to which ownership of land and growing control of labor by the land owner were developed in connection with the rise of the new çiftlik system. In addition, we are now more aware that the spread of market-oriented large farms coincided with a parallel expansion of land reclamation and improvement activity in the marginal lands, pastoral and flooded lowlands in particular. We also now know that most of the new çiftlik with their plantation-like structures came into being on such lands beyond the old miri lands with their traditional small-sized çift-hane units.

Here we shall take up the region of western Anatolia in order to more closely examine çiftlik formation in the eighteenth century. Detailed lists concerning the çiftliks of two great ayans, Hacı Mehmed Agha, *mütesellim* of Teke in Southwest Anatolia and Kara Osmanzade Hüseyin Agha, mütesellim of Saruhan in western Anatolia shall be examined here. Drawn up in the years 1815 and 1816 respectively, these lists from the estate books show the private properties left by the two ayans upon their deaths.[25] The çiftliks entered in these lists of inheritance can not be state-owned lands or muqata'as leased out by the treasury though originally they might have been so.

Both men were agents, or mütesellims acting on behalf of the governor or treasury in collecting revenues and performing some other financial and administrative functions in the *sancak*.[26] Mütesellims were usually selected from among the local notables with influence and wealth, and they, in turn, used their connections with the government in increasing their local influence and wealth, especially in terms of land. In both cases, the total value of their hereditary properties reached approximately a quarter of a million *guruş* (253,000 guruş for Hüseyin Agha and 251,000 guruş for Mehmed Agha) which represents a large fortune for the time. The composition of their fortunes was similar. It consisted of arable land, livestock, buildings, equipment, and crops.

The annual profit rate in relation to the capital invested was much higher in Hüseyin's çiftliks (1/10, 1/6, 1/3) than in Mehmed's (1/50, 1/10, 1/7). The highest rate was realized by cash crops (cotton production in the çiftliks Kara-Ağaçlı, and Ulu-Bara in Hüseyin's estate and rice grown on Mehmed's çiftlik, Çeltükci). The high profit rate must have been due to the fertility of soil as well as to closeness to the İzmir market in the case of Hüseyin's çiftliks.

The value of the land in Hüseyin's çiftliks varied between approximately 11 and 30 guruş per dönüm (1 dönüm equals 920 sq. meters). In Mehmed's çiftliks, it was much lower (2–4 guruş per dönüm). The value of land suitable for cotton and maize growing was highest (in the çiftlik Kara-Ağaçlı 33 guruş per dönüm).

The size of çiftliks varied between about 600 and 1,700 dönüm in Hüseyin's and between 700 and 13,000 in Mehmed's estates. In the latter the average size was 8,000 dönüm or 734 hectares while in the former about 1,000 dönüm or 90 hectares. According to Christo Gandev, çiftliks in the Vidin region on the Danube varied between 30 and 500 hectares.[27]

Evidently, high productivity and high value of land in Western Anatolia accounted for the smaller size of çiftliks. Hüseyin's estate was made up of eight çiftliks, while Mehmed's was twelve çiftliks of various sizes. It is to be noted that in some çiftliks uncultivated fields were quite numerous as in çiftliks Mihaili and Ulu-Bara. The estate of Hüseyin included three types of çiftliks: those with fields in which the produce belonged entirely to the landlord, those combining fields of the former with fields rented to the reaya and those çiftliks which were simply leased to tenants.

It appears that the first type of çiftliks was the standard type with all the features of a plantation-like large farm. Since the share of labor was not deducted from the yield in the final accounts, we assume that the produce in these çiftliks belonged entirely to the landlord, and that labor was wage-labor. With the second type of çiftlik, part of the fields were rented to the reaya who met the rent by surrendering part of the produce at the rate of 1 *ölçek* (i.e. measure or *kile* equal to 25.656 kg.) of barley and 1/2 ölçek of wheat per dönüm. In the çiftlik Kayışçılar, the rent was paid in cash at a predetermined rate. The first type of çiftlik comprised everything to make it a complete production unit: animal power for ploughing, threshing, and transport, ploughs, wagons, and other tools, stables, storehouse for crops, simple houses and shacks to accommodate agricultural workers (*çiftçi odaları*), and even a grocery shop. Horse breeding also seemed to have been an important occupation on most of the çiftliks of Kara Osmanzade Hüseyin. In the capacity of mütesellim, Hüseyin had to maintain a small security force, and during the wars, had to increase their number and join the Sultan's army.

After land, pairs of oxen for ploughing proved to be the most important and costly component of a çiftlik. It can be said that each çiftlik in Hüseyin's estate employed one pair of oxen for every 140 or 160 dönüm of land. (Mihaili and Ulu-Bara were not typical in this respect since there existed too many uncultivated fields at the time of recording). In Mehmed Agha's estate, the ratio shows too great a difference from one çiftlik to another to give any example. Apparently in the çiftliks Hacılar and Çeltükci, cattle breeding was an important occupation. Epidemics appear to have caused great losses of oxen with disruptive consequences for agriculture. Mehmed Agha lost twenty-six oxen out of forty on the çiftlik İmhan before the listing.

Because of the high costs of maintaining agriculture and the shortage of agricultural labor in many areas, çiftlik owners preferred to convert their farms into cattle ranches or dairy farms (*mandıra*) supplying oxen for neighboring villages and dairy products to nearby towns. The rate of profit was much higher in such çiftliks and most of these çiftliks were found near cities. Examples can be given not only for the eighteenth and nineteenth centuries, but as far back as the sixteenth century. At any rate, cattle and sheep breeding had always been an important activity in the large çiftliks unlike the ordinary reaya çiftliks.[28] Yegen Mehmed Agha, voyvoda of Tire, had several çiftliks devoted predominantly to cattle breeding.[29] In the çiftlik Kara-Yunuslu, for example, there were 113 cattle and 28 horses, but little agriculture.

In the çiftliks directly exploited, we find a diversified agriculture with wheat, barley, cotton, and maize being the main crops culti-vated. In Hüseyin's two çiftliks (Kara-Ağaçlı and Ulu-Bara), cotton, however, made up the greater part of the income. Even there, though, we can not speak of a monoculture. Cotton was one of the principal export items of the region since the fifteenth century.[30] There were also vineyards and orchards which made up only a small part of the çiftliks.

The greater part of the land on the majority of the çiftliks of Hüseyin were rented to the reaya or free peasants. Usually, the rent was paid in kind from the produce of the land and sometimes in cash as in Kayışçılar. The third type of çiftlik leased by Hüseyin brought an important income as down-payment made at the moment of leasing, i.e., *muaccele* and as yearly rent or *icar*. This type of çiftlik was of relatively small size, 150, 250, or 1,200 dönüm. In the directly ex-ploited fields (first type), hired hands seem to have been the standard form of labor, with the landlord supplying all the means of produc-tion: land, seeds, plough, oxen, beasts of burden, as well as accom-modations. The totality of the yield belonged to the landlord. Men-tioned in the çiftliks of Hasan Agha in Central Anatolia, in the lists published by Yuzo Nagata,[31] sharecropping was a traditional form of agrarian labor, and seems to have been replaced by hired labor on the more advanced market-oriented çiftliks in western Anatolia.

Most of the çiftliks of the Kara Osmanzade family had the physi-cal features of a typical çiftlik as portrayed by western travellers. Our estate lists include costly mansions (*konaks*) with kiosks and coffee rooms with separate watch towers of stone or earth. In addition, there were rooms for farmers, or çiftçi odaları, stables, and storehouses.

Big *Çiftliks* in the Vidin Region

In a study published in 1943, I examined the emergence of the big çiftlik owners in the Vidin region and concluded that the Bulgarian peasant insurrection of 1850 broke out primarily as a result of the socio-economic conflict between peasants and çiftlik owners.[32] The key process which gave rise to the emergence of big çiftlik owners in the Vidin region of northwest Bulgaria was the leasing out by public auction of state-owned lands to individuals. This type of lease was applied from the earliest times in the Ottoman Empire to the state-owned arable lands which were not actually in the possession of the reaya and not under cultivation. The treasury leased such lands, wherever available, to increase state revenues. Such lands, referred to as muqata'a, were given to individuals on the basis of perpetual lease inherited only by direct male lineage, as was the case with the reaya çiftlik possession. The possession document was called *tapu*. At the time of the lease, the lessee made a down-payment to the treasury called *icare-i muaccele*. This corresponded to tapu paid by the reaya to get possession of miri land, and it amounted to only one year's income of the land in question. Anyone willing to pay the rent, or *icare*, could take possession of such land.

This general practice was known as far back as the fifteenth century when it first appeared in Ottoman land surveys. Urban people willing to make profitable investments acquired muqata'a lands. For them, profitability was a decisive factor, and when such muqata'a lands proved to be profitable, producing such marketable crops as rice, cotton, and sesame, as well as favorably located for transportation, they usually found lessees among city-dwelling investors. In Vidin, there was nothing new in this respect. What was new was that in the period 1760–1850, Central European markets began to offer higher prices for the agricultural products of this Danubian province with easy transportation possibilities.[33] The vast uncultivated arable land belonging to the treasury now became an attractive investment area. The treasury, however, leased the land only to the Muslim *agha*s since the area was a strategically sensitive one. Such landholdings, each comprising the entire area of a village was called a çiftlik. According to one document,[34] the Christian peasants did not have land in their possession because the Vidin province was located on the frontier and the Muslim population consisted of only a few thousand. So, in order to encourage their concern with the safe-keeping of the fortress of Vidin, each village in the area was given with a tapu to an agha, notable or commander of a garrison unit. Furthermore, a special regulation forbade the sale of the miri lands to Christian peasants.

Another innovation in the system was the growing tendency to consolidate possession rights of the aghas on the muqata'a lands, thereby making them actual proprietors. This tendency was reinforced by the liberal views on land ownership introduced by the reformers of the nineteenth century under Western influence. When, in 1839, the Rescript of Tanzimat abolished *corvée*,[35] the Bulgarian peasants did not want to perform *corvée* services which actually were regarded as corresponding to rent. The aghas argued that the rent was to be remitted, because the Ottoman subjects are "lawful possessors and proprietors (*malik ve mutasarrıf*) of their land, no one can occupy and cultivate someone else's land without consent and compensation."

It was through renting from the aghas that the Christian peasants were able to obtain and cultivate the land on these çiftliks. On the other hand, the lands still directly under state control were farmed out, first to tax farmers who, as a kind of middlemen, rented them to the peasants. Thus, in both cases peasants were simple rent-paying tenants. After the declaration of the Tanzimat reforms in 1839, the state tried to stop the sale by tapu of state lands to aghas. The Sultan's special order was required for such sales to be valid, but still the aghas managed to obtain possession of twenty villages after that date. Also, conversion of commons, pasture land, and forest areas (the possession of which was acquired by the tapu system) into çiftlik land seems to have gained momentum during this period.

The rent on the aghas' çiftlik lands or *ücret-i arazi* was not a simple rent but involved various payments and services which were actually the combination of some old feudal customs. The peasant had to perform for the agha *corvée* services for two months a year, and deliver a certain portion of his produce, namely 25 *okka* or 31 kg from each crop he grew, 30–40 okka of maize per cart, one okka cheese for every ten sheep in addition to one cartload of wood or 12 guruş instead, and 3/10 guruş per dönüm of vineyard.

There were additional dues paid to aghas for beehives, pasture land, etc. The total sum of all the payments made by the peasant was estimated to be equal to or even greater than the taxes paid to the state. The obligations established by custom for the stewards or agents of the aghas were to be added to all this. In sum, the so-called *aghalık* or *gospodarlık* regime in the Vidin region was characterized by a combination of the new çiftlik system with the old Ottoman feudal customs. The continuation of the feudal services and dues made the conditions particularly onerous for the peasants of this region. The Bulgarian *knezes*, notables who coveted the position of Muslim aghas on the prospering çiftliks, provided leadership for peasant rebellions in the region in the 1840s. The peasant protest was primarily against *corvée* services, and feudal customs and dues in particular, since the declaration of the Tanzimat reforms promised to put an end to the old Ottoman regime throughout the empire.

The reaction of the Tanzimat administration to the situation is particularly interesting. The administration first abolished the corvée. The aghas protested, however, arguing that they had the ownership of the land, and the *corvées* corresponded to the rent (*hakk-ı arazi*). The government asked both sides to come to an agreement. The aghas were not willing to give up a source of labor without which çiftliks could not continue. The ultimate goal of the peasants and even more so of the knezes was to get possession of land which originally belonged to the state. For these reasons, a real reform could not be worked out. Only the *corvée* service for cultivation was abolished in return for an increase in the proportion of the produce to be delivered to the agha. The Tanzimat administration, under the influence of the western view of land possession and proprietory rights, eventually espoused the view of the çiftlik owners, while the Christian reaya were aware of the original state ownership of the çiftlik lands. In other words, Tanzimat liberalism, though against the *corvée*, confirmed and reinforced the rights of the landowners on land. Under the Tanzimat, the old Ottoman tapu system or leasing state lands on a permanent basis was in the process of turning these lands into real property for the aghas. Later, the hereditary rights on such lands were further extended and the aghas' exploitation of peasant labor worsened. In 1850, a government report[36] confessed that the aghas "reduced the peasant almost to slavery" on their çiftliks. The inspector sent to investigate the situation proposed as the only radical reform to prevent the renewal of the insurrection, the abolition of the gospodarlik regime and the leasing of the land to the peasants. The down-payment (*muaccele*) made by them would be used to compensate the dispossessed aghas. The proposal became law, but the government confirmed the state's proprietary rights on all such lands. As under the tapu system, the peasant was now to acquire permanent tenancy rights by making a preliminary down-payment (muaccele). This simply meant the return to the old çift-hane system, and the replacement of the aghas by the reaya on state lands.

The reaya, however, did not want to recognize the state's rights either, and claimed a pure and simple transfer of the land without having to pay any rent or lease money. These details from the Vidin region can illustrate how explosive the social implications of the çiftlik system were in the Ottoman Empire.

Christo Gandev, who studies the çiftlik regime in the same area through local sources from the *kadı* court records of Vidin, gives more details about the internal organization of the çiftlik and the relationship between the Christian farmers and Muslim landowners.[37] According to the more typological interpretation of this historian, the new çiftlik system which emerged in this region under the economic incentive of the central European market by the second half of the eighteenth century had all the characteristics of a "capitalist mode of exploitation." In other words, the new çiftliks were created by urban investors of every social background with the purpose of producing export crops for the Austrian market. The uncultivated state lands or waste lands were bought, and transformed into freehold properties. The labor force was supplied by the growing numbers of landless proletarianized peasants who worked in the çiftliks as paid agricultural workers or sharecroppers. Seasonal wage labor was also hired at harvest time. Profit being the only concern of these capitalist landlords, the rent was increased and inferior working conditions were imposed upon the workers, while in the typically feudal çiftliks, regulations and customs put restrictions on the exploitation of labor. The agricultural workers on the new "capitalist" çiftliks constituted a mass of serfs cruelly oppressed and exploited. In the Vidin region, Gandev continues, the average size of a çiftlik varied between 30 and 500 hectares. Besides the landlord's mansion and a large courtyard, a typical çiftlik included shacks for workers, storehouses, stables, mills, slaughterhouses, presses, and other facilities. On these çiftliks, the number of oxen for ploughing varied from five to twelve, while large herds of sheep, cattle, and horses were bred. Thus, the new "capitalist" type çiftlik was a plantation-like farm in its purpose and organization.

Gandev's observations on the organization of the çiftlik in terms of physical arrangement, employment, and the relationship between landlord and labor suggest similar features in the çiftliks in Rumelia and Anatolia. But I can not agree with his theory about the origin and evolution of the new çiftliks which were due more to the transformation of miri and muqata'a than reclamation of new lands.

Postscriptum

In his important paper based mainly on French consular reports, Gilles Veinstein rightly emphasizes that "if the two ayan (Kara Osmanoğlu Mustafa and Araboğlu) indeed owed their fortune to wheat and cotton, this was not because they were producers. Rather, according to Consul Charles de Peyssonnel, they profited due to their status as administrative and fiscal authorities, as governors. Neither here nor elsewhere in his dispatches does the consul show them to be the propietors of vast çiftliks employing a servile labor force or even of large-scale feudal-type "domains" specializing in export crops in response to European trade, as they are sometimes portrayed."[38] Yuzo Nagata's article[39] on the çiftliks of the Kara Osmanoğlu family came only one year after Veinstein's.[40]

The list of the çiftliks privately owned by Mustafa's successor Hüseyin Kara Osmanzade did not, of course, include the state-owned lands under tax farming (*miri muqata'a*s); but they still amounted to a large landed property, obviously organized, at least in part, into certain farms in several villages, the organization of which appears quite different from the traditional peasant family farm.

I still fully agree with Veinstein on the point that Mustafa Kara Osmanzade, founder of the family fortune, called by Peyssonnel as "the richest and the most greedy of the Ottoman Empire,"[41] owed his fortune mainly not to the production of his çiftliks but to his financial operations as usurer, tax-farmer and controller of trade between European merchants and Turkish producers.

While Veinstein says that "we must definitely dispense with the image of these aghas as large landlords"[42] and distinguishes them from the ayans of Rumeli (those of Serez)[43] they nevertheless can be compared, in their capacity to control land and production—and trade—under the system of *muqata'a-iltizam*, with the ayans in the other parts of the empire. In the rest of his paper, Veinstein gives ample evidence of this from the reports of de Peyssonnels.

The second important point Veinstein makes on the basis of the evidence provided by the French consular reports covering the period 1748–1778 is that the increasing importance for the rising cotton industries in France of the cotton of Western Anatolia, in addition to the traditional wheat exports, constituted the basis of the economic-financial activities and wealth and power of these ayans.[44]

It is safe to say that in the eighteenth century changes were definitely taking place, under the impact of Europe, in certain coastal areas of the Ottoman Empire, which ultimately led to the reorganization of agrarian production. I believe the evidence supplied by the French consular reports do not contradict but rather confirm the characteristics of these changes which we tried to demonstrate in our paper.

Also, mention should be made of a typical situation which Veinstein stresses in his paper. It is extremely interesting to observe through consular reports the peculiar conflict of interest between the ayans who were trying to maintain their control or "monopoly" on the export trade of principal staples—cotton and wheat—from Western Anatolia and the French who were trying to break this "monopoly" by attempting to penetrate into the producing areas in order to buy these goods at lower rates.[45] At times, the French tried to reach their goal by approving the Porte's centralization policies against the ayans. But, in general, foreign trading nations found the ayans more cooperative and useful for their trade for the very reasons the Porte had allowed them to survive. In other words, the ayans had a long term interest and concern in protecting agriculture and trade in their respective areas while governors and tax-farmers with short-term tenure were, as a rule, trying to realize quick gains without being concerned with long-term prosperity of the area under their authority.

Undoubtedly, the key mechanism which gave the ayans their share of control in foreign trade in agricultural products was the muqata'a-iltizam system. Now, we all agree on this point. The real struggle among the ayans centered around the question of who was getting the muqata'as in an area.[46]

2

On the Çiftlik Debate

Gilles Veinstein

We wish to discuss the various ways of analyzing the genesis, nature and socioeconomic significance of *çiftlik*s in the Ottoman Empire, meaning by çiftlik an extensive arable holding, one of its usages in Ottoman terminology.[1] In fact, some of these modes of analysis are recent, others older, but they were all elaborated largely by scholars who were not "Ottomanist" historians. These views were put forth at an early stage of historical research in the field and these scholars had at the time very limited documentation at their disposal. They were tempted to generalize on the basis of scattered data, and were not always aware of the true significance of the data or of the complexity of the problems involved in the analysis. We intend to confront these stimulating, but probably premature, "theories" with both the findings of recent historical research and our understanding of deeper Ottoman realities. For the time being this confrontation is at most a first approximation, since historical research on the subject has really only just begun. Many documents need still to be located and studied before we can get a more precise and complete view of the phenomenon.

The first such theory may be styled the Marxist theory. In this view, the emergence of the çiftlik on the ruins of the old *timar* system is interpreted as the passage from feudalism to capitalism in agriculture. This would be an instance in the Ottoman context of the general process affecting modern societies. A concrete illustration of this view was provided in a study that the Bulgarian historian Gandev devoted to the çiftliks of the Vidin area in the eighteenth century on the basis of documents from the *sicils* of the concerned *kadıs*.[2] The accent was put first on the changes in the social origin of the new landholders, urban capitalists taking the place formerly occupied by landed seigniors, and secondarily on the new relationship between the landowners and the peasantry—*reaya*. The reaya was no longer a freeholder subjected to a rent payment, but had become a proletarianized wage-laborer (*valet de ferme*).

A second kind of interpretation shares many features with the first, but the accent is shifted: trade opportunities, which was merely one factor in addition to the local factors in the Marxist scheme, is now seen as the very origin of the constitution of the çiftlik. In this view, the growing needs of central and western Europe for certain commodities such as corn, rice, maize, and cotton led Ottoman landlords to look for ways to maximize their profits, and to get rid of the old forms of land tenure and agricultural labor in favor of more intensive and more market-oriented production. Their efforts resulted in a phenomenon very similar to the second serfdom evolving in the same period in Germany east of the Elbe, Poland, and Bohemia, characterized by large-scale monoculture, and harsh enserfment of peasants. This view was based originally on geographical studies of the Balkans, especially those of Busch-Zantner.[3] It was subsequently asserted by Stoianovich, Braudel, and Sadat.[4] As Braudel stated categorically: "Cereal-growing in Turkey, as in the Danube provinces or in Poland, when linked to a huge export trade, created from the first the conditions leading to the 'second serfdom' observable in Turkey."[5] More recently, Wallerstein's "peripheralization theory" gave a new boost to this conception of the 1950s and 1960s. Here too, the emergence of the Ottoman çiftlik is considered as the result of the integration of Ottoman agriculture in the capitalist world-economic system of modern times. It is a consequence of the trade of western Europe, center of the system, with the Ottoman Empire acting as one of its peripheries. Several articles by Wallerstein, Keyder, İslamoğlu and Keyder, and Sunar are examples of this interpretation.[6] The "second serfdom" theory and the "peripheralization theory" have two major implications: not only does the çiftlik present the character of a rationalized and export-oriented exploitation (which had already been postulated by Marxist theory), but the factors of its genesis are purely external, the impact of international trade being the necessary and sufficient condition for its emergence.

However, when dealing with the "çiftlik debate," we should not ignore a third set of interpretations, much older in its origins, which may be labelled the "Ottomanist theory" since it was first expressed by Ottoman chroniclers and political thinkers themselves and exerted a great influence on Ottomanist historians until the present day. According to this analysis, the emergence of the çiftlik is the product of the corruption of the classical Ottoman institutions related to the timar system. This idea was first expressed by Ottoman writers like Selaniki, Ali, Ayn-i Ali, Koçi Bey, Sarı Mehmed Pasha, and the unknown author of the *Kitab-i Müstetab*.[7] It is more or less present through the works of different contemporary historians such as İnalcık, Akdağ, Cvetkova, Özkaya, even if their explanations of the subversion of the ancient order are not always the same. Furthermore, the "Ottomanist theory" may be combined with the Marxist one, as for instance in Cvetkova's work.[8] This theory is concerned not so much with the socioeconomic nature and significance of the phenomenon as with its genesis, which it treats in terms of purely internal factors, and with its institutional implications. The emergence of çiftlik corresponds to the transformation of the former state land (*miri*), traditionally allocated under special conditions simultaneously to reaya as holdings (*çift*) and to state officers as prebends (tımar), to large freehold properties or quasi-properties in the hands of a newly emerging stratum of private individuals. This process is stigmatized as an illegal one, a disruption of the ancient order, linked to the various crises of the Empire in its late period.

To evaluate the different assumptions in the three sets of interpretations mentioned above, several questions must be examined: what do we know about the genesis of the çiftliks, in particular about the role of internal and external factors operating in the process and its presumably illegal character? What can we learn from the documents about the çiftliks themselves, their size, location, chronology, and organization? Finally, what can we establish about the assumed connection between the çiftliks and the export trade of the Empire?

Genesis of the *Çiftlik*s

We must not consider the formation of the çiftliks in too general a way. There were in fact multiple processes, different in their characters and results. We may start by distinguishing three possible origins of a çiftlik. The tımars contained within them a large number of reaya holdings. The çiftlik could be constituted top-down, by transforming the tımar (one or several) into a çiftlik. Or it could be constituted from the bottom-up, by consolidating a certain number of çifts. In the latter case, the çiftlik proprietor remained subject to the tımar-holder.

İnalcık has recently drawn attention to a third possible source, very important and completely different in its nature.[9] It was a tradition of the Ottoman Empire, as well as of previous Islamic states, to allot to wealthy individuals—predominantly members of the ruling elites—large, waste, or abandoned (*mevat*) lands. They were state-owned lands not then in the possession of the reayas and not under cultivation. They did not belong to the land tenure system generally utilized—miri lands, the tımar, the *çift-hane*. In exchange for these grants, the beneficiaries had to undertake the necessary improvements such as irrigation works. From the state's point of view, the aim of the operation was land reclamation (*ihya*, or *şenlendirme*). Consequently, the big estates originating from this process were by no means illegal appropriations. On the contrary, they were granted by the sultan by way of official acts: appropriation acts (*temlikname*) and delimitation acts (*sınırname*). When not awarded as freehold properties, they were given as farms (*muqata'a*) with perpetual leases. Furthermore, the phenomenon had nothing to do with the decay of the old system since it was from the beginning outside of it. The practice existed as far back as the fifteenth century, but it survived and even developed during the whole of Ottoman history. İnalcık described a very significant project for rice cultivation in Anatolia, near the village of Yenice, proposed by two statesmen in the position of contractors, Feridun Ahmed and Sokullu Mehmed Pashas, in the second half of the sixteenth century.[10] Other examples of this practice no doubt will be discovered by further research in the archives. I have come across in the *defter*s concerning the Ottoman North Black Sea provinces in the same century a striking extension and even systematization of this practice.[11] In this area, where the Porte confronted rich but uncultivated and sparsely populated vast lands, such çiftliks were multiplied. In 1542, we find eighteen çiftliks of this kind around Kefe. But it was in the low Dniestr valley, around Akkerman, that this method of colonization was by far the most developed. In 1570, the *kaza* of Akkerman contained 193 of these çiftliks. They were very large exploitations, subdivided over time between several holders, the extent of whose holdings were regularly fixed by certificates (*hüccets*) of the kadı. The beneficiaries, all Muslims, belonged to widely varying categories: officers and soldiers of the local garrisons, local or external agents of the state (including one pasha, some individuals related to pashas, and an interpreter of the Porte), Tartar chiefs, as well as *ulama*, craftsmen, and the population of surrounding villages. These beneficiaries had to pay an annual "çiftlik tax" (*resm-i çiftlik*) as well as the normal dues on production. The actual agricultural work was probably performed by peasants settled on the çiftlik itself or in the neighborhood, in the form of sharecropping. In some cases the relatives of the holder temporarily employed nomads or slaves did the work.

Certain developments of the eighteenth and early nineteenth centuries that were commonly considered as a novelty of their periods and consequently interpreted as a product of the evolution of the Empire are in fact not essentially different from these earlier practices, even if they were stimulated by the contemporaneous expansion of central European markets. For instance, the çiftliks of the Vidin area in the eighteenth century described by Gandev, which he called "çiftliks" proper as opposed to "villages seigneuriaux", were in fact very similar to the çiftliks of the North Black Sea steppes. They too were regularly established by an official act in marginal lands included in sultanic or vizierial hass outside of the çift-hane system, in favor of more or less the same kind of mainly urban individuals. İnalcık correctly understood the nature of these Bulgarian large landholdings of the eighteenth century, which did not depend on the destruction of the "feudal order," since the same practice existed already at the apogée of this order, albeit external to it.[12] Moreover, İnalcık argues that the çiftliks closest to the "theoretical picture" of these big estates have to be linked not so much to the late evolution of the Ottoman land tenure system as to this permanent method of land reclamation: "Large agricultural lands organized as production units under a single ownership and management and usually producing for market came into being mostly on mevat . . . outside the areas under çift-hane system."[13]

Nevertheless, çiftliks also appeared in the framework of the old Ottoman land tenure system as a result of its corruption, although in these cases the final product seems to have kept some features of the previous structures and consequently would provide a less perfect final result. A common view among Ottoman observers and modern historians is that çiftliks were constituted at a relatively late period, starting from the end of the sixteenth and beginning of the seventeenth centuries, by dispossession of the peasants. The çiftlik owners accumulated in their hands a number of çifts formerly cultivated and possessed by the reayas. This evolution, whatever means might have been used, must have been a usurpation, i.e., an illegal process, since according to the law (kanun), the reaya holdings, transferrable to the heirs of the legitimate owners in an indivis manner, could in no way be alienated. As McGowan reminds us, the kanun forbade "that reaya holdings be sold, given away or willed in gift, left in trust, loaned, pawned in return for a loan, leased, exchanged or transferred to a neighbor of a deceased reaya on a preferential basis."[14] This model which I shall discuss below, is undoubtedly valid, but there were aberrations—cases in which the gathering of çifts under single ownership does not seem to have been illegal at all.

First, as McGowan himself emphasized, most of what was in principle forbidden by the kanun concerning the alienation of the çift was in fact tolerated, as long as it was done with the knowledge and permission of the responsible *timariot* on whom the çift in question depended, i.e., if the operation was made *be marifet-i sipahi* or *sahib-i arz*.[15] As Faroqhi pointed out, "this arrangement could lead to a fairly active land market, where debts not infrequently caused the sale of agricultural land."[16] A possible illustration of such a mechanism, was an important çiftlik constituted *marifet-i sipahi ile* by a rich Jew of Avlonya (Albania) Çaçari David, in the late 1560s: it included no less than twenty-eight fields (*tarla*) one of them bought from the son of Hasan Çelebi, as well as several vineyards and orchards. Half of this çiftlik was duly transferred to his son as a gift, with the agreement and validation of the local kadı.[17] Moreover this application of the classical law paved the way to further enlargement of the *sipahi's hassa çiftlik* by appropriation of reaya holdings located on his own tımar.[18] The rigid provisions of the çift status could be evaded legally with the agreement of the tımar-holder under certain circumstances; furthermore, these provisions did not apply to all situations. In principle, the çift being the property of the state, the reaya had only usufructuary rights (*tasarruf*) on his land, with all the limitations mentioned above. However we sometimes encounter in Anatolia, even in early periods, arable fields designated as freehold properties (*mülk tarla*). Barkan noted this puzzling phenomenon, apparently contradictory to the Ottoman land regime, as did Faroqhi in the context of Ankara and Kayseri regions at the end of the sixteenth and the beginning of the seventeenth centuries. Being mülks, these fields could be freely sold and bought by anyone in a position to do so. The origins of this development have not yet been elucidated, and Faroqhi, suspecting a connection with proximity to urban areas, wondered whether it "was of purely local importance, or whether parallel developments (could) be encountered in the districts surrounding other large trading cities."[19]

In the case of Crete, the presence of mülk tarlas, as well as the inclusion of tarlas and çiftliks among the items registered by the kadıs in probate inventories—a way of legitimating their character of freehold properties—are obviously related to the special land tenure system of this late Ottoman conquest, where the concept of miri land was categorically rejected, in order, so they argued, to return to the true Islamic conception.[20]

Furthermore, reaya land did not consist entirely of arable soil—of fields whose possession was reduced to usufructuary rights. It also included other categories of land such as orchards and vineyards, which everywhere and always had a status of freehold properties and consequently could be legally sold. In certain districts where commodities like olive oil, fruits, wine, and silk were predominant, often a type of large estate had already been constituted on a perfectly legal basis by consolidating small units at a quite early period. Such a development can be found, for example, in the 1560s in the Avlonya area, where well-to-do Jews collected several vineyards in their hands.[21] In the eighteenth century there were many examples of large-scale land patrimony originating from the same category of land. For instance, in 1757 the biggest part of the landed interests of a Panayot Benakis, the famous *kocabaşı* of Kalamata, were made of fifty-seven gardens (*bahçe*) amounting to a total of 57 hectares, including olive trees, orchards, and mulberry trees (to which later on he added an additional eleven "çiftlik" villages).[22] Stoianovich mentions the similar case of Çey (or Çay) bey of Coron, in the Morea, who possessed nearly half the olive groves of the territory of Coron in the eighteenth century.[23] The land holdings of Müridoğlu Hacı Mehmed Agha around Edremid, in the land of olives, described by Faroqhi in this volume, belonged to the same category.

A dispossession of the reayas, then, could come about in the framework of the classical land regime without violation of its conventions, nor was it always a late development linked to its decay.

Nevertheless, we should not discard the commonly held opinion expressed by the Ottoman authors mentioned above that starting from the end of the sixteenth and the beginning of the seventeenth centuries the sipahis themselves and other powerful individuals (usually among the military class, including the *kapı kulu*) took advantage of the circumstances to usurp the reaya land, the çifts themselves, as well as the pastures, woods, and other lands customarily used by villagers in common. In these cases, the process was definitely illegal; the Porte condemned it through its edicts and sent *fermans* to the kadis to forbid them to make certificates (hüccets) legitimating these practices.[24] As a matter of fact, McGowan distinguished two forms of dispossession: the first case was "titular dispossession" which "leaves the cultivator in place but generally imposes new and harsher conditions upon him." In this form the reaya had to satisfy not only, as before, the demands of the state and the timariot but also those of a newcomer called *sahib-i alaka* (interested party) or more explicitly *sahib-i çiftlik* (possessor of the çiftlik). A second case was that of a "physical dispossession," a seizure of holdings left vacant by the flight of peasants, for one reason or another, or by the compulsory expulsion of the reayas. New cultivators, recruited among fugitives, worked the land under new and worsened conditions, different from the traditional reaya status.[25] These evolutions are explicitly described by contemporary sources, in particular the *adaletname* of 1609 published by İnalcık, or the *Kitab-ı Müstetab*.[26]

To explain the two crucial factors—flight and migration of the peasants and the consequent vacancy of land as well as the growing freedom of action of local potentates—we must unravel a complex of interacting elements connected with the various crises undergone by the Empire during the period. The fiscal crisis of the state—due to the increase in military expenses, the fall of war profits, and some economic developments, such as the fall of customary profits in the Middle East as a consequence of the increasing competition of new trade routes, and the impact of American silver—led to the debasement of currency, inflation, and ultimately overtaxation of the reayas by the state, the local governors, and the sipahis. Faced with such indebtedness, the peasant was compelled to surrender his tenure and to flee; if not, he was at least ready, after having pawned his çift or having sold it, to alienate his rights in exchange for the privilege of remaining on his land and obtaining the protection of a local notable against new exactions.

The political crisis of the empire was also a factor. The weakening of the central power and of its control over both its local representatives and the local potentates, greatly favored the general trend toward overtaxation. It became impossible for the reaya to fight against abuses, exactions, usurpations; flight once again remained the only viable response.

The effects of the military crisis could be observed at different levels. On the one hand, the disturbances created by the war had the same result as indebtedness: flight of the peasants or their seeking the protection of their local potentates. On the other hand, changes in the technology of war played a role in the departure of reayas: as a consequence of the obsolescence of the old sipahi army and the need for new troops with firearms (especially infantry), the state let young reayas enter in the army. The attractiveness of these new possibilities for the landless and even for the young peasants with landholdings contributed strongly to the vacating of reaya land. According to İnalcık, who emphasized this cause of desertion ignored by more traditional accounts, "the more direct and effective factor drawing peasants away from agriculture in this period [i.e., end of the sixteenth and beginning of the seventeenth centuries] seems to be government's increasing demand for mercenary men."[27] In addition, the negative effects of this phenomenon were supplemented by the unrest that these new troops (called *sekban* or *saruca*) provoked in the countryside when dismissed after the campaigns: they became uncontrolled troops (*kapusız levend*) and harassed the peasantry. The *celali* movement which gave rise to the great flight (*büyük kaçgun*) of the peasants in Anatolia at the turn of the century, has to be discussed in the light of this mechanism.[28]

More controversial but also important in the process through which the old reaya lands became available were demographic factors, particularly the apparent demographic catastrophe of the seventeenth century, the extent of which has not yet been precisely calculated.

Some of the factors creating new conditions in the countryside and providing opportunities for usurpations of the reaya land were perennial in the years of Ottoman decay, from the end of the sixteenth to the nineteenth century, whereas others were more closely linked to the effects of wars and their impact was more conjunctural. There is no doubt that the troubles of the celali period, the wars against Austria at the end of the seventeenth century, and the wars against Russia at the end of the eighteenth century paved the way for particularly great waves of flight and dispossession of the peasantry, as described above.

What about the specific characters of the çiftliks built on the basis of the usurped reaya land? At least at the end of the sixteenth century—for instance, through the stipulations of the already cited adaletname of 1609—because of the general shortage of labor, çiftlik owners frequently turned to livestock raising, using slaves or hirelings. Nevertheless, both then and later, when we consider the units devoted strictly to arable production that were constituted by the consolidation of former reaya holdings, the question remains whether the old structure was totally transformed by the emergence of new relations of production and a complete reorganization of labor within the framework of the large landholding, or whether, on the contrary, the previous çift-hane system survived, merely altered by an aggravation of the peasants' burden. Gandev himself admitted that in the "seigniorial villages" originating from peasant holdings (to be distinguished from the genuine çiftliks established on marginal lands), there was no substitution of capitalist for feudal relations but only a worsening of the previous feudal relations.[29] In the example of the Serbian çiftliks described by Stoianovich, the çiftlik owner appeared only as a new claimant beside the traditional timariot. The peasant had to pay him, outside of the labor services, a second tenth (to be more precise, a ninth) called *deveto* collected by the *çiftlik sahibi* or by his agents, "on the portion of the crop that was left after the payment of the tenth to the local holder of the state benefice or tımar." Stoianovich concludes: "One of the main grievances of the Serbs against the Ottoman administration at the opening of the Serbian insurrection of 1804 was against the deveto."[30]

On the other hand, many çiftliks may have emerged without an exceptional economic incentive. The opportunity for usurpation created by the internal crises of the Empire, even if these crises may have had some external causes, is sufficient to account for their appearance. In McGowan's words: "the prevailing level of revenues was quite enough to justify the struggle," without resorting to the rise in external market demand to explain the development.[31]

In the case of the çiftliks generated by the subversion of the crumbling tımar system, usurpation took place not at the level of the reaya holding but at the level of the former prebendal unit. The initial prebends were called "hass," "*zeamets*," and "tımars" according to their respective size. In the classical system they were only conditional, non-hereditary possessions closely linked to the fulfilment of a fixed duty. Now, in total disregard of the law, they were transformed into a more secure form of tenure, becoming private property *de jure* or *de facto*.

Some historians such as Cvetkova, emphasized the particular importance of this development in the emergence of the çiftliks:

> The transformation of the old military fiefs into private, hereditary domains were the basis upon which the *çiftliks*—the new forms of feudal landed property in the conditions of emergent capitalist relations—would later come into being.[32]

At the origin of this evolution, we find the same general causes, expressed in the formula of financial, political, and military crises, which have already been mentioned, to explain the dispossession of the reaya. However, there were, in addition, factors in the process under consideration that involved state responsibility directly.

Due to the growing place of venality and of all kinds of abuses in the attribution of the timars, these prebends were no longer held by competent, deserving persons and tended to lose their military character. Moreover, a great part of the timars reverted to the Treasury to be transformed into hass retained by the Sultan or offered as appanages or property grants (*arpalık* or *başmaklık*) to members of the ruling elite or to people close to the court, without any military or administrative responsibilities. On the other hand, Kunt draws attention to another state practice, one that went against the rationale of the prebendal system, which was known as early as the end of the fifteenth century but which seems to have become much more common by the end of the sixteenth century: the granting to some governors of a small part of their hass as permanent estates or, to translate the expression in use, "as an estate" (ber vech-i çiftlik), which the holder retained after leaving his office. He probably kept such a çiftlik throughout his lifetime, though he may not have been able to pass it on to his heirs.[33]

Following the comments of Koçi Bey and other observers of Ottoman decay, historians denounced these practices as the origins of the decline of the tımar army, until then the backbone of the Ottoman military power. However, these developments should be considered as more consequence than cause. The obsolescence of the sipahis, who proved to be unable to adapt themselves to the new conditions of war, encouraged the Treasury to take over a part of the tımars (only a part, since the system did continue to exist into the nineteenth century), the usefulness of which had become doubtful. In the meantime this massive transfer of revenues yielded the funds necessary to pay the new troops which were better able to meet the Habsburgs' military challenge.

To understand how the hass of the Treasury and other prebends assigned to pashas, beys or other officials tended to become quasi-property in private hands, one must consider the widespread application of the farming-out (iltizam) system in the collection of these has revenues. The reasons for this practice, according to İnalcık, were mainly "the technical, economic and bureaucratic difficulties . . . the government had to come to grips with in controlling and collecting the tax revenues."[34] A new development decisively strengthened the power of the leaser (mültezim) on the land and populations. This was a category of life-term tax-farms, established in 1695 for a better management of the resources, termed "malikane."[35] Not only did the leaseholder have total freedom of management during his life, but after his death the Treasury gave preferential rights to his heirs in the bidding, which tended to confer a quasi-hereditary character to these malikanes.[36] Under these conditions the transformation of the prebends into farmed-out units (muqata'as) and especially into life-term farms was generally considered as a major factor of the emergence of the çiftliks. İnalcık expressed this opinion strongly:

This new practice known as mālikāne virtually gave the mültezims quasi-proprietary rights over extended territories, villages included. Thus, the mālikāne system made a major contribution to the rise of a new landlord class with the rights, as free holders, over large tracts of state lands (*mīrī*), and it is in this practice that one has to look for the origins of the *çiftlik* system, and the rise of the village *aghas* (landlords) and the renowned eighteenth century dynasties with large *muḳāṭa'a* estates in their holding.[37]

In later studies, as previously mentioned, İnalcık points out other possible sources of çiftliks, in particular the legal attributions of mevat lands. Moreover, in a further stage of his work he appeared fully conscious that the estates originating from an appropriation of the former prebends did not necessarily represent a radical change in the previous agricultural structure and consequently did not correspond to the ideal scheme of the çiftlik. In this respect he established a distinction between the appanages (muqata'as, and malikanes) on the one hand, and the genuine plantation-like çiftlik on the other, "since the appanages were simply the fiscal administrative rearrangement in the possession of the lands which did not necessarily bring about a change in the çift-hane system." In the first type of estates:

> The *çift-hāne* system continued to prevail and the relationship between the farmer-*re'āyā* and private individuals . . . was the same as under the *tīmār*-system. As before the new-comers were simply collectors of the rent in the form of dues, and as a rule did not attempt to reorganize the labor and the production on these lands[38].

So he came to the same conclusion already drawn for the çiftliks born from the appropriation of the reaya land. In both cases, when çiftliks came into existence, one need not resort to market factors to explain their development. The prevailing level of rents as well as the possibility of making these revenues permanent were sufficient inducement.

The çiftlik, when it was established, did not tend in fact to correspond to a plantation-like estate. Moreover, it is somewhat problematic that most malikanes even evolved into çiftliks. When we assert that the malikane naturally led to a situation of quasi-property, we tend to omit the fact that these life-term tax-farms were generally not managed directly by the recipient, but were in return granted to secondary mültezims. Under these circumstances who were the agents of their transformation into property, the former or the latter? The secondary mültezims, drawn from among the local notables and in direct contact with the land, seem to have been in a better position to operate this appropriation. As a matter of fact, the dynasties of ayans mentioned above were mostly these secondary mültezims. The initial ones were more likely to belong to the ruling elite and to the favorites

of the Court remaining in the capital. However, as was not the case
with the initial leases, their leaseholds were extremely short and unstable. This fact is illustrated by the example of Kara Osmanoğlu Hacı
Mustafa in the Manisa area by the middle of the eighteenth century
who had to struggle each year to retain his muqata'as, and was not
always successful. He confronted all sorts of obstacles, compelled to
fight at one and the same time against the malikane holder, his competitors, and the reaya who complained to the Porte about his abuses
and attempts of usurpation.[39] All these factors lead us to calculate
that a change in the status of the malikane was not so easy to achieve,
and it remains uncertain how much change had occurred in this
regard before the fundamental Ottoman land law was promulgated in
1858.

To conclude, the genesis of the çiftliks, contrary to the "Ottomanist theory," was not always an illegal process related to the subversion of the traditional order, but could occur even at an early period in
consonance with this order, in the interstices of the village network or
even in the core of the old system. In other cases, the emergence of
the çiftliks was only a byproduct of this subversion, either by dispossession of the reaya or by the appropriation of the former prebends. In any case, the internal factors are sufficient to account for
these developments. The demands of the external market, assumed
by more recent theories, appears as a possible stimulant (we shall
come back to this point in further detail) but not as a decisive one.
Furthermore, the radical change in the relationship between owners
and workers and the reorganization of labor in the framework of the
new estates alleged by the same theories, seem to have been very
limited, since the solidity of the çift-hane system throughout the
whole period has been underestimated. In order to confirm and develop these evaluations we must now consider what we learn from
the documentation on the nature of the çiftlik itself.

Nature of the Çiftlik: Theory and Reality

The various theories concerning the nature and significance of
the çiftlik were built on the basis of an interpretation and systematization of scanty data. Recently, some empirical studies and archives
have been published, especially by McGowan, Nagata, Faroqhi, and
Cezar, but there is still much to do in this direction. The Ottoman
archives, in particular the numerous series of the registers of Muslim
courts (the sicils of the kadıs) need to be scrutinized from this point of

view. Nevertheless, at the present stage of research some discrepancies have already emerged between the results of these pioneer publications and previous theorizing.

In spite of the scarcity of the available data concerning the magnitude of the çiftliks, it appears that they were not invariably, or even predominantly, the sizeable estates they were generally assumed to be. For instance, McGowan came to the conclusion that most çiftliks of southern Europe were still small-scale in the seventeenth and eighteenth centuries. In particular, he wrote: "Studies of late Macedonian conditions show that . . . although there were some medium and large *chiftliks*, most *chiftliks* were small, 25 to 50 hectares being typical."[40] According to Kiroski's study on the çiftliks of Polog, in Macedonia, in the late nineteenth century, 46.8 percent of the çiftliks were under 25 hectares, with an average size of only 14.[41] On the other hand, McGowan calculated from a Manastır (Bitolj, Bitola) *tevzi defteri* of 1710, that at that time in this district the mean number of adult males on one çiftlik was 3.5, the modal number being 2.[42] No more than a dozen sizeable estates existed in this district.

The Bulgarian çiftliks described by Gandev were of very different sizes, between 30 and 500 hectares. The same conclusion is to be drawn from the documents published by Nagata on the big farms of western Anatolia in the eighteenth century.[43] Whereas those of Hacı Mehmed Agha, the mütesellim of Teke, varied between 700 and 13,000 dönüm with an average of 734 hectares, the çiftliks of Kara Osmanzade Hüseyin Agha, the mütesellim of Saruhan, were more modest in area, varying between 600 and 1,700 dönüm with an average of only 1,000 dönüm, or 90 hectares.

Likewise, what we discover about the commodities produced in these çiftliks does not correspond to the theoretical picture of market-oriented production exclusively devoted to export crops such as cotton and tobacco. If specialization sometimes did exist, it was in those çiftliks engaged in cattle-breeding. On the contrary, the agricultural enterprises exhibited an extremely diversified production pattern, where commodities for consumption such as wheat, barley, maize, and fruits, played a predominant part. That is true for the Bulgarian çiftliks described by Gandev as well as for the west Anatolian ones documented by Nagata. It is to be noticed that in 1816, among the total of 9,650 dönüm owned by Kara Osmanzade Hüseyin Agha, only 279 dönüm or 2.9 percent, were devoted to cotton (*pembe tarlası*), 10 dönüms of them remaining uncultivated. Furthermore, one is struck by the importance of unexploited arable land (*hali tarla*) in these estates, which consequently can not be considered as intensively cultivated. We are aware that certain Western sources may give an entirely different impression. For instance, Stoianovich mentioned that "an İsmail bey and later his son Yusuf expanded their already extensive cotton plantation in the region of Serres," but this statement is based on a report by the French consul Félix Beaujour.[44] In the same way, Peyssonnel styled Kara Osmanoğlu at the middle of the eighteenth century as "the master of cottons" in the İzmir area.[45] We shall have to come back to the ambiguities of the consular formulations which may make them misleading. In any case, plantations of this kind are not yet documented by primary sources of Ottoman origin.

Likewise the Ottoman documents under scrutiny, which were actually very limited in number until recently, show clearly that slave labor or wage labor, either seasonal or annual, did exist in the framework of the çiftliks, (kul, hademe, and ırgad are mentioned), but were by no means the only or even the predominant forms in use. On the contrary, sharecroppers (ortakçı) working under various conditions, seldom precisely described, seem to have played a preeminent role, even in cattle-raising. As McGowan put it, "Most chiftliks of southern Europe were . . . characterized by share-cropping," and, he added, in very explicit terms, with the çiftliks of janissaries in Serbia and those of the Muslims of Bosnia in mind: "The average Balkan chiftlik was a rental operation, far closer in its character and its scale to the Grundherrschaft past from which it evolved, than to the Gutsherrschaft character which has frequently been imagined for it."[46]

The Anatolian examples of the nineteenth century also devised a great variety of solutions. The çiftliks of Kör İsmailoğlu Hüseyin in the district of Havza and Köprü included both servants (hizmetkar) and ortakçı.[47] As far as the estates of Kara Osmanzade Hüseyin Agha are concerned, İnalcık distinguished three kinds of arrangements: 1) all the produce going to the landlord, with the workers being paid in kind or in cash; 2) a mixed regime, with fields of the first type and fields rented to reaya, the rent being in kind or in cash in the form of a lump sum; 3) all the fields of the çiftlik leased to tenants. Still, he concluded that "the greatest part of the land on the majority of the çiftlik of Hüseyin was rented to the reaya or free peasants. Usually the rent was paid in kind from the produce of the land, sometimes in cash."[48]

These observations illustrate the permanence of the old pattern of relations (rent-payer/rent-receiver) in contrast to the newly-emerging capitalist relationships. Generally speaking, there is no radical transformation of the traditional status of the reaya as expressed by the çift-hane system, no reorganization of labor, and no significant intensification of production. According to McGowan, this practical conservatism explains why the Ottoman government never had to acknowledge and legitimate by official dispositions a new social and legal status for the peasants, something tantamount to the second serfdom spelled out in edicts by central European governments. Contrary to the assumption of Stoianovich and Braudel, such an evolution did not occur in the Ottoman Empire, neither *de facto* nor *de jure*.

Another postulate of the "second serfdom" as well as the "peripheralization" theories concerns the location of the çiftliks—the map of the phenomenon. It was assumed to be linked to areas directly open to the external market—coastal plains and interior basins along the routes of communications—such as Thessaly, Epirus, Macedonia, Thrace, the Maritsa valley, Danubian Bulgaria, the Kossovo-Metohija basin, the coastal plains of Albania, parts of Bosnia, and the coastal plains of southern and western Anatolia, Egypt, and Syria.[49] While this general view contains a large part of truth, it has to be tempered. When testing its value for southeastern Europe, McGowan did accept that location near the sea could be a critical factor in the diffusion of çiftliks. However, he came to the conclusion that in this area the phenomenon was in fact a two-tiered development, first in the south, later in the north: "Zones located near the Aegean, Adriatic and Black Sea shores had their *chiftliks* long before the opening of the straits," whereas "the entire north-tier, comprising Danubian Bulgaria (and parallel with it to the north, Walachia and Moldavia), as well as Serbia and Bosnia, were not much developed for other than pastoral exports . . . until after the opening of the Straits and the associated development of traffic on the Danube, or in the case of Bosnia, until the demand peak of the Napoleonic period."[50]

Moreover, a further detailed study of the various regions would show a strongly unequal development of the çiftliks as well as differences between the respective shares of internal and external markets among the factors involved. Given the internal causes of the genesis of the çiftliks it follows that many of them, either in these areas or in others much further removed from the arteries of communications, may have arisen without any connection to foreign trade or even to the market represented by a large town in the vicinity of the grower. They arose "because the opportunity for usurpation was there rather than because the market demanded their appearance" as, for instance, in the case of the pastoral holdings of the celali period.[51]

Another way to approach the basic question of the connection between market demand and the emergence of the çiftlik would be to ask whether the traditional Ottoman land system could not and actually did not coexist with the impact of foreign trade. To answer the question, let us first examine the example of the "boom" of the Turkish wheat in the years 1548–64, as described by Aymard and

Braudel.[52] During this period, a significant amount of wheat was shipped from the Ottoman Empire to Venice and Ragusa; this traffic developed within the framework of the traditional land tenure system, i.e., the tımar and çift-hane systems. Exports were supplied both by the hass of the Sultan and of various pashas, including the Grand Vizier, Rüstem Pasha, and by the reaya çifts (delli poveri according to the Venetian sources). No shifts in the structure of the estates appeared, only some internal reorganization, such as a regulation by which the state seized the opportunity to maximize its receipts by limiting strictly the shares of the exports originating from the reaya. Moreover, sometimes a priority was given to the sales from the Sultan's estates, and after 1552, all the regularly exported wheat was required to come from the state hass.[53]

This example, borrowed from the classical period, would suggest that the impact of trade was not enough by itself to provoke structural changes before the necessary historical preconditions would have allowed them. But still, by the middle of the eighteenth century we find, for instance through the reports of the French consul in İzmir, that the production of the villagers, that is to say commodities originating from the old pattern of small independent holdings worked by the reaya continued to supply the Western trade.[54] Even Stoianovich, generally not inclined to minimize the importance of the çiftliks, considered that the major part of the cotton exports from Salonika in the eighteenth century did not derive from big estates but both from the "manorial reserve" of the aghas (kantar cotton) and from the tenth levied from the smallholders (öşür cotton).[55] This connection between export trade and rent collection is another confirmation of the permanence of the traditional system.

Now if we examine in more detail the relationship between the growing class of local ayans and the export trade, we must first keep in mind that export revenues were not the only source of their fortunes. Other activities such as the farming out of state revenues, the collection of the salgun taxes, the recruiting of troops and collection of provisions and livestock for the army, credit transactions, usury were certainly at least as important. More to the point, when they did take advantage of the market, it was more in their role as deputy governors (mütesellim, voyvoda), tax collectors, and tax farmers than as producers of marketed goods. Their abuses in the collection of taxes, such as the "right of aghalık" mentioned by Peyssonnel, was a convenient way to maximize their profits.[56]

Nevertheless, they did possess çiftliks, and the existence of big estates in the hands of the Kara Osmanoğlu family, as revealed, for instance, in the documents published by Nagata, might appear to be evidence against the above expressed opinion. However, these documents pertain to the nineteenth century: 1816, for the estates of Kara Osmanzade Elhac Hüseyin Agha; 1841, for those of Kara Osmanzade Yetim Ahmed Agha.[57] In addition to that, these landed interests seem to represent only a small part of the fortune and investments of the family. For instance, the total value of Hüseyin's çiftliks, 250,000 guruş, was lower than the sum paid by his predecessor Hacı Mustafa to farm out the *voyvodalık* of Manisa for the single year 1752.[58] Moreover, these çiftliks were not primarily devoted to the production of export commodities.

Furthermore, these estates remained precarious. The ayans had to confront many discouraging obstacles in constituting their landed patrimony, among them the double opposition of the primary mültezims and the reaya in question, the complaints of the latter being abundantly documented: for instance, in February, 1755, Kara Osmanoğlu Hacı Mustafa had already leased the muqata'a of Turgutlu for four years, but the peasants were complaining about his many-sided and endless exactions and abuses. Consequently they wanted a new mültezim to be appointed, and made their own choice in favor of a certain Seyyid Mustafa.[59]

The main opposition probably came from the state itself, which seriously jeopardized the development of the çiftliks by its widespread practice of confiscations.[60] In this respect, a large part of the available descriptions of çiftliks are nothing but inventories in view of a confiscation, after the death or the punishment of the usurper, as is the case of the lists concerning Kara Osmanzade Hüseyin.[61] Not infrequently the confiscated estates were left by the state to the heirs in exchange for a cash payment (*bedel*). In other cases the various çiftliks of the deceased were sold to bidders and scattered about, as was the case in 1808 for the estates of Kör İsmailoğlu Hüseyin, the former ayan of Havza and Köprü.[62] Faroqhi has mentioned a çiftlik formerly owned by Tekelioğlu Mehmed Pasha, bought by the *tekke* of Abdal Musa in Elmalı after the punishment and death of this ayan.[63] Unavoidably, these threats had consequences for the economic behaviour of the local notables of the eighteenth and nineteenth centuries, as Western observers also noted. These ayan tended to transform their estates into inviolable pious endowments (waqf), the administration of which was passed on to their heirs according to the provisions of the donation act. Likewise there was a certain attraction to the mülk estates—for example, houses and shops in the cities— perhaps partly because these types of property did not face the same jurisdictional problems. For instance, we learn from Peyssonnel[64] that Kara Osmanoğlu Hacı Mustafa had bought "most of the houses in

İzmir." Furthermore the best way to have a chance to evade the consequences of what Olivier called "the tyrannic law of confiscations"[65]
was to invest preferentially in movables like currency, gold and silver
jewels, and precious furs and clothes, which were easier to transport
or to hide. Under these conditions, it is not surprising that the value
of the çiftliks and fields was only 19 percent of the total fortune of the
ayan of Havza and Köprü.[66]

   If the existence of çiftliks and the impact of export trade on the
Empire are two certain phenomena, their connection is much more
questionable. First, the genesis of çiftliks is much more complex than
has frequently been assumed, and the role of internal factors, not
deriving from market expansion must not be overlooked. Secondly,
the capacity for resistance and adaptability of the old agrarian structures and labor relationships was much greater in the Ottoman empire than has been imagined. And even when the çiftlik did exist, it
did not necessarily indicate a radical change in those older structures.
Conversely, export commodities were by no means always and everywhere supplied by it. These first impressions would have to be confirmed by a more extensive study of the available historical sources,
mainly the Ottoman ones.

Part II

3

Peasants, Commercialization, and Legitimation of State Power in Sixteenth-Century Anatolia*

Huri İslamoğlu-İnan

Recent research on Ottoman agriculture suggests that commercial expansion in the peasant economy did not set into motion a trend towards concentration of land or towards the formation of large estates.[1] Nor was there a general tendency toward peasant dispossession and conversion of peasants into enserfed or wage labor on large holdings. Instead, production for the market, to a large degree, took place on small plots worked by free peasants. This pattern held true for periods of commercial growth both before and after Ottoman agriculture was exposed to increased European demand for its products. In this article I will primarily deal with the response of Ottoman peasant economy in north-central Anatolia to increased commercial demand in towns and to population growth in the sixteenth century.[2] First, however, I will discuss a number of conceptual problems relating to the dynamics of Ottoman peasant economy.

A central issue confronting students of Ottoman agriculture is that of explaining the underlying mechanisms that were responsible for the persistence of independent peasantry. The explanations given derive from the high land/labor ratio and from the fiscal considerations of the state, which relied on the extraction of peasants' sur-

*A slightly different version of this article appeared under the title: "Les paysans, le marché et l'Etat en Anatolie au XVIe siècle" in *Annales E.S.C.*, XLIII, 5 (September–October 1988), 1025–44.

pluses, in the form of taxes, for its primary source of revenue.[3] I will argue that these explanations are based on an essentially economic logic and present a picture of the Ottoman state as a maximizer of revenues. The political dimension is thus reduced to a taxation function.[4] As such, the economistic view is inadequate in accounting for political mechanisms that subsumed such variables as land/labor relations, population growth, and commercial expansion, and influenced the way in which these factors affected changes in land distribution, organization of production, and labor control. Put differently, in order to understand why changes in economic factors did not lead to the dispossession of the peasantry and to the formation of large estates, we require a more adequate conception of the political logic of the Ottoman economy and society than the taxation function alone provides.

Political Authority and its Relation to the Agrarian Economy

Important to the political logic of the Ottoman system was a legitimizing notion,[5] by which I mean that state actions were informed by the belief that such actions were enforcing traditional rights and norms. Furthermore, practices of the state carried out by its agents were to a large degree supported by the consensus of the society. Hence, it is possible to detect, in the intervention of *timar*-holders in the production and appropriation of peasant surpluses, as well as in the principles underlying the organization of markets, a concern for maintaining the subsistence economy of free peasants, a concern for preventing accumulation on land through limits imposed on commercial production, and, finally, a concern for directing agricultural surpluses to specified markets so as to ensure the provisioning of non-agricultural populations. Implicit in these concerns was a paternalist world-view premised on the role of the state as dispenser of justice and perpetrator of eternal order.[6] A paternalist *weltanschauung* was universalistic in that it presupposed the application of the principle of justice to all subjects regardless of their religion or creed, and it assumed an undivided centralized polity. This world-view was embodied in legal documents and in the principal institutions of the system of revenue grants (or the *timar* system), *kadı* courts, market regulations and organization, and in the principle of the state ownership of land. These institutions are all too familiar, and I will not discuss them here,[7] but I will point to those aspects that are immediately relevant to the legitimation process.

First, it is important to note that the paternalist model in the context of the timar system describes a separation of juridical and administrative practices whereby the tımar-holders as extractors of peasants' surpluses exercised no jurisdiction over the person or the land of peasants on their timars. Such jurisdiction lay with the central state, which exercised it through a hierarchy of judges or kadıs, who were responsible for administering both the Islamic Law (*shari'a*) and the sultanic law or the *örf*. This meant that kadıs oversaw the activities of the tımar-holders and made sure that the latter did not step beyond their rights in their interaction with the peasants and performed their administrative duties in accordance with the precepts of state legal codes.[8] The presence of kadıs together with tımar-holders in a given locality was, in turn, to provide the peasants with recourse to justice. As such, the paternalist model assumed a consensus by the ruled over the principles of justice and order. Rescripts of justice, or *adalet-names*, on the other hand, provided a means through which the central state could respond to the grievances of the ruled.[9]

The second feature of the paternalist model largely derives from the consensus aspect and defines the central state as the source of legitimation. All claimants to revenues, including those who were not state officials such as the recipients of revenues from *waqf*s, pre-Ottoman ruling groups, and later the local notables (*ayan*) and tax farmers, derived their rights over peasants' surpluses from the juridical and administrative practices of the central state.[10] Juridical-ideological institutions of the state served to legitimize revenue collection in the eyes of the peasantry. The central state, however, intervened to support the claims of revenue holders provided that surpluses were produced by independent peasants. As such, from the point of view of the central state the independent peasantry not only constituted its fiscal base but also the basis of its political legitimacy.

The paternalist model I have just outlined pertains to an ideal image the political authority had of itself and of the society over which it ruled. As such, it parts company at many points with realities even in the sixteenth century when the state authority was at its zenith. Yet the model had a reality as the legitimating principle of political authority; it provided the idiom of domination and a vocabulary for political expression of different groups within the society. In this capacity the paternalist precepts manifested a certain degree of resilience in the face of changes occasioned by the internal dynamic as well as by a new world-historical dynamic after the seventeenth century. This is not to say that the legitimating principle remained stationary; it, too, was transformed and was gradually undermined especially in the eighteenth and nineteenth centuries as the Ottoman Empire was integrated into the world market and the practices of the central state under external and internal pressures increasingly contradicted its own ideal. On the other hand, the resilience of the paternalist idiom, especially in relation to rural producers, may in part be accounted for by its adherence to the right of producers to subsistence and the obligation of the political authority to ensure the conditions of that subsistence. For instance, when the central authority impinged on this right in Bulgaria during the nineteenth century, by recognizing the private property rights of Muslim *aghas* on peasant lands, the peasants rebelled and demanded a return to state ownership of land.[11] In doing so the Bulgarian peasants were expressing their right to subsistence in terms of the paternalist ideology.

At the same time, especially in the nineteenth century, it appears that the central authority, in its struggle for survival under adverse internal and external conditions, clung to the precept of preserving the subsistence economy of the peasants. Legitimacy concerns as well as fiscal considerations, and the political conflict with the landed classes dependent on the world market, played a part in this struggle. Consequently the central bureaucracy took a contradictory stance in the application of the Land Code of 1858 that was passed under British pressure.[12] On the one hand, property rights of peasants on land were codified, and titles were granted to peasant families. On the other hand, introduction of private property made the land alienable, which, if the law were fully implemented, would result in peasant dispossessions in the event of indebtedness. The central state moved to impose such customary restrictions as prohibitions on confiscation of peasant plots in cases of indebtedness, or as the reassertion of peasants' rights to own farmsteads on private property. As such the state sought to protect the peasantry from the adverse effects of commercial development. The contradictory attitude of the central bureaucracy in relation to the land code may in part explain the absence of peasant rebellions in Anatolia during the period of commercial expansion. This pattern of development is in sharp contrast to that in Egypt where the state increasingly identified with the interests of landed classes and applied the law of private property in land, and, in so doing, undermined its legitimacy in the eyes of the peasantry.[13] One consequence of the Egyptian pattern of development was the peasant uprisings in the 1870s which culminated in the British occupation. Viewed in this perspective, the ability of the Ottoman state to maintain its political independence may in part have been a result of its ability to maintain a semblance of its legitimacy vis-à-vis the rural population in the Ottoman heartlands.

To account for this specificity requires a re-formulation of the nature of political authority in the Ottoman empire. This involves a conception of state power not merely as a site of coercion or surplus extraction but as a combination of coercion and hegemony or consent, that is, the legitimacy concern.[14] Central to this conception is the assumption that state power requires consensus that both encompasses and conceals coercion. Consensus, in turn, depends on the effectivity of juridical-ideological practices that legitimate political authority.

In the Ottoman context the dominant ruling coalition of central (*Enderun*) bureaucrats, janissaries, and members of the juridical-religious scholars (*ilmiyye*) sought to reconcile the interests of peasants, merchants, artisans, tribal groupings, and pre-Ottoman ruling groups around the paternalist world view. This world view, however, had a dual focus. First, was that of Islamic precepts embodied in the Islamic Law (shari'a) which provided the organizing principles (or ideology) of social life. The second focus of the paternalist ideology was the Sultanic law (or örf); its basic premise was that the ruler was responsible for the welfare of his subjects.[15] Örf provided the organizing principle for the relationship between the rulers and the other groups in the society. But the consent of the ruled to rulers was mediated through institutions (e.g., *tarikat*s, guilds, *medrese*s, or institutions of higher learning) organized around the Islamic ideology.

Central to this complex legitimation matrix were the religious scholars (*ulama*). First, the ulama in their capacity as judicial functionaries were responsible for mediating the relationship between the ruling class and the other social groups through the application of the örf principles. Secondly, they mediated the relationships within the society in their capacity as waqf administrators, as judges responsible for the application of family law. Finally, the ulama played a role in mediating the paternalist ideology through the educational system. Thus, the ulama can be characterized as "organic intellectuals" whose activities were directed towards the reproduction of dominant social relations. The ideological unity that made possible the reconciliation of the interests of the ruling coalition with those of other classes in the society was to a great extent the result of the ulama's intellectual activities.[16]

Peripheralization undermined this scheme of legitimation of state power. First, with the centralization measures and the reforms enacted to fulfill the requirements of economic integration into the world market, came the formation of a new ruling class of bureaucrats. This class was characterized by its inability to reconcile its interests with those of other classes in the society, primarily because its very existence came to depend increasingly on global linkages and interests often in contradiction with the interests of indigenous classes. The alliance of the central bureaucracy with "foreign" merchants or their minority agents is a case in point. Concomitant with this development was the undermining of the universalistic world view that forged the interests of different groups. The new role of the central bureaucracy as an agent in facilitating the operations of the world–economy meant the adaptation of Western principles in organizing the state and its relation to the society.[17] For instance, granting of special privileges to Christian subjects through the establishment of separate commercial and penal courts came into conflict with the old organizational principle that focused on the role of the Sultan as the protector of all his subjects.[18] At the same time, in order to meet the expenses incurred by the adoption of new reform measures, the central state resorted to more coercive means of surplus extraction (or taxation).[19] Put differently, the concern of the central bureaucracy to legitimate itself within the inter-state system often came into conflict with its concern to legitimate itself inside the empire.[20] In the event that the ruling class that held state power was unable to reconcile this conflict, it resorted to "coercion."[21] Hence, it is in this context that one could talk about rule without consent, or Ottoman "despotism" that the nineteenth-century writers were so keen in observing. Again, in this historical context, one could view the "weakening" of the Ottoman state structure incumbent on the "peripheralization" process in terms of the undermining of the legitimacy of the Ottoman ruling class and of its alienation from other classes.

Consensus in this context describes the process whereby the paternalist world view spoke to the genuine aspirations and requirements of rural producers. One such aspiration was the right to subsistence. Consensus over that right largely took the form of a passive act in which the main features of the social order were accepted as givens. Yet this passive posture should not suggest that the peasantry was totally isolated from the dominant ideology and institutions and that whenever it expressed itself politically it did so in the idiom of its local cultures.[22] That is, just as the peasant economy that is centered around village communities can not be considered to be entirely autonomous of the institutions of the central state which affected patterns of production and distribution in that economy, the "local" culture of the peasantry can not be viewed as totally autonomous. The paternalist idiom and its symbols were to some degree internalized by the peasants, and as such these and not necessarily the folk forms, provided the vocabulary of resistance to the central state—as the Bulgarian case shows.

This is not to suggest, however, that the perpetuation of the independent peasantry was a smooth, non-conflictual process, given the consensus matrix and the institutional framework of surplus extraction and distribution. It involved a continual struggle on the part of the central authority to impose its administrative-juridical institutions and precepts on local claimants to revenues, especially at times of commercial expansion. The central state sought to limit commercial production to reclaimed wastelands where large estates were indeed formed,[23] and to state farms as was the case with rice production.[24] This dynamic was further complicated by the existence of organic links between groups that formed the ruling coalition and the commercial and landed interests within the society. The central bureaucracy and the ulama controlled large stretches of land and both of these groups, and the janissaries (infantry corps) participated in trade. Hence, one can not view the state as a monolithic class of surplus extractors. Not all members of the ruling coalition were at all times interested in maintaining the integrity of peasant holdings. Here, for analytical purposes, a distinction needs to be made between the class content of the state and its institutional aspects. It was primarily through the intervention of administrative-juridical institutions in the class relations between the extractors and the producers of surplus that the independent peasantry was maintained. The effectiveness of this intervention varied of course, but it is in the context of these institutions that peasant production and limited commercial development in peasant economy took place.

Viewed in this perspective, peasant economy can not be treated as an invariable or as being merely subject to cyclical variations deriving from economic variables internal to it. Here I refer to Malthusian[25] and Chayanovian[26] formulations on the nature of peasant economies. The Malthusian view assumes that, given the absence of technological change, agricultural production in pre-industrial societies is essentially stagnant. As such, changes in the population factor explain the changes in the organization of production and rural class relations. The Chayanovian view, on the other hand, points to the size of the peasant household and its level of self-exploitation as determinants of the levels of production. While these approaches point to two dynamic elements in the peasant economy, namely, demographic factors and self-exploitation of peasant households, they fail to relate these elements to the political-social context in which peasant production takes place.[27] Put differently, these frameworks tend to explain the changes in the peasant economy in terms of factors internal to that economy. I will argue that both the perpetuation and changes in the peasant economy were largely a function of external structures, i.e., power relations and the political-juridical institutions in which these relations were embodied.[28] In doing this I will stress the externality of the population factor[29] and point to the extra economic determinants of demographic growth such as conditions of political stability, migration, and forced sedentarization of nomadic tribes. At the same time, other external determinants of agricultural production, such as state taxation demands, will be admitted into the analysis. Thus, once these external linkages of the peasant economy are established, it is no longer possible to treat the peasantry as either autonomous or invariant. Its perpetuation or disappearance becomes incumbent on the larger political-social context.

Agrarian Relations and the State: Ottoman Anatolia

In the light of these general observations I now turn to specific structures of the Ottoman agrarian society in north-central Anatolia. In doing this I will first focus on the relations between extractors and producers of the surplus and the relations of these groups to central authority. Tımar-holders were not the only claimants to peasants' surpluses. In north-central Anatolia after the Ottoman conquest in the fifteenth-century, pre-Ottoman system of surplus extraction relations were largely left intact. This meant the recognition of the claim to peasants' surpluses of the former Turkish military rulers (*ümera*) and the members of religious establishments including the ulama at mosque-*medrese* complexes, and *shaykh* families who were the custodians of dervish hospices (*zaviyes*). This religious elite controlled large stretches of lands as their waqfs. At the same time, the interests of the religious elite and the umera were intertwined, as it was not uncommon for the umera to convert their properties into waqf. Under the *malikane-divani* system which was the predominant form of surplus-extraction in this region, the pre-Ottoman ruling groups retained the ownership rights to land, and revenues from land were divided between the legal owners (or the *malikane*-holders) and *divani*-holders who were entitled to revenues as part of the tımar.[30] As such, state ownership of land as a central precept of the paternalistic idiom of rule was not enforced in this region. In the second half of the fifteenth century the Ottoman central administration was content to appoint the members of the pre-Ottoman ruling groups with claims to divani revenues as tımar-holders.[31]

Throughout the sixteenth century the Ottoman central authority was engaged in a continuous struggle with the local elites to establish its political-juridical framework and to control a larger share of the surplus from this region.[32] Ottoman tax registers[33] suggest that in the sixteenth century the ümera families were gradually replaced by direct state appointees as claimants to divani revenues and as tımarholders. In this period there was also a rise in the share of waqf in total revenues. Under the malikane-divani system freehold properties could be sold or divided among heirs resulting in discontinuities in ownership and in extreme fragmentation of holdings. In order to prevent fragmentation and to escape confiscation by the central state, the pre-Ottoman umera increasingly converted their properties into family waqfs. At the same time, the Ottoman central state in the sixteenth century allotted a significant part of the revenues that directly accrued to it, to mosque-medrese complexes.[34] Thus, it appears that the central state was seeking an alliance with the local religious scholars (ulama) who as teachers, judges, and reciters of sermons at mosques controlled the ideological-juridical institutions. These institutions had formed the basis of legitimacy of the local Turkish dynasties. As such, alliance with the ulama was a means of coopting that legitimacy and therefore further undermining the domination of local dynasties. On the other hand, it is not unlikely that the central administration appointed the judges (or kadıs) in this area from the ranks of the local ulama who then would be in a position of implementing the juridical precepts that constituted the basis for the legitimacy of state power. This, in turn, could explain the prominence of ulama as claimants to surpluses in the sixteenth century.

But what were the implications for the organization of agricultural production and for rural class relations of the introduction of the tımar system on the one hand, and of co-optation of local ideological-juridical structures, on the other? In general terms, increased application of the timar system and appropriation of the local ideological-juridical apparatuses allowed the central state to intervene in the class relation between the owners of land and the direct producers. Concrete manifestations of this intervention, in turn, defined the character of rural structures under the malikane-divani system. First, under this system, legal owners of land were entitled to a rent but neither the condition nor the amount of this rent was determined by them. The amount of rent was specified in state legal codes as a single tithe (one-tenth of peasants' total output) on grains and other produce and as one-half of the dues from beehives and mills. Legal owners were not free to cultivate their lands, nor could they intervene in the production process undertaken by "free" peasants with usufruct rights to small plots and whose rights and obligations were specified in state codes. All matters relating to the person and the land of the peasant were outside the purview of legal owners (or malikane-holder); these were the responsibility of tımar-holders who formed the administrative cadres and whose powers could be revoked by the central state. Tımar-holders received the divani share of revenues which consisted of another single tithe on grains and other produce and the other half of dues on beehives and mills. In addition, however, tımar-holders were responsible for the collection of all *resm-i çift*[35] or land cum personal taxes, sheep tax, and penal fines. Moreover, peasant holdings could not be sold or purchased without the permission of tımar-holders who were responsible for the drawing of title deeds and who saw to the dispensation of holdings that fell vacant. Secondly, neither legal owners of land nor tımar-holders exercised any jurisdiction over peasants; as was the case on state-owned lands, legal matters relating to peasants and their land were settled at the tribunal of the kadı appointed by the central state. Finally, there were legal sanctions against accumulation of land in the hands of legal owners; though malikane-holders could sell or purchase lands, such transactions were subject to validation by the central state.

In brief, direct intervention of the administrative (political) and juridical practices of the central state in the "internal nexus" of surplus extraction or class relations between the legal owners and peasant producers, deprived the former of any local power base and reduced them to the status of a "rentier" class. As such, the malikane-holders, though they held the ownership title to land, were dependent on the administrative-juridical apparatus of the state for appropriation of rural surpluses. This was tantamount to the establishment of the political domination of the central state and resulted in the gradual undermining of the claims of the pre-Ottoman ruling elite— both to revenues and to political domination. In the sixteenth century, those tımar-holders who did not belong to this group, and the local ulama, co-opted by the state, emerged as the two major claimants to revenues in north-central Anatolia. On the other hand, the state's intervention in surplus extraction relations aimed at preserving the integrity of peasant holdings and at preventing any control by surplus extractors over the peasant production process. In doing this, the central state was not merely seeking to secure its own fiscal base, but—perhaps more importantly—fulfilling its ideological role as the protector of the peasantry and the preserver of "eternal order." Embodied in juridical structures, this ideology served to legitimize state controls over the production and appropriation of surpluses, and constituted the basis of the state's political domination. In the next section I will discuss how this specific structure of surplus-extraction relations in north-central Anatolia affected changes in the organization of production and in rural class relations during a period characterized by population growth and commercial expansion.

Population and Production Trends
in the Sixteenth-Century Peasant Economy

In the second half of the sixteenth century, north-central Anatolia witnessed phenomenal increases in population and commercial growth.[36] Yet population growth did not result in Malthusian scissors and in a subsistence crisis, nor did commercial demand in towns lead to peasant dispossessions. Can we explain the absence of these developments in north-central Anatolian agriculture simply by high land/labor ratios that the aggregate figures for Ottoman agriculture may suggest?

First of all, population growth did lead to a deterioration of the land/labor ratio; there is evidence of extension of arable lands, of fragmentation of peasant holdings (*çifts*), and of conversion of *mazra'a* or uninhabited cultivated lands into full fledged villages.[37] But scarcity of land does not appear to be a main constraint on peasant production, and it does not appear justified to talk about a Malthusian type subsistence crisis arising from population pressure on land. Contrary to Malthusian expectations, peasants in north-central Anatolia responded to population growth by intensifying production. They did this by employing techniques of intensive land utilization which they mobilized in response to changes in demand patterns. This took the form of introducing new crops into the rotation—such as legumes with nitrogen-fixing properties[38] and opening forest assarts[39] cleared by fire and axe which frequently provided fertilization so as not to require draught animals. Of course, peasants were always aware of such techniques, but because they were labor intensive and required the peasants to work harder, it appears that they were not employed before population growth and increasing demand for peasant's produce made their employment absolutely necessary.

Population growth, which was largely a result of immigration into this area from the more turbulent regions of eastern Anatolia, was accompanied by a rise in the numbers of landless peasants (or the new migrants) listed as *caba*s in the late sixteenth-century registers.[40] The availability of labor made possible the use of intensive techniques in the production of the two major crops—wheat and barley. Yet the increases in the production of wheat and barley lagged behind population growth.[41] To close this gap it appears that peasants increased the production of other foodstuffs: fruits, vegetables, legumes, and dairy products, which as we will see later, were also marketed.[42] The cultivation of these goods required significant labor outlays made available by increased population. In brief, north-central Anatolian peasants escaped the Malthusian scissors not because of the fact that land was infinitely available, but because increased numbers in the later sixteenth century made possible the intensification of agricultural production.

Secondly, since there is nothing to suggest that peasants of north-central Anatolia were actually suffering from food shortages, urbanization in the sixteenth century can not simply be explained in terms of the subsistence crisis.[43] To the extent that urban population growth was an outcome of migrations from the agricultural hinterland, it was probably more in response to increased employment opportunities in towns. One such opportunity was joining the entourage of provincial administrators.

Finally, in the later sixteenth century distribution of land was somewhat more egalitarian than the pattern of fragmentation suggests. Thus, for instance, survey data show that in districts around Tokat many çifts entered in the name of a single person were in fact shared. More significantly, there is also evidence that tenures that came up for disposal tended to go to the landless as were forest assarts listed in the later surveys.[44] While the availability of assart lands and mazra'as that were converted into villages in the later sixteenth century suggest that land was not scarce, this could not have been an effective barrier against enserfment. Nor did the availability of land provide the peasantry with infinite options for setting up independent farms.

It was of utmost importance to the Ottoman administration how land was utilized and who was utilizing it. The fact that available lands were cultivated by independent peasant farmers was not so much a function of the supply of land as the effective exercise of political authority. Thus, timar-holders were assigning assarts and lands that came up for tenure when a peasant died without leaving an heir or when the lands were not cultivated for five years to landless peasants and not to, say, urban notables, nor did they establish estates on such lands. Lastly, timar-holders also controlled some lands that they rented out to peasants.[45] This practice afforded peasant production some flexibility whereby the producer could vary the size of his holding according to the size of the household; more importantly, in the later sixteenth century these lands were leased to new immigrants. Although, timar-holders were leasing these lands under favorable conditions at a time when demand for land was high, they were still leasing them to peasants, and they did not convert their domains into large commercial estates to benefit from the commercial opportunities. Labor shortage was not a significant barrier to such a development. I have mentioned earlier that the presence of a significant number of cabas, the use of labor intensive techniques, and increased rice cultivation on state farms worked under sharecropping arrangements, all point to the availability of labor.

Though peasants in sixteenth-century Anatolia were able to provide for their subsistence, not all peasant production was for subsistence. Surplus production in this period was largely in response to state demands for wheat and barley. These demands took the form of the grain tithe collected in kind and of extraordinary levies at times of emergency or war. The tithe represented as much as one-fifth of the peasant's total output in the areas under investigation where a double tithe was extracted. Extraordinary taxes were also levied in kind (*nüzul*), requiring two-thirds or four-fifths to be paid in wheat and one-third or one-fifth in barley. Sometimes, though, they took the form of forced government purchases (*sürsat*).[46] However, it is not possible to determine the magnitude of these impositions for the period under study, since they were not recorded in the fiscal surveys, and separate records are not available prior to 1590.[47] Yet, state demands for such tax deliveries from areas in north-central Anatolia must have increased considerably in the later sixteenth century when the imperial army repeatedly traversed these areas *en route* to Iranian campaigns. Thus, it can be argued that taxation demands siphoned off a significant part of peasants' grain surpluses, and that the increases in total grain yields[48] were to a large extent stimulated by increased state demands to meet the requirements of an army on the march.[49] This may, in turn, explain the higher rates of increase in barley yields, a staple food for army horses.

Peasants also produced a surplus for sale on local markets which in north-central Anatolia, a region including as many as twelve towns, meant urban markets. It is true that market involvement of peasants was limited by the state's appropriation of tithe and levies in kind. Yet increases in the later sixteenth century in the production of fruits, especially grapes used in winemaking, vegetables, and livestock suggest an increase in the commercial production of peasants for town markets.[50] Since this was not a closed rural economy, peasants required markets to obtain the cash necessary for the purchase of manufactured goods they themselves did not make and for the payment of money taxes. There is also evidence of increased production of cotton[51]—which was not a very significant crop in this region—

possibly in response to the demands of rural weavers and spinners as well as of urban craftsmen. The increased tax revenues from the rural dye house in Karahisar-ı Demirli—a region that also witnessed a rise in the cotton production—suggests an increase in the activities of domestic cloth and yarnmakers in the later sixteenth century.[52]

A major commercial crop produced in north-central Anatolia was rice. The extent to which there was a shift to rice cultivation in response to increased market demand is not clear from the data included in the surveys. The Ottoman central government was well aware of such a tendency and tried to protect other peasant produce from the onslaught of rice. In doing this, it attempted not only to ensure the production of subsistence goods but also to preserve the integrity of small peasant producers. Judging from the extent of government regulations limiting rice cultivation and the measures against those who cultivated more than the specified amount of seed, it may be concluded that the state was engaged in a continual struggle with the local officials as well as other notables who wanted to extend lucrative rice cultivation on their holdings. To maximize their profits, these personages made illegal impositions of *corvée* labor.[53] Hence, given the considerable temptation to increase rice yields, the production of this crop may have also taken place on a "contraband" basis; therefore the actual yields may have been greater than those recorded in the surveys. By the same token, the tendency toward the "enserfment" of the peasants on rice fields may also have been more significant than in other spheres of cultivation.

On the other hand, we know that rice was exported from north-central Anatolia to the Crimea and possibly to İstanbul, but this export production largely took place outside of the peasant economy. Rice, requiring considerable investment in irrigation, was produced on large state farms by sharecroppers, who were under a different legal status than ordinary peasants. A legal framework allowed large scale commercial production of rice to take place.[54] This legal framework also sought to contain the infringements on the free status of the peasantry and threats to the integrity of peasant holdings likely to arise in commercial rice cultivation. The extent to which sharecropping relations were generalized and peasant cultivators participated in such relations, largely depended on the state's ability to enforce its measures and on the willingness of local administrators and notables to abide by those measures. The surveys, unfortunately, are not very helpful in shedding light on this aspect of the rural dynamic.

Lastly, there was a considerable increase during the later sixteenth century in the number of sheep raised by peasants in north-central Anatolia.[55] That such increases were especially pronounced in the hinterland of towns suggests that they took place in response to increased urban demand. In addition to supplying the urban upper classes with meat, sheep were also the source of wool. Part of the wool produced by peasants went to supply urban weavers, while at least some was used by rural craftsmen.[56]

Despite increased urban demand for the products of sheep farming, there is little reason to suppose that a significant shift to pastoral activity occurred in the peasant economy resulting in conversion of fields to grazing lands. Grain cultivation, safeguarded through state measures, remained the dominant form of agricultural activity during the sixteenth century. But the importance of sheep husbandry as a supplementary activity seems to have increased. From the perspective of the peasant household economy, this meant that either certain lands were set aside for grazing or, if animals were grazed on fields, longer fallow periods were required. In the latter case, animal droppings on fields must have contributed to increased soil fertility.

Grazing lands were not recorded in the surveys in any systematic manner,[57] therefore it is not possible to establish whether these lands were preserved or reclaimed in the later sixteenth century when peasants sought to increase grain yields. On the other hand, sheep farming was a much less labor-intensive activity than crop cultivation; the prospect of more work if grazing lands were converted into fields—at a time when peasants were already working harder—might have stopped them from reclaiming these lands. This consideration, coupled with favorable market conditions, could in part explain the rise of sheep farming in this period. At the same time, the rise in sheep husbandry may also suggest that at least part of this activity was carried out by local ruling groups on their freehold properties or on reclaimed wastelands, or by timar-holders on mazra'as that were not assigned to peasants.[58] As sheep raising did not require large outlays of labor, such commercial activity could be carried out without uprooting the peasantry or impinging on their free status.

Conclusions

The model of social-economic transformation revealed through the detailed study of a single Ottoman region in the sixteenth century suggests the following conclusions. First, rural economic development—i.e., increases in productivity and changes in technology—was to a large extent stimulated by taxation demands and not, in any significant way, by market demand patterns. By leaving the organization and control of the actual production process in the hands of direct producers with hereditary cultivation rights over the land, the Ottoman system afforded the peasantry the minimal space to increase yields in response to changes in demand patterns. That is, the system offered possibilities of economic development, but this development was largely dictated by extra economic structures that described surplus extraction relations and legitimization concerns, and *not* by economic decisions of individual producers responding to favorable market demand patterns.

Thus, this study rejects views of development that ascribe the stagnation of pre-industrial economies to the intervention of non-economic factors into the "economic" sphere. Instead, I have argued that Ottoman economy largely owed its dynamism to state intervention in the form of taxation demands. As such, this study stresses the political rationality of economic development in the Ottoman empire. Secondly, and as a result of the above pattern of economic development, commercial expansion in the form of increased demand for agricultural goods did not result in any significant commercialization of agricultural production. In the later sixteenth century market involvement of peasants was limited, though not totally absent. In contrast, increased commercial demand signaled an intensification in the market participation of revenue holders or groups with a claim over peasant surpluses; in the period under study, these groups were the timar-holders and ulama. Given that the grain tithe collected in kind was calculated as a fixed proportion of total yields, increases in the aggregate supply of grains were translated into increased marketed surpluses by these groups. A rough estimate indicates that nearly two-thirds of the total grain tithe from areas under study— after allowances are made for consumption needs of individual groups—found its way to local town markets in the second half of the sixteenth century. This amounted to nearly 13 percent of total wheat and barley yields from these areas.

It can thus be argued that food requirements of local towns were to a large degree met from the surpluses marketed by revenue holders who absorbed the price effects resulting from increased commercial demand for foodstuffs. On the other hand, more than half of the total income that accrued to revenue holders from sales of tithes and from money dues was, in all likelihood, spent locally.[59] Both the ulama and the timar-holders were major consumers of urban finished goods; their increased incomes, coupled with the expansion in their entourages in the later sixteenth century, could be expected to provide the primary stimulus for the expansion of urban craft production. Hence, the regional urban development that characterized this period appears to have been largely an outcome of increased market involvement of revenue holders who were the principal beneficiaries of increased commercial demand for agricultural goods.

Thirdly, increased commercial demand, given the limited market involvement of the peasantry, did not lead to an increased specialization between urban and rural areas. One indicator of such an increase would be the changes in the extent of rural craft production, which in sixteenth-century north-central Anatolia largely consisted of weaving and spinning of wool and cotton produced by the peasants themselves. The only evidence that the fiscal surveys provide of these activities is taxes levied on dye-houses.[60] Of the three dye houses recorded in the rural areas under study, only one—and that in the tribal district of Karahisar-ı Demirli—shows a substantial increase in its revenues in the period between 1520 and 1575; the one in Kafirni near the city of Tokat shows a sharp decline in revenues, while income from the third dye house in Yıldız (again near Tokat) remained constant during the same period.

These trends, in turn, suggest that at least in Kafirni and Yıldız, peasants might have diverted some of their time and labor away from craft production to intensive production of grains and of non-grain crops.[61] The latter activity, coupled with rising demand for cloths as population increased, might have led to increased peasant purchases of cloths and yarns in towns. But this tendency toward increased market involvement of peasants was restricted by the "limited commercialization" of agricultural production and the absorption of peasants' surpluses through taxes. This, in turn, imposed limits on the amount of cash the peasant had at his disposal (especially after the payment of money taxes) and therefore on the peasant's ability to purchase urban manufactures.

On the other hand, in Karahisar-ı Demirli considerable increases in dye house revenues point to an intensification of weaving and spinning activities in this region, where both cotton and wool production, as evidenced in the rise of sheep farming, also rose during the sixteenth century. But it is not clear whether it was the peasants or nomads who increased their weaving and spinning activities; if it were the nomads, were they responding to increased peasant demand? At present, we know very little about the interaction between the peasants and the economy of pastoral nomads; but peasants of this region—as more of their labor and time was absorbed by intensive methods of agricultural production—might have increased their purchases of finished goods from nomads. Moreover, since they could enter into barter exchange relations with the nomads, peasants probably preferred nomad-produced goods to those of urban craftsmen, who demanded cash. In sum, "limited commercialization" of peasant production, largely dictated by the mode of surplus extraction that characterized the Ottoman society, meant that increased urban demand in the later sixteenth century did not lead to increased specialization of production between urban and rural areas. Though peasants might have purchased more finished goods both in urban markets and from nomads in the later sixteenth century than in earlier periods, rural craft production remained an important activity of the peasantry.

Fourthly, commercial expansion did not have the effect of disrupting the organization of agricultural production based on small peasants holdings. As I have discussed earlier in relation to the impact of population growth on rural economic and social structures, there is no evidence that peasant dispossessions increased in the later sixteenth century, nor is there any indication of widespread formation of large commercial estates. Appropriation of peasants' surpluses in the form of taxes in kind on grains, coupled with legal sanctions against the sale and subdivision of peasant plots, ensured the cultivation of staple goods for peasant subsistence and for the provisioning of the army and the towns. Also, the political-legal structures of the state appear to have been effective in significantly limiting capital accumulation in the countryside and, therefore, differentiation among peasant households. More importantly, these structures also imposed constraints on the amount of surplus that was extracted by different groups of revenue holders and on their claim on the peasants' land and labor. The concern of the central state for maintaining the integrity of the peasant household economy is particularly pronounced in the restrictions on commercial production of rice. These restrictions were primarily aimed at preventing the expropriation of peasant lands and the recruitment of peasants as sharecroppers or corvée labor on rice fields by revenue holders who sought to expand the cultivation of this highly lucrative crop.

Finally, in describing the structure of surplus extraction relations in north-central Anatolia I have tried to show how the incorporation of pre-Ottoman ruling groups into the political-legal framework of the central state ensured their dependence on the state for extraction of surpluses and therefore, their subjection to the state's political authority. This structure of dependency of revenue holders on the administrative (coercive) and ideological (legitimating) apparatuses of the state, in turn, largely explains why population growth and urban commercial expansion in the sixteenth century did not result in the destruction of the peasant household economy, i.e., fragmentation of peasant holdings, peasant dispossessions, formation of large estates, and increased social coercion of labor. Consequently, the timar-holders and the ulama at mosque-medrese complexes—who were the two major groups with a claim over peasants' surpluses—did not benefit from increased commercial demand for agricultural goods through forcefully converting peasant holdings into units of commercial production. Instead, revenue holders enriched themselves through marketing of the tax on the output at favorable market prices.

The later sixteenth century also witnessed the decline of the timar system as changes in war technology shifted the balance from provincial cavalry to foot soldiers. From the point of view of provincial administrators or timar-holders, this signalled the breakdown of the administrative framework that enforced their claim to surpluses. Thus, faced with the prospect of losing their privileged status, these soldiers took to plundering the countryside and resorted to illegal extortions of peasants' surpluses. This reaction, which broke out in local disturbances throughout Anatolia and came to be known as *celali* uprisings, represented not so much a resistance to the state's political-juridical structures that prevented commercialization of agriculture and therefore capital accumulation in the hands of provincial administrators, but a resistance by this group to the prospect of being excluded from the political-juridical framework of the state that enabled them to appropriate agricultural surpluses.

Once the timar system was effectively replaced by tax farming as the dominant form of taxation in the seventeenth century, agricultural production undertaken by independent peasant producers on small plots appears to have been reconstituted. Tax-farmers then enforced their claims over specified shares in the context of the political-legal practices of the state. Tax-farmers belonged to the ranks of local notables—ulama and merchants—and the economic trends of the later sixteenth century no doubt contributed to their ascendancy in the subsequent period. These developments remain outside the scope of this study and information relating to seventeenth- and eighteenth-century developments in north-central Anatolia is scarce. Yet recent research on European territories and for Anatolia in the nineteenth century[62] strongly suggests that in response to increased European demand for agricultural goods, tax-farmers did not undertake to radically transform the rural social-economic structures and to bring about a commercialization of agricultural production. Instead they responded to increased commercial demand by claiming a larger share of the surplus either through squeezing the peasants for more taxes or by not delivering to the state what was its due. While this signalled increased economic power of tax-farmers—who sold these surpluses on lucrative markets—and a decline in the actual amounts received by the state, these developments do not appear to have eliminated the political-juridical dependence of tax-farmers on the state in most Ottoman territories.

Thus, the pattern of social-economic development described here has certain generalizable features. Shaped by the evolving structures of the Ottoman society, it is a pattern premised on regional economic development encouraging the rise of local power nodules which remained dependent on the state for enforcing their claim over surpluses produced by "free" peasants. Such a model of rural development, of course, requires further elaboration in the light of micro-historical studies of different Ottoman regions at different time periods. But, I believe, it may provide a framework for research on patterns of rural development under conditions of commercial expansion, both prior to and after the period when the impact of European demand was felt.

4

Wealth and Power in the Land of Olives: Economic and Political Activities of Müridzade Hacı Mehmed Agha, Notable of Edremit

Suraiya Faroqhi

The present study forms part of an inquiry into the extent and limits of locally based power, as it was exercised in Ottoman Anatolia during the period generally described as "post-classical," beginning with the 1570s or 1580s and ending in the 1830s. It focusses on the political initiatives available to *reaya* and low-level provincial dignitaries.[1] This approach may help remedy our tendency to consider "politics" as an exclusive appanage of the Ottoman ruling group. Certainly, the upper levels of the Ottoman bureaucracy like other ruling groups, tended to see themselves as the only political actors on the scene, and would scarcely have admitted the possibility that reaya or even locally based intermediate groups might have legitimate political aims of their own. On the other hand, Ottoman reaya possessed considerable resources when they wished to engage in passive resistance. As a result, the central government's options were in fact more circumscribed than was readily admitted, namely by the amount of taxes that provincial society was able and willing to pay. Under these circumstances, there is something to be learned from looking at Ottoman politics from the provincial or even local viewpoint; for thus we can escape, if only for a moment, the purely government-oriented view of our sources.

In this context, the provincial notables play a crucial role as intermediaries between the state apparatus and the reaya. As yet, we possess no systematic study of the *ayan* of the Ottoman realm, although the literature on this subject has already reached quite impressive proportions.[2] As a precondition for such an undertaking, one would need to compare the notables of eighteenth or early nineteenth-century Anatolia with similar "intermediate" groups that functioned during the same period. As examples, one might mention the *kaids* of Tunisia who operated in a partially tribal context, or the notables of the Damascus area who seem to have monopolized control over the land in a fashion that Anatolian notables were never able to achieve.[3] And beyond the Ottoman realm, it would be worthwhile to see in what way the notables of, for instance, a small state of northern Italy (who profited from absolutism at the same time as they limited its scope), differed from their Anatolian counterparts, and what features they may have had in common.[4]

But to return to the Ottoman realm and the monographs covering it: Halil İnalcık and Bruce McGowan have analyzed the ayan's role in the Ottoman taxation system.[5] In this context they have dwelt upon the power that these notables derived from enjoying the right to distribute the taxes assessed as lump sums in İstanbul, over the towns and villages of their district. This political aspect of ayan power has been considered so important that the economic activities of these provincial notables have been pushed into the background. However, in real life the political power and economic strength of Ottoman notables were interconnected. Certainly, the origin of ayan power was political. Equally, when ayan fell from power and lost their lives, as was the case with the hero of our story along with many others, it was never because they went out of business due to the bankruptcy of a debtor. (Readers of Balzac's novels will recall that this constituted the socially approved way in which businessmen fell from power and glory in early nineteenth-century Europe.) This fact is worth noting because certain ayan did engage in large scale moneylending. Ottoman ayan often also fell from power in rather a spectacular manner, but this was because they had lost political support in İstanbul, and in many instances their estates were regarded as welcome additions to the ever-empty treasury. But between the dates of their rise to and fall from power, economic activities might contribute a great deal toward cementing an ayan's power base, and I shall try to reconstruct how he might balance the political and economic sources of wealth and power.

Hacı Mehmed Agha and Edremit

Very little is known to date about the biography of Müridoğlu Hacı Mehmed Agha. The name would seem to indicate more than routine religious commitments; his father was probably the disciple of some dervish *şeyh* (*mürid*), and he himself had undertaken a pilgrimage to Mecca. While Müridoğlu's base of operations was undoubtedly Edremit and in nearby Kemer-i Edremit (modern Burhaniye), toward the end of his life he was also deputy governor (*voyvoda*) of Mihaliç (Karacabey); the area of his official activity also included nearby Gönen. At one point in his career, Müridoğlu had moreover served as voyvoda of Edremit. From the foundation registers of the sixteenth and twentieth-century published research, it appears that Edremit did not possess many public monuments,[6] and Hacı Mehmed Agha does not seem to have tried to remedy this situation by constructing mosques or endowing foundations. Or if he did, these structures did not survive him.

Müridoğlu Hacı Mehmed rose to power in a district which, then as today, was a major producer of olives and olive oil. Nedim Göknil, who observed Edremit and the neighboring towns of Burhaniye and Havran in the early 1940s, has left a graphic description of the cultivation of olive trees and the manufacture of olive oil at a time when the traditional olive presses (*mengene*) had just been replaced by small factories.[7] At that time, olives and olive oil were produced largely for the domestic market, as indeed they are today. However, even during the war years observed by Göknil, there was some exportation to Italy: high quality oil from Edremit was apparently mixed by Italian manufacturers with low quality domestic types to produce olive oil of a standard quality. But it would seem that İstanbul was the principal market because communications with the interior of Anatolia were poorly developed and the widespread consumption of olive oil in the towns of central Anatolia is comparatively recent.

From the data contained in the Müridoğlu estate inventory, it would seem that the economic orientation of the area did not change all that much between 1820 and 1940. The olive groves, which were to assure many inhabitants of Edremit a considerable degree of prosperity in the mid-twentieth century, were already in existence in 1820. Moreover, while French merchants of the eighteenth and nineteenth centuries bought large quantities of olive oil in Crete and Tunisia for use in the soap industry of Marseilles, the olive producers of Edremit remained unaffected by this demand.[8] Olive oil is not even mentioned among the goods that French merchants of the time usually purchased in İzmir. Thus it would seem that the olive oil and soap produced in Edremit and Kemer-i Edremit were largely sold to İstanbul. Moreover, since Ayvalık, Edremit's predominantly Greek neighbor, was in difficulty due to the involvement of its inhabitants in the Greek War of Independence, the position of the predominantly Muslim growers of Edremit was presumably enhanced.

When describing Edremit during the early 1940s, Göknil dwelled upon the tendency toward the concentration of wealth and property that could be observed at the time. However, and in this his observations are confirmed by other scholars who have dealt with western Anatolian society, such as Xavier de Planhol,[9] these concentrations were never permanent: what had been accumulated in one generation was readily dissipated in the next. Göknil invoked moralistic explanations for this state of affairs, particularly the presumed unwillingness of the second generation to secure their position by hard work. But it would seem that we are dealing here with a more permanent feature of Anatolian society. Müridoğlu Hacı Mehmed Agha also acted as an engrosser of land and olive trees; however, according to the time-tested method of the Ottoman administration in dealing with all too powerful ayan, after his death his son was granted only a small share of his father's property.[10] In this case, the dissipation of the family's wealth was not due to any incompetence on the part of Hacı Mehmed Agha's son, but obviously to the intervention of the Ottoman central administration. However, even after the practice of inheritance confiscation ceased, a permanent elite of prominent families in many sectors of Anatolian society was not established for a considerable time; therefore a more comprehensive explanation is required. This should take into account the effects of the Islamic Law (*shari'a*), locally applied rules of inheritance, and governmental policies. Whether other factors were involved as well must remain a topic for future investigations.

Müridoğlu's Activities as a Moneylender to Administrators and Taxpayers

Due to the social relationships that it reveals, the section of Müridoğlu's estate inventory reflecting his activities as a moneylender can be used as a "guidebook" that permits us to reconstruct the manner in which he attempted to maintain his power on a local level. The inventory does not contain any references to interest-taking, although it is of course possible that some of the sums mentioned as debts consisted of both capital and interest.[11] Nor does the inventory contain any data on the deceased's cash, jewelry, or debts. Now it is improbable that Müridoğlu possessed none of these things. But jewelry and cash were easily spirited away. As far as the debts are concerned, it is true that Müridzade Hacı Mehmed was a very rich man, but even so, there must at least have been some goods ordered on behalf of his household and not yet paid for. In principle, the Ottoman treasury, in confiscating most of the deceased's possessions, should have assumed responsibility for paying his debts. But given the rather terroristic conditions often accompanying the confiscation process, it is not clear how many creditors were bold enough to present themselves, nor does one dare guess what happened to their claims.

Among the more than sixty-five cases in which money was owed to the deceased, I will first treat the instances in which the credit extended was visibly connected with taxation: tax debts owed by villagers and townsmen, tax farms acquired by residents of the area, and payments to functionaries in charge of the Ottoman postal service. In the second instance, I will look at the cases in which more directly economic transactions would seem to have been the cause for the debt. Our task is somewhat complicated by the fact that we possess not one but two lists of debts: a list forming part of the inventory, presumably compiled by treasury officials in İstanbul and a list of debts, added on as an afterthought, compiled according to the documents sent to İstanbul by the *vali* of Kütahya immediately after the execution of Müridoğlu Hacı Mehmed.[12] There is some overlap between the two lists, as was in one case officially acknowledged by the scribe. But since in a number of other unacknowledged cases it is certain or else highly probable that the same debt has been referred to more than once, it has seemed prudent to regard only the debts recorded in the first list as documented with a reasonable degree of certainty.

Müridoğlu Hacı Mehmed Agha had lent money to a member of the powerful Kara Osmanoğlu family of the İzmir-Manisa region; the debtor mentioned in the estate inventory is a certain Mehmed Agha. According to a document concerning the estate of Kara Osmanzade el-hac Hüseyin Agha, who died in 1231/1815–16, there was at that time a member of the family named Mehmed Agha acting as tax collector (*muhassıl*) in the province of Aydın.[13] It is possible that this was the same person who had borrowed money from Müridoğlu. In addition, the voyvoda of the neighboring town of İvrindi, another tax-collecting official, still owed Müridoğlu, 5,300 *guruş* from a tax-farming contract (*kaza-i mezbur bedel-i iltizamından baki*).[14] It is not quite clear how this latter expression should be interpreted. Either Müridoğlu had lent the voyvoda of İvrindi the money with which the latter had purchased his tax farm, or else the voyvoda had farmed the İvrindi taxes as a subcontractor of the wealthy Edremit *agha*. In the list compiled according to the evidence sent to İstanbul immediately after the execution of Müridoğlu, the voyvoda's debt is recorded as 18,000 guruş. However for this latter figure the compilers of the inventory were unable to find documentary evidence and thus based themselves only upon the unsupported testimony of the voyvoda's servants. Therefore it is not possible to determine whether the difference between the two sums of money was due to the fact that during the intervening period, the voyvoda of İvrindi had paid part of his debts. Or else the estimate of 18,000 guruş was simply unrealistic and had to be modified when better data became available.

However the most important "political" debt owed to Müridoğlu Hacı Mehmed was recorded for Mihaliç (Karacabey), where he held office as a voyvoda in 1822–23. Not only did the inhabitants of this district owe back taxes which the Ottoman treasury undertook to collect, but Hacı Mehmed Agha had paid almost the entire tax known as *kalyoncu bedeliyesi* on the inhabitants' behalf, which amounted to 45,000 guruş. Apparently, it was not quite easy to determine the exact amount of money actually paid over; for the vali of Kütahya when putting together the documents which he sent to İstanbul seems to have questioned the seamen serving as kalyoncu instead of consulting the appropriate registers. According to a *kanun* promulgated by Sultan Selim III in 1804–06, the kalyoncu bedeliyesi was to be paid on behalf of 9,275 seamen at the rate of 100 guruş per person.[15] If the same rate was still applied in 1822–23, the inhabitants of Mihaliç should have been paying the equivalent of 450 seamen, or somewhat less than 5 percent of the total revenue expected from this tax. In addition Müridoğlu was owed 10,581 guruş by the inhabitants of Edremit and Burhaniye for so-called *memleket mesarifi* (local expenditures). According to the explanations given by İnalcık, this expression should refer to the expenses of provincial administrators and, more specifically, to the costs of tax collection.[16] In addition, the non-Muslims of the area owed Müridoğlu at least 19,500 guruş for the tax known as *hizmet-i mübaşiriye;* two wealthy traders known as Lazoğlu Anton and Mali zimmi from Havran had taken up this loan in the name of the local *millet.* But when Lazoğlu Anton defaulted, it seems that the Ottoman fisc demanded payment of the debt from the local Greek community. Moreover it is probable that the debts owed by the *kadıs* of Edremit and Burhaniye to Müridoğlu (2,750 and 393 guruş respectively) were also in one way or another connected with their appointments to these positions, or else to the fulfillment of the kadıs' official duties.

Two other debts owed to Müridoğlu Hacı Mehmed Agha were connected with *tımars* located in the area. While at the beginning of the nineteenth century the tımar had long since lost all significance as a means of financing the Ottoman army, the institution was by no means dead; in fact, during the reign of Selim III, there were even suggestions to restore some significance to the tımar if not in the financing of the army, at least in that of the bureaucracy.[17] The provincial governor (*mütesellim*) of the *sancak* of Karası, in which Edremit was located, owed Müridoğlu 750 guruş in connection with a tımar, while the list of the Kütahya vali refers to a debt owed by the voyvoda of İvrindi and called *tımar akçesi* (tımar money). It is not clear what exactly was meant by these expressions, but the yearly revenues from these tımars may have been transferred to Müridoğlu to secure repayment of a debt, a proceeding not unknown even at the end of the sixteenth century.[18] If not, the mütesellim and the voyvoda collected all state revenues in their respective territories, and were supposed to then transfer to Hacı Mehmed a sum of money corresponding to the two tımars that had been assigned to the latter. Other types of financial relationships can doubtlessly be imagined.

Debts from Commercial Transactions

The aforementioned distinction is convenient, but probably not altogether appropriate. It is very possible, and indeed probable, that some of the trade relations that Müridoğlu engaged in were only possible because the latter, as tax collector and wealthy man, was able to put pressure on people to trade with him. Moreover for the majority of all transactions, the register gives only the name of the debtor, without telling us anything about the preceding relations between Müridoğlu and the people who owed him money. Only in one instance does the inventory specify that 10,496 guruş were owed to the deceased because he had supplied villagers of the district of Kemer-i Edremit (Burhaniye) with grain to bridge the difficult months preceding the new harvest. It is quite possible, however, that the other sales were of a similar kind. Thus the villagers of Papazlı (modern Altınoluk?) in the district of Tuzla still owed the agha of Edremit 300 guruş for wheat, and an unspecified group of semi-nomads (*yörük*) had purchased barley for him. One would like to know more about this latter transaction, for the debtor recorded in the inventory was a certain Mustafa Agha from the village of Güre, located on the road from Papazlı to Edremit. Did this Mustafa Agha undertake to guarantee the yörük's debt, and if so, for what reason? And if this assumption is true, what services were the yörük expected to render in return? At present, these questions can only be posed, but not answered.

In other instances, it is obvious that Müridoğlu must have had relations with traders. We do not know what he had sold to a group of unnamed Bergama merchants, but it is certain that they owed him 3,000 guruş at the time of his death. Some more information is available about the merchant from Kemer, Lazoğlu Anton, who had borrowed money on behalf of the local non-Muslim community. Apart from the hizmet-i mübaşiriye already mentioned, Lazoğlu owed Hacı Mehmed Agha 11,000 guruş for olive oil purchased, and another 10,000 guruş under the somewhat enigmatic heading "veterinarian in charge of mules" (*"hekim-i eşter,"* followed by an unidentifiable word).[19] Lazoğlu was in some way involved in the Greek uprisings of the 1820s and fled Ottoman territory—to where we do not know. Therefore the 695 olive trees he owned in the Edremit area were seized, in partial payment of his debt to the fisc. Moreover he had a (non-Muslim) guarantor whose trade is not known but who was in İstanbul at the time the inventory was being prepared; the latter was called upon to discharge Anton's debts to Müridoğlu, which had been transferred to the Ottoman fisc due to the latter's death.

Lazoğlu Anton was not the only debtor of Müridoğlu's who was deeply enough involved in the Greek uprising that he had to flee the country. A personage identified as Bali the scribe (Yazıcı Bali) was in the same position; originally he came from the village of Güre but possessed olive groves in Havran-ı Kebir. Yazıcı Bali was in debt to the tune of 6,500 guruş, and the same applied to Manolaç (Manolakis ?), a resident of Molova district and probably a trader, who had disappeared without discharging a debt of 6,000 guruş to Müridoğlu. In his case, an Ottoman official was ordered to seize Manolaç's property on the island of Lesbos.

On the other hand, by no means were all Greek merchants of substance in similar political difficulties. Mali of Kemer, who had borrowed money along with Lazoğlu in order to discharge the millet's tax debts, still resided in the Edremit area when the inventory was being compiled; like Lazoğlu Anton, he had also purchased olive oil from Müridoğlu. Yorgi, the partner (*şerik*) of a certain İsmail Efendi, was equally a substantial man who paid a debt of 5,000 guruş, incurred under what circumstances is unknown. Yorgi also seems to have remained in Edremit or the immediate vicinity. One wonders how the relations between Müridoğlu and his Greek trading partners were affected by the political vicissitudes of the times; a number of possibilities come to mind, but the inventory is unfortunately completely silent on this matter.

Debtors Everywhere

In most cases, we know very little about the reasons which prompted people to apply to Müridoğlu for money; usually the small loans were least well documented. The reasons for contracting most of the larger loans are somewhat better known. Out of a total of 333,884 guruş outstanding at the time of Müridoğlu's death,[20] 103,601 guruş (31 percent) were loans made in connection with tax collection and other official business. (These figures do not include debts documented only in the vali of Kütahya's list.) On the other hand, 83,838 guruş (25.1 percent) appear to have been connected with commercial transactions. Given the difficulties in categorization, these figures should be taken as approximations, but Müridoğlu Hacı Mehmed Agha apparently did try to strike a rough balance between maintaining political influence and making money.

It is of some interest to compare the size of the loans recorded. Almost one half of all loans contracted are in the lowest category; moreover twenty-seven out of these thirty-two cases involved loans up to 500 guruş (40 percent of the total). As an olive tree was officially considered to be worth 15 guruş and a jug of olive oil to be worth 6.7 guruş,[21] loans up to 500 guruş were probably small, and presumably had been made to people of modest means. About one quarter of all loans were in the category of 1,000–5,000 guruş which left only slightly over 25 percent for truly important transactions. Among the latter the largest items were clearly political in nature: the taxes that the inhabitants of Mihaliç were to pay Müridoğlu Hacı Mehmed as their voyvoda (56,000 guruş), and the loan made to a certain Valizade Süleyman Agha, who almost certainly had held an official position at one point. Lending for political purposes was evidently risky: tax-

Table 1: Loans Extended by Müridoğlu

Size of Loan*	Number of Cases	Percentage of Total
– 1,000	32	47.8
1,001– 5,000	18	26.9
5,001–10,000	8	11.9
10,001–15,000	4	6.0
15,000–20,000	2	3.0
20,001–	3	4.5
	67	100.1

* in guruş

payers might take flight and public administrators fall from power—a misfortune that Valizade Süleyman Agha was apparently unable to avoid. But at least in the case of Müridoğlu, his "political loans" were probably a *conditio sine qua non* for obtaining a position in which he was able to amass the wealth that he did.

The Olive Economy

A substantial number of debts owed to Müridoğlu were apparently due to his selling olive oil on credit. Although some of his customers, as we have already observed, were Greek, Müridoğlu also sold to Muslim dealers; thus the inventory names a certain Balyalı Hacı Ahmed who settled a debt of 930 guruş. However, the most important among the Muslim dealers was Mehmed Ali Agha, whom the inventory specifically identifies as a "trader in olive oil" (*rugan-i zeyt tüccarı*). He owed one debt of 16,023 guruş and another of 7,500 guruş. The first was discharged without further complications; the second had a more involved history. At the time that Müridoğlu was paying a visit to İstanbul (or had been called to the capital in order to account for his doings?) a certain Manolaç, probably the same who was later to flee the country, sent a bill of exchange to the capital. This bill of exchange, possibly after having changed hands a number of times, finally resulted in the second debt of Mehmed Ali's to Müridoğlu. Whether Mehmed Ali was willing to pay, however, is not too clear. While the inventory normally states that a given debt had been discharged, or else that drastic steps had been undertaken to secure payment, there is no information whatsoever on the manner in which Mehmed Ali's second debt was settled. Possibly the matter was still pending at the time the inventory was compiled.

Where did all this olive oil come from? According to the inventory, Müridoğlu was at first assumed to have owned 18,118 olive trees. Later, another 1,091 trees were added to the list, which gives us a total of 19,209 olive trees. Obviously, not all these trees were at their maximum stage of productivity. The estate inventory records 1,646 trees described as *dikme*, that is young trees, and if these are substracted, we get a stock of about 17,500 trees. According to the anthropologist Altan Gökalp, the olive trees grown by comparatively inexperienced growers in the 1960s, under conditions that were probably not too different from those prevalent in early nineteenth-century Edremit, produced between 20 and 25 kg. of olives per tree.[22] Thus Müridoğlu Hacı Mehmed should have harvested between 350 and 440 tons of olives per year. After treating their olives in rustic village presses, which Gökalp observes have not changed much since Roman times, the villagers of Sofular (province of Aydın) in the 1960s obtained a liter of oil for each 4–6 kg. of olives.[23] Thus, assuming that Müridoğlu had his entire harvest converted into olive oil, he should have obtained between 87,500 and 109,000 liters of olive oil a year.

It would seem that Müridoğlu took charge of pressing his own oil, for the inventory records the existence of presses (*mengene*), one of which was quite elaborate containing seven storage vessels (*küp*) and two kettles (*kazgan*). Some of the oil was converted into soap, for Müridoğlu owned four workshops for the preparation of this commodity. Two of these were not in usable condition, but one of the workshops in active use seems to have been quite large, with thirty-five storage vessels and two kettles. Moreover, Müridoğlu probably used the services of other people, mostly Greeks, in preparing some of his olive oil. At the time the inventory was compiled there was a total of 5,406 jugs (*testi*) of olive oil belonging to Müridoğlu in the possession of six people, one of whom held 2 jugs and another 3,632 jugs. Since the document does not mention any sale in connection with these people, it would seem reasonable to regard them either as paid employees or possibly contractors. Moreover on Müridoğlu's different properties was found a stock of 4,982 jugs of olive oil.[24] Thus the olive oil in the possession of Müridoğlu and his agent amounted to 10,388 jugs, which probably had been produced mainly from the harvest of 1822.

While we have no idea as to the amount of olive oil an Edremit jug may have represented, we can estimate the monetary value of these supplies, for we know that Müridoğlu Hacı Mehmed during his lifetime had sold a total of 23,230 jugs to the purveyor of the Ottoman Arsenal in İstanbul and to the latter's son-in-law. This amount was sent in three different batches; the value per jug amounted to 6.45, 7.27, and 6.39 guruş respectively; the average was 6.7 guruş (23,230 jugs being worth 154,646 guruş). If this figure is multiplied by 10,388 the number of jugs not yet sold, we arrive at 69,600 guruş, an approximate measure for the value of the stock of olive oil still remaining in Müridoğlu's possession in the İstanbul market. The price paid by the arsenal may have been lower than the market price. Moreover, the manner of expression employed in the inventory does not permit us to determine whether the sum of money paid over constituted the arsenal's entire debt, or whether an unpaid balance yet remained. But even so, the figure arrived at can at least be regarded as a low estimate. The inventory does not mention any stocks of soap, and the fact that two of the workshops intended for the manufacture of this commodity had ceased operations indicates that soap manufacture was not very lucrative during the last years of Müridoğlu's life. But still it is probable that 70,000–75,000 guruş could be realized every year out of the sale of olive oil and soap.

The problem of determining the market value of the olive trees themselves remains. No mention is made in the inventory of the land on which these trees stood; it is probable that just as in the case of the villagers whose olive groves Altan Gökalp was to observe about 140 years later, the land belonged to the public domain. Nor does the inventory make any attempt to estimate the value of Müridoğlu's 19,203 olive trees. But we know that the fugitive Lazoğlu Anton's trees had been valued at 15 guruş a piece when they were confiscated; by that token Müridoğlu's trees should have been worth 288,045 guruş. However this is almost certainly an undervaluation, for the treasury had an obvious interest in assigning the trees as low a value as possible, as this would have permitted the seizure of other property belonging to Lazoğlu and/or his debtors and guarantors.[25]

What is remarkable about Müridoğlu's olive groves is that in spite of the total number of trees involved individual units were small; at most a few hundred trees in a given locality, but in most cases far less than one hundred. Accordingly the number of plots was high, amounting to more than 120. This would not have been particularly surprising in hillside villages, where the rugged terrain may have permitted only small plantations, but many of these plots were located in the immediate vicinity of Edremit, which is completely flat. Moreover, while some of these plots are characterized by the name of the place in which they were located (Ilıca *kurbunda, dere ağzında*, etc.), the majority were called by the name of a man.[26] Normally, one would expect the only personal name to be attached to a property in such a fashion to be the name of the former owner. Under these circumstances, one begins to wonder about the manner in which Müridoğlu may have acquired all these trees. To give an idea of the magnitude of his holdings, one might mention that in the late 1960s, the villagers observed by Gökalp were able to live on 300–400 trees per family, supplemented by some sheep, cattle, and wage labor in the cotton fields.[27] Thus it would seem that even by twentieth-century standards, Müridoğlu possessed enough olive trees to ensure the livelihood of about 50 farm families.

In the early nineteenth century, when cash demands upon a peasant family were lower, this number should have been higher still. It is not improbable that Müridoğlu's strategy of making loans to villagers for purposes of survival or the defraying of taxes allowed him to foreclose; this would explain the frequency with which the names of persons other than himself were attached to Müridoğlu's olive groves. Or else he may have demanded that peasants indebted to him graft shoots of olive trees onto unproductive "wild olives," the trees which thus were converted into fruit-bearing ones becoming the property of the creditor. But that would amount to the same thing, for at least on the southwestern coast of Anatolia, customary law assigns a "wild" olive converted to a fruit-bearing tree to the person that has done the grafting.

Grain Production

Twentieth-century Edremit is not known for its abundance of grain. Even during the difficult years of the Second World War, local farmers preferred to specialize in olives and buy their grain in the market.[28] Probably, however, the dominance of the olive tree was not as strong in the early nineteenth century as it was to become 150 years later, and in this context it is not surprising that Müridoğlu should have grown both wheat and barley in addition to his olive trees. Apart from feeding his family and retinue, the grain he produced was sold, which allowed the agha of Edremit to establish relations of patronage with villagers in the area.

The land on which this grain was grown was not technically freehold property (*mülk*), but belonged to the state and was rented to Müridoğlu on what was, in principle, an inheritable lease (*betemessukat-ı tapu*). But long before the law of 1858 legalized the practice, *tapu* holding had begun to resemble freehold property in many respects.[29] Tapu holdings could be sold; in fact, 10,549 guruş were owed to the estate of Müridoğlu on account of certain fields that the latter had sold during his life time. Moreover the sheer fact that Müridoğlu's tapu holdings were enumerated in the estate inventory is in itself suggestive, for this means that they were considered the property of the deceased, while similar estate inventories compiled during the sixteenth and seventeenth centuries had taken exactly the opposite view.[30]

Müridoğlu's holdings of grain fields amounted to 4,239 *dönüm;* if we assume that the dönüm intended here was approximately the size of the modern official dönüm (939.3m²) this would have amounted to about 400 hectares. Again this land did not constitute a compact holding, but was distributed over a number of locations. Fields are all identified by the name of a locality and not by that of a person as in the case of olive groves. There is no indication of the manner in which

Müridoğlu may have acquired these lands, but we can make some assumptions about the amount of saleable grain which they may have produced. From the harvest of 1823, which was the last to occur before the preparation of the inventory, the storehouses of the agha of Edremit contained 5,065 İstanbul *kiles* of wheat (about 130 tons), and 7,420 kiles of barley (165 tons), in addition to smaller quantities of fodder, vetches, beans, and chickpeas. This figure does not include the grains which Hacı Mehmed Agha had accumulated as tax collector of Mihaliç (Karacabey).

From the previous year 1822, Müridoğlu's storehouses contained 13,697 kile of grain (about 340 tons), that is, a slightly larger quantity than had been stored in 1823. Nevertheless, the real harvest of 1822 must have been considerably larger, since part of the grain had certainly been consumed and the seed grain for 1823 must also have been taken out of the storehouse prior to the compilation of the inventory.[31] It is tempting to use these figures as a starting point from which to compute yields per hectare, a kind of data so much sought after and so rarely found by historians of agriculture. But the uncertainty as to the size of the dönüm involved, and more importantly, the fact that we do not know whether the grain found in the storehouses constituted the entire harvest, make such an undertaking unfeasible. It would appear, however, that at the end of each of the two years covered by the inventory, about 250–300 tons of grain could be made available for consumption.

One can also assume that by the 1820s, most of the wheat and barley produced on Müridoğlu's property was not sent to İstanbul or even smuggled abroad, although the latter may have happened during the grain boom of the Napoleonic wars. In the beginning of the nineteenth century, the Edremit region stood out because of its production of olive oil and also because legumes (broad beans, chickpeas) constituted a secondary specialty crop. This would imply that grain was produced mainly for local consumption. Evidence of the fact that Müridoğlu's grains were indeed consumed locally can be found in his estate inventory: the agha owned two mills in Edremit itself, and baking ovens in Edremit, Kemer (Burhaniye) and the nearby village of Zeytinli. None of these baking ovens was apparently located in the vicinity of Müridoğlu's own residence in Edremit. Thus it seems that these ovens were used, probably against payment of a fee, by people who were not satisfied with bread baked in the ashes of a domestic fire. Whether Müridoğlu put any pressure on householders in order to make them use his mills and baking ovens remains unknown.

Houses and Other Built-Up Properties

At the time of his death, Müridoğlu owned four residences, one of them in ruins, important enough to be considered a *konak*. The family's main residence was located in Edremit's old town quarter of Gazi Celal. From the description it appears that this dwelling possessed an outer courtyard which was used for the reception of male visitors and also for certain domestic or even agricultural tasks.[32] An inner courtyard contained the residential quarters. The house possessed an upper floor, its own supply of running water and was embellished by a pond,[33] which according to the fashion of the times, may have been fitted out with a fountain of some kind. In addition, Müridzade shortly before his death had undertaken the construction of a second large konak in another part of Edremit. A third, probably smaller konak was located in the *mahalle* of Hacı Tuğrul. This building, which also possessed two courtyards, a *hamam*, and its own water supply, had been donated by the deceased to his son Mustafa Agha, who thus must have been an adult at the time of his father's death; this was the only property left in the hands of Müridoğlu's family after the *müsadere* had been completed.

In addition to these buildings, meant to house the family and its retainers, Müridoğlu also owned real estate producing rent. This included a *han* and at least four shops in Edremit, and there was also a coffee house in Edremit and another in Kemer (Burhaniye). In the village of Zeytinli, Müridoğlu owned several houses (*menzil*) inhabited by Greeks. One of the latter bore the name of Manolaç, a man known by this name who held positions of trust in Müridoğlu's entourage may have been the same person. Müridoğlu may have housed some of his married servitors in accommodations that formed part of his property; whether these people were expected to pay rent is impossible to determine. In addition to references to full-scale houses, Müridoğlu's inventory also mentions ten "rooms" (*oda*), all located in the village of Zeytinli. Under the circumstances, these "rooms" were probably very simple shelters to house temporary workers.[34]

While we do not know whether the four Zeytinli dwellings described as menzil were equipped with the auxiliary buildings needed for a farm, certain other houses are explicitly described as farm houses. In the vicinity of Edremit, there was the so-called *çiftlik* of Kazdağlı, which must have been a peasant dwelling, for apart from the indispensible cowsheds and storage spaces, it contained only two rooms. The same applied to two further dwellings in or close to

Edremit, which moreover possessed but one inhabitable room each. It is unlikely that Müridoğlu had gone to the trouble of putting up these structures to house tenants or sharecroppers; for if such had been his habit, and given the size of his properties, one would expect to find rather more of such farmhouses than the three çiftliks recorded in the inventory. It seems more probable that these buildings had once belonged to peasants who had been forced to abandon them; Müridoğlu may well have acquired the çiftliks by foreclosure on account of unpaid debts.[35]

How Müridoğlu Used His Fortune: An Evaluation

In a sense, the inventory of Müridoğlu's properties allows us to make certain guesses with respect to the aims their owner pursued during his lifetime and the strategies he employed in order to achieve these aims. But for that we need an overall balance of his assets; unfortunately, as has been explained previously, we know nothing at all about his liabilities. Even among the assets there are certain gaps, particularly where real property is concerned; for the inventory does not contain money valuations, and while it is possible to estimate the value of olive oil and grains, that is not possible in the case of houses, mills, or olive presses. Thus all the figures involved must be considered minimum estimates which give a distorted picture of reality. Even so, a rapid overview of Müridoğlu's assets would seem to be of some interest.

Let us begin with the item, which due to the lack of published data on İstanbul grain prices in the 1820s, is particularly doubtful, namely the value of Müridoğlu's holdings of wheat and barley (for this reason the latter have been excluded from Table 2). For wheat, the closest approximation to an İstanbul price per kile to be found in the published literature is a consular report from the year 1845 that states that the price of grain had recently risen from 18–22 guruş a kile to 23–27 guruş.[36] If for the the sake of argument we assume that 18 guruş was a possible price in İstanbul in the 1820s, the 20,202 kile of wheat that were found in Müridoğlu's possession should have been worth 363,636 guruş, to which one would still have to add the value of barley, vetches, and other crops.[37] Thus if the price adopted for wheat is unrealistically high, one can only hope that this overestimation somewhat makes up for the omission of the other crops. Under these circumstances, Müridoğlu's recorded fortune, apart from ready cash, jewelry, and real estate, must have surpassed the 1,000,000 mark.

Table 2: Müridoğlu's Assets

Assets		Value in Guruş	% of Total Value
Loans		333,884	48.2
loans connected with public business	163,601		(15.0)
loans connected with commerical transactions	83,838		(12.1)
Olive trees		288,045	41.7
Unsold olive oil (Istanbul prices)		69,600	10.1
Total		691,529	100

Certainly Müridoğlu's wealth did not compare with that of the really rich ayan of the time, such as that of Tepedelenli Ali Pasha, who was in a position, when called upon, to make contributions to the tune of 500,000 guruş to the Sultan's war chest.[38] But on the other hand, compared to the ayan of Havza and Vezirköprü (near Amasya) who in 1808 left a fortune of about 20,000 guruş and whom Cezar considers as typical among Anatolian ayan, the agha of Edremit was a very wealthy man indeed.[39] Among the elements of Müridoğlu's fortune which we have been able to estimate with a degree of confidence, almost one half (48.2 percent) consisted of loans. The value of his olive trees amounted to 41.7 percent of his known fortune.

Müridoğlu Hacı Mehmed had made a fortune out of three sources: money-lending both political and commercial, grain cultivation, and the sale of olive oil. He was a sophisticated commercial farmer, far removed from the rusticity of the Havza-Vezirköprü ayan whose portrait has been drawn by Yavuz Cezar. By the same token, if Kör İsmailoğlu Hüseyin of Havza and Vezirköprü was typical of the Anatolian ayan of the early nineteenth century, then Müridoğlu Hacı Mehmed most emphatically was not. But even considered as an individual, the network that he had succeeded in building up can tell us a great deal about the relationships that made up the provincial society of which he formed a part. By way of a conclusion, we can now summarize the lessons to be learnt from Hacı Mehmed's estate inventory.

Conclusion

At first glance, it would seem that one of Hacı Mehmed's main aims, if not the foremost one, was to become and stay rich. A considerable part of his money-lending activities were probably directed toward this aim: Müridoğlu seems to have made a considerable number of small loans in the hope of later foreclosure. Moreover, while at least part of his grain production may have been intended for domestic consumption, to specialize in the production of olive oil meant orientation toward the market—in this particular instance, the domestic rather than the foreign market. Thus, while it would certainly be anachronistic to call Müridoğlu Hacı Mehmed Agha a "capitalist"—the sociopolitical environment was scarcely propitious for capital accumulation—he seems to have viewed money as a means not of procuring objects for use, but as a means of earning more money. To use Eric Wolf's expression, Müridoğlu's activities may be classed under the heading of "money begetting money."[40]

On the other hand, Müridoğlu's political ambitions were modest and did not go beyond local tax collecting or loans to people influential at the provincial level. He never played a major political role. In spite of the importance of the loans involved, it would seem that Müridoğlu's limited political activities were mainly directed toward survival, and in this, he ultimately failed. The fate suffered by Müridoğlu was certainly not unique during those years when Sultan Mahmud II was consolidating his power prior to his attack on the janissaries. A similar fate befell the Cabbarzade or Kara Osmanoğulları, who held an incomparably larger share of political power than the wealthy small-town agha whose story emerges from the Müridoğlu inventory. Perhaps no strategy could have saved Hacı Mehmed Agha, for his defeat was due to structural reasons.

In his analysis of the inventory of Kör İsmailoğlu Hüseyin, ayan in the area of Havza and Vezirköprü, Yavuz Cezar has pointed to one of the key structural facts by which the central government remained, in spite of everything, stronger than the ayan: the institution of confiscation (*müsadere*) which gave rise to a redistribution of the sources of wealth that had been controlled by a deceased ayan.[41] From this, the central administration benefitted in two ways: first, because of the financial advantage to the Treasury, as the lands and goods of a former ayan were redistributed against payment of cash; secondly, because of the political disadvantage that a confiscation brought upon the sons and nephews of the deceased ayan who might attempt to perpetuate their predecessors' political power. Not that such perpetuation was impossible, as the example of the Kara Osmanoğulları shows. But Cezar is certainly right in seeing the müsadere as one of the crucial institutions by which the Ottoman central administration, even without the benefit of a modernized army, managed to retain its hold over the provinces. This was particularly true since in certain cases müsadere was practiced even though the owner of the property was by no means dead,[42] or else the death of an ayan might be hastened along to provide an occasion for müsadere. From the Ottoman Sultan's point of view, the abolition of müsadere in the course of the Tanzimat came just at the time when the institution was no longer essential from a political point of view. The great ayan of the preceding period had been shorn of their power in the context of the Empire, even though some of them might retain an important position at the local level.[43] If Müridoğlu Hacı Mehmed Agha had flourished a generation later, he would probably have been left in peace to make money among his olive plantations and bills of exchange.

5

The Trade of Cotton and Cloth in İzmir: From the Second Half of the Eighteenth Century to the Early Nineteenth Century

Elena Frangakis-Syrett

Cotton

In the second half of the eighteenth century, İzmir experienced an unprecedented economic growth that made it the most important port in the Ottoman Empire's trade with the West. During that time France was the dominant economic power in the Levant, and, through its port of Marseilles, the principal trading partner of İzmir. By then the Egyptian and Syrian ports had fallen behind. Salonica and İstanbul, although major ports, could no longer compete with İzmir, which kept its position until the early nineteenth century. The predominance of cotton among the exports of İzmir coincides almost to the year with the predominance of İzmir as the biggest exporting port of the Empire. Cotton remained the principal export of İzmir until the beginning of the nineteenth century, after which it declined.[1] Massive exports of cotton reflected the further orientation of İzmir's agricultural production to external commerce and its integration in the world-economy.

Unlike mohair yarn or Ottoman silk, which were transported to İzmir from Ankara and Bursa, cotton was produced in the immediate vicinity of the port-city. It was cultivated in the plains of Bakır, Gediz, Kırkağaç, Akhisar, Bergama, Kasaba, and Manisa, along the valleys of

97

the rivers Küçük and Büyük Menderes, and in the neighborhood of the cities of Bayındır, Tire, Ödemiş, Aydın, and Denizli. Cotton from these areas was considered by European merchants to be better than that of Adana or Syria. There were eight types of cotton varying in quality and taking their names according to the place of production. Top quality cotton was produced in Aydın and Subatça.

Due to a lack of data, it is impossible to quantify total production of cotton and the proportion exported to the West, but it is possible to calculate the exports of cotton to Marseilles, the principal trading port of İzmir. Taking the average for every decade in the second half of the eighteenth century, we have the following figures: in the 1750s, 8,270 bales[2] were exported annually; in the 1760s this increased to 12,285 bales annually—an increase of 48.5 percent; in the 1770s, the annual average dropped slightly to 12,235 bales and in the 1780s it rose to 20,279 bales—an increase of 66 percent.[3] In 1750 alone exports amounted to 7,319 bales; in 1788, a peak export year, they more than trebled, reaching 26,402 bales.[4]

There was a substantial increase in the export of cotton at the end of the eighteenth century which carried over into the nineteenth century. From 1788 to 1820, cotton exports trebled to almost 70,000 bales.[5] The considerable growth of cotton exports, at least until 1820, reflects the dimensions of commercial growth of İzmir. In the early nineteenth century we have the following breakdown of the export figures: Güzelhisar and Subatça sent for export to the market of İzmir 8,000 bales; Kırkağaç, a seat of the Kara Osmanoğlu, the biggest cotton producer and local administrator, sent 25,000 bales of second quality cotton to İzmir annually. Akhisar, Bergama, and Kınık furnished İzmir with another 25,000 bales of third quality cotton. Kasaba furnished the city with 10,000 bales of lesser quality cotton annually and Manisa with 4,000 bales.[6] Manisa cotton was also of low quality and was used mainly in local production of cloth; very little was exported to the West.[7]

In the second half to the eighteenth century, the share of cotton in the overall value of exports of İzmir to France varied from 30 to 59 percent. A peak year for cotton exports was 1788 with a share of 72 percent of total exports. In the 1780s, although cotton exports continued to grow in absolute value, their share in relation to the exports of İzmir averaged 49 percent annually. In 1782 İzmir's cotton exports represented 60 percent of all Ottoman cotton exported to France; this share dropped in the next two years, but in 1785 it rose to 65 percent. At that time its greatest rival, Salonica, had an average share of 19 percent, with all the other Ottoman ports providing the rest.[8] Despite the absolute increase in the production of cotton, its share in total exports of the western Anatolian port dropped by the early nineteenth century. In 1820, for example, cotton represented 12 percent of İzmir's exports to France, as France was importing American cotton instead of cotton from the Levant. In 1832, cotton ranked fourth in value among İzmir's exports to Austria; it accounted for 12 percent of İzmir's exports to Russia and only 2 percent of the port's exports to Great Britain.[9]

Great Britain had been importing cotton from the United States even before American independence, and the invention of the cotton gin in 1793 resulted in greater imports of American cotton. Great Britain imported cotton from the United States even in the years 1812–13 when the two countries were at war with each other, as İzmir was cut out of the British market.[10] In 1857, according to British sources, cotton's share of İzmir's exports to the West was a mere 1 percent in value; raisins, valonia, madder, and wool represented the top export items of İzmir with shares of 14 percent, 13 percent, 12 percent and 11 percent respectively.[11] In 1858, according to French sources, cotton and wool exports together represented 8 percent of İzmir's exports to the West, with valonia and alizari topping the list with a share of 37 percent of the exports.[12]

In the second half of the eighteenth century, cotton production in İzmir mainly served the needs of the textile manufacturers in the south of France.[13] France, however, did not at any time have the monopoly of cotton purchase: the Dutch and other western Europeans in İzmir and non-Moslem Ottoman merchants—Armenians, Greeks, and Jews, who were mainly established in the Italian ports—were buying cotton and distributing it to the rest of Europe.[14] By the end of the eighteenth century and the beginning of the nineteenth, Switzerland and Germany were importing cotton, either directly from İzmir or through Holland.[15]

During the eighteenth century, the French would not permit merchants other than French nationals to import İzmir cotton into France. It was only during the Revolutionary and Napoleonic Wars that the French started to use non-Moslem Ottoman merchants as their agents or partners in İzmir.[16] By 1815, they had opened their trade in Marseilles to non-French merchants. Non-Moslem Ottoman merchants in İzmir, and in particular Greeks, started to export cotton to their compatriots who had, since the 1780s, established a commercial base in Marseilles.[17] Well into the 1820s, French merchants trading in the Levant, whose particular interests were hurt by the policy of *laissez-faire*, protested against this policy and sought its revision. Yet at the same time they were aware that British and American merchants were their biggest rivals, not the Greeks.[18] Finally, with France starting to import American cotton, French merchants in İzmir were left without an important merchandise they could purchase in exchange for the cloth they sold.

From the middle of the eighteenth century, the more liberal policy of the Dutch state allowed non-Moslem Ottoman merchants to export cotton to Holland and to set up commercial houses there. Some of the biggest names of the Greek trading community in İzmir also figured in Amsterdam—namely Mavrogordato, d'Issay, Rodocanachi, Petrocochino, Ralli, and Vlasto.[19] In the 1780s Greek merchants taking advantage of the international economic and political situation expanded their trade activities in the Italian ports as well. As was reported:

> The trade of Trieste with the Levant is practiced mainly by Greeks whose principals are in the Ottoman Empire. Until recently their trade was limited; their capital outlays were not very considerable and their activities were limited to the Morea, Salonica, Smyrna and the Islands of the Archipelago. The growth in their trade activities that has taken place in the last two to three years is due to the Dutch who have been bringing to Trieste the silk and cotton that they had bought in the Levant. From there they take them by land to Holland, Germany and Switzerland. They use the same route for exporting cloth to the Levant from Europe.[20]

The Dutch were using a land route because the British had imposed a tight blockade of their ports in the years 1781–82.[21] In 1782, all Dutch shipping had ceased.[22]

The best time for the Western merchants to buy cotton was in December, January, and February when most of the cotton still remained in the hands of the producers. The western Europeans also sent their brokers, non-Moslem intermediaries, to the environs with money to purchase it for them. A fortnight after the money was paid, the goods were sent to the city.[23] On the eve of the French Revolution, £15,000 were sent weekly by the Europeans to the environs of İzmir for the purchase of cotton. Starting with the first week in January, this amount decreased weekly. The whole procedure went on for five months until the entire crop was sold.[24] A large part of the cotton production was bartered against goods imported from Europe and occasionally against bills of exchange at an extraordinary discount. For instance, a Western merchant would pay for cotton with a bill of exchange that he had received *in lieu* of payment for some coffee or indigo he had sold to an Ottoman buyer. If the Ottoman buyer were honest and paid the cotton seller by the set date, the latter not only recovered his money but made a profit too, for the western European merchant had sold him the bill at a discount. On the other hand, he ran the risk of never recovering his money.[25]

Apart from the growing demand in the international market for cotton, and competition amongst Western merchants for its purchase, another factor that contributed to the rise in the price of cotton was local consumption by Ottoman manufacturers. In 1749, all the western European merchants banded together and declared a temporary boycott in the purchasing of cotton as a protest against a rise in prices. The result was that Ottoman merchants bought all the best cotton for the manufacturers in the interior of Anatolia and the Europeans had, in the end, to buy what was left at a still higher price.[26] The Ottoman price of cotton continued to go up throughout the second half of the eighteenth century; but, the high rate of devaluation of the Ottoman coin, which increased as the century drew to a close, eliminated the rise in price in the international market, making cotton marketable at all times.[27]

In the 1770s, there were in İzmir factories dyeing cotton yarn and printing cloth and muslins for export to Switzerland, Germany, and Great Britain, and they also catered to an internal market.[28] Western merchants became involved in both processes. The French experimented with buying cotton yarn and having it dyed in İzmir before exporting it to Marseilles, and, in the middle of the nineteenth century, the British imported British cloth which was then printed locally and sold. But, they found that printed Swiss cloth was underselling them.[29] One reason for this was that local Ottoman officials insisted on collecting two sets of duties on the cloth—one on the import of the cloth and another on the sale of the finished product. Workshops producing coarse cloth and lesser quality silk stuffs existed in İzmir and Chios, catering mainly to the lower end of the internal Ottoman market. These low-quality products could be potentially competitive since no duties were levied.[30]

Information on the relations of production for the cultivation of cotton as well as of other goods in the hinterland of İzmir in the eighteenth century is scant.[31] From references made by European consuls, mainly British and French, on these issues, it would appear that there existed in western Anatolia both small-scale peasant proprietorship[32] and large-scale landownership,[33] both connected to the external market, either directly or indirectly. Large-scale landowners, referred to in the documents as *agha*s, but in reality were lesser *ayan*s, sold the produce of their land to western European merchants, sometimes through an *homme d'affaires* who was usually an Armenian.[34] The most powerful ayan in the area, the Kara Osmanoğlu, with their rivals the Araboğlu, were known to apply any measures possible in order to increase the price of their produce. For instance, they might not allow the peasants to use their animals to transport the crop, hoping that the delay thus incurred would force the Europeans to offer higher prices.[35]

Another favorable development, fully exploited by the ayan, was the increased demand from the interior for cotton,[36] usually due to a failure in the crop production either in the immediate environs of İzmir or in the interior of Anatolia.[37] Whereas lesser aghas seemed to be participating in the market directly, Kara Osmanoğlu and Araboğlu did so usually through their peasants. As for the small peasant producers, the question was whether they could afford the cost of transportation to İzmir's market at all. Western merchants did not yet venture inland; so, rather than waiting for cotton to be brought to the İzmir market, they preferred to send their agents inland. Non-Moslem merchants usually bought the cotton on the spot and brought it to the city's market, either independently or in order to fulfill an order placed by a Western merchant. In fact this was seen as the best way to guarantee the purchase of first quality cotton.[38] This practice, intensified in the nineteenth century, prompted the British consul to note:

> Roads should be constructed to lessen the current cost of transport which inhibits many times the grower from sending his produce to the market. Instead he sells on the spot to speculators at prices unfavorable to him.[39]

Although there were certainly large-scale landowners, *de facto* if not *de jure*, it is less clear whether they could qualify as feudal landowners.[40] As late as 1792, the province of Aydın is recorded to have supported 110 *zaim* holders, 4,235 *timariots*, and one *beylerbeyi* whose annual revenue was 923,000 *akçes*.[41] In other words, the classical Ottoman feudal land system was still, at least partly, in force. Some landowners did have extensive jurisdiction over their lands, as did Kara Osmanoğlu Hacı Mustafa Agha, who had changed the boundaries of the peasants' plots.[42] Yet "opulent landowners" in the environs of İzmir were collecting their rents in money from their peasant cultivators. In the face of rampant inflation and depreciation in the first decade of the nineteenth century, an obliging government arbitrarily adjusted the rate of exchange in favor of the Ottoman coin and of the landowners' revenue.[43] This would indicate that these peasants were either sharecroppers or tenant farmers leasing their plots of land from the landowner under various forms of tenancy. Sharecroppers were, on the whole, Greek immigrants from Morea and from the Aegean islands who came from the 1770s onwards, settled in the lands of Kara Osmanoğlu, and cultivated cotton.[44] By the beginning of the nineteenth century, 3,000 Greek cultivators were settled around Kasaba as well as in the area surrounding the city of İzmir.[45] Bringing cultivators from outside was one method used by Kara Osmanoğlu to combat scarcity of manpower and depopulation of the countryside.

Small peasant proprietorship in western Anatolia, which was prevalent in the nineteenth century, seemed also to be current in the eighteenth. The European consuls speak of great oppression being suffered by such proprietors:

> the great oppression of the aghas has determined the proprietors to cultivate their lands every third year, a period beyond which they cannot go under pain of forfeiting their lands to the aghas.[46]

These aghas were in a position to oppress the peasants, either in their capacity as administrators, as tax farmers, or as providers of protection in a time of continuous anarchy created by peasants turned bandits or by feuding ayans.[47] At the end of the eighteenth century, and at the height of the power of the ayans, the British consul made the following observation of what was happening in the countryside:

> The population is reckoned to increase here [in the city of İzmir] considerably which is to be attributed in a great measure to the interior parts of the country being much depopulated by the extortions and oppressions of the numerous aghas appointed to the government of extensive districts which include many small towns and villages and who levy greater taxes on the inhabitants than are legally due.[48]

Lending to the peasants at usurious rates; so that the peasants could then meet their ever-increasing tax obligations to them and letting them slide into growing indebtedness, was another method used by these aghas to extract surplus and increase their power over the peasants. Inflation and depreciation, endemic in the Ottoman economy from the third quarter of the eighteenth century and continuing into the nineteenth, made usury widespread.[49] Depreciation of the Ottoman currency also took away a large part of the gain realized by the peasant in selling his produce, despite the continuous increase in international demand for cotton. Another labor relation was wage labor; either seasonal labor or on a daily basis.[50] The scarcity of manpower increased the need for migrant/seasonal labor.

Sources refer to Kara Osmanoğlu, the most powerful ayan in the area, both as "a proprietor of the grounds where cotton is planted . . . and (where) immense riches have been accumulated by the great demand for that article"[51] and as "an extraordinarily good administrator (where) trade is flourishing."[52] Certainly Kara Osmanoğlu was a landowner of considerable scale, with lands and titles his family had amassed through service to the Sultan. He was influential in the cultivation of cotton in the area by bringing in additional labor, owning the means of transportation, not being overtly extortionist, and protecting all peasants.[53] He owned the largest number of camels in the caravan trade between İzmir and western as well as eastern Anatolia.[54] He was also involved in large-scale international commerce. Western merchants were, at times, duly appreciative of his actions.[55] Although he was all-powerful in his own region, his position was still precarious. He had to fight palace intrigues that aimed to undermine his position, or that of his supporters.[56] This precariousness made him vulnerable as a landowner. Ultimately, perhaps, it was as administrator and tax collector that he was most influential in the area.[57]

In the nineteenth century, following the destruction of the power of the ayans and the abolition of the *corvée*, small-scale peasant proprietorship became even more prevalent, although large-scale landownership continued to exist alongside it.[58] Want of capital and manpower were probably the two most important factors that inhibited productivity and sometimes even dictated the type of production. For instance, in 1863, despite the four-fold increase in land prepared for cotton seeds, a large part of American and Egyptian seeds available to the cultivators were not being used. The reason for this was that American and Egyptian cotton required more labor than the local variety, and "the native farmers, however desirous to increase cotton cultivation . . . can not calculate upon the amount of labor required to make it productive and remunerative."[59] Large-scale landowners were successfully planting American cotton seeds for they had the capital to hire extra labor.

Defective tillage, deficient manure, and high transportation costs were other factors that plagued agricultural production and resulted in low productivity during the eighteenth and nineteenth centuries.[60] Agricultural implements remained rudimentary, and cotton gins, in existence since the nineteenth century, were mostly owned by British or American capital.[61]

Cloth

From the early seventeenth century to the early twentieth century, cloth was the most important export of western Europe to the Levant.[62] İzmir was no exception. The export of raw materials— cotton, cotton yarn, mohair yarn, wool, and silk in the eighteenth century, and wheat, raisins, figs, and other foodstuffs in the nineteenth century—was complemented by the importation of manufactured goods, namely cloth. Of the European cloth exported to İzmir, in terms of popularity and sales French cloth was the most important in the eighteenth century and British cloth in the nineteenth.

In the second half of the eighteenth century, over 180 French manufacturers from Languedoc sent cloth to İzmir, ranging from very expensive varieties to competitively priced types of cloth.[63] Strict classification was imposed on this cloth in order to maintain standards and credibility in the Levantine market. A large number of different types of cloth were sold in the market of İzmir, the most popular of which were the *Londrins seconds*. Though not a luxury cloth, it was above average quality and sold well in İzmir. It was not always bartered, but could be sold for cash. In fact, there was a direct correlation between the market for wheat and the sale of Londrins seconds in İzmir. For when wheat sold well, the cash available was used by the Ottoman merchants to buy Londrins seconds. When wheat sales were on the decline, French merchants avoided sending too large a quantity of Londrins seconds for fear that it would be left unsold, and sent instead lesser quality cloth.[64] When the buyer had nothing to exchange, the seller was forced to sell him cloth on credit, which could be extended as long as two years. The European merchants were not the only ones selling cloth on credit to shopkeepers and dealers in the bazaar. Non-Moslem Ottoman merchants, who were themselves importers of cloth into İzmir, did so as well. Around 1820, such European and non-Moslem merchants formed an association to protect themselves from fraudulent debtors and impose on them stricter terms of payment.[65]

There were three types of Londrins seconds, which took their name from the place of production in the South of France— Carcassonne, St. Clermont, and St. Chinian. They first appeared in the Levantine market as an imitation of the British cloth—hence the name Londrins. By the 1730s, British cloth was ousted from the Levantine market by the French Londrins. There were two qualities of *Londrins seconds de Carcassonne,* both of which did well. The St. Clermont and St. Chinian were also popular, though more for their color than for their quality.

Londrins seconds totally dominated French cloth exports to İzmir. In the late 1750s, they represented 77 percent of all French cloth exports; in the 1760s, they represented 85 percent; in the 1770s, 93.5 percent, and in the 1780s, 95 percent. Between 1783–88, of all Londrins seconds exported to the Ottoman Empire, İzmir's market absorbed 39 percent.[66] The reason for the predominance of Londrins seconds was that İzmir supplied a large but middle-range market in Anatolia and Persia. Unlike İstanbul, İzmir had no group of officials or rich dignitaries who would buy very expensive luxury cloth. Expensive cloth was usually consumed within the city of İzmir and in its immediate environs, such as Chios.[67] Second in marketability came the cheaper *Londres larges*, which did particularly well in the Persian market. The Ottoman-Safavid wars greatly affected the sales of this cloth in İzmir. Other kinds of French cloth that came to İzmir were in small quantities.[68]

For most of the second half of the eighteenth century, the French authorities strongly believed in controlling the market and influencing prices. For instance, they only allowed a limited quantity of high quality cloth to be sent to İzmir, in order to prevent the oversupply from being sent to İstanbul where it would compete with the wares of other French merchants. Thus, it was by accident that luxury quality gold and silver thread cloth reached the market of İzmir in any quantity.[69] Another way to regulate the price of cloth was through the system of *répartitions*. A merchant was only allowed to sell a certain number of bales of cloth within a specified period of time and within a set price range. This way he could not try to undersell his compatriots. In the second half of the eighteenth century, this restriction was practically abandoned, as the French authorities realized that whatever they gained by keeping the prices from falling too low, they lost by the limited amount of goods they sold.[70] Other nationalities came in to fill the gap in the market left by the French, for there was always competition in İzmir both among the buyers and among the sellers of cloth.

When introducing a new type of cloth, they usually bartered it against mohair yarn, until it became popular. They were not alone, however, in dealing with mohair yarn. French merchants established in Ankara also bought mohair yarn, usually for cash. When considerable amounts of cash were thus deployed, the French in İzmir found themselves unable to barter their cloth.[71]

Other incentives were then placed on the price of the cloth to make its sale attractive. In such cases, the price usually included an *agio*, or discount, based on the expected depreciation of the Ottoman currency between the time of the purchase of the cloth in İzmir and the time it took to transport it to its final destination for sale. So that the Ottoman merchant would not carry the loss from the depreciation of the currency, or pass it on to the local consumer and risk pricing the cloth out of the market, the European merchant agreed to carry part of the loss himself. This practice became current especially after the 1760s due to growing inflation and depreciation of the Ottoman currency. The exact amount of agio was decided periodically by the European merchants and the Ottoman authorities, though not necessarily in direct consultation with each other. If no agio was agreed upon in İzmir, the Ottoman merchant went to another city—İstanbul, Salonica, or Bursa—where there was agio in force, to trade there in cash.[72] İzmir not only lost out on cloth sales, but ran the risk of having its market drained of capital.

If the market were particularly depressed and the European merchants were finding it difficult to sell their cloth for cash, they were prepared to give credit. Credit could be extended from three times thirty-one days to three times eighteen months. The longer the terms of credit, the lesser was the agio included in the overall price. The agio was also used as an added incentive in the following way. British merchants declared an agio of 2–3 percent on payments of debts, if these payments were made in "good money," that is, in European currencies. Other Europeans had to follow suit, at least as long as the British were giving this incentive, in order not to have their own payments made in Ottoman *para*, which, with the rate of depreciation of the Ottoman currency at that time, was rapidly losing its value.[73]

It is difficult to establish the trends in the prices of the cloth imported into İzmir: French statistics tend to group several types of cloth into one, citing a total value only, or else they give the price of a type of cloth on the basis of different measurements.[74] Nevertheless, if we compare the index of the volume with that of the value of cloth imported into İzmir, we find that initially there was a constant fluctuation between the two indices.[75] After 1766, the index in value rose perceptively higher than the index in volume, showing a rise in the price of imported cloth.[76] In the late 1780s, the gap between the two indices started to close as the increase in price slowed down. These trends are also reflected in the share of cloth that the market of İzmir claimed in relation to French cloth exports to the Levant as a whole. In the years 1750–70, İzmir accounted for 22 percent in value and 30.4 percent in volume of all French cloth exported to the Ottoman Empire. In the years 1771–89, this share increased to 35 percent in value and 34 percent in volume.[77]

The volume of cloth exported to İzmir from France during the years 1750–70 averaged 1,972 *ballots* or 986 bales per year.[78] In the years 1770–80, annual cloth exports averaged 2,191 ballots per year, for an increase of 82 percent. The years of peak consumption were 1779–83, with an average of 2,911 ballots per year. In 1750, cloth represented in value 48.4 percent of all the exports of France to İzmir; in 1760, its share was 73 percent; in 1770 it dropped to 33.5 percent; and in 1780 it rose again to 51 percent. In the years immediately preceding the French Revolution, cloth exports fluctuated between 21 percent and 28 percent. In absolute terms İzmir imported 836,410 guruş worth of cloth on an annual average between 1750–70. In the years, 1771–89, it absorbed 1,323,355 guruş on an annual average, or an increase of 37 percent. In the peak years of French cloth exports, cloth worth 1,706,966 guruş was imported annually.[79]

Although trade between İzmir and France increased until the French Revolution—İzmir's highest exports to France for the century, both in volume and value, were recorded in 1787—the trade in cloth dropped off in the early 1770s and again in the late 1780s. British cloth, more competitively priced than the French and of a far better quality, had already started to compete with French cloth: in the 1770s, 64 percent of British exports were made up of cloth and in the 1780s, 56 percent. From the 1780s onwards, much British cloth was reaching İzmir via Italian ports.[80] Between 1777 and 1782, there was a recovery in French exports due to the American War of Independence (1776–83).

As France and later Spain entered the war against Great Britain, Britain ceased sending goods to the eastern Mediterranean in convoys; only private individuals sent goods at their own risk. As a result British trade with İzmir was constricted.[81] During the Napoleonic Wars, British cloth started to reach İzmir through Malta, and by 1812 through British-held Ionian Islands, Corfu in particular. These trading networks were not exclusively in British hands. Greek merchants also went to Malta or Corfu to get British cloth for distribution in the ports of the eastern Mediterranean, including İzmir.[82]

At the height of popularity of French cloth in the market of İzmir, in the 1750s and 1760s, the mere label indicating that it was made in Languedoc was enough for a bale not to be opened.[83] But, even before the political upheaval of the French Revolution and the subsequent years of warfare between Great Britain and France in the Revolutionary and Napoleonic Wars, which swept away most of the infrastructure of French trade in the Levant, French manufactures had already fallen into trouble. Keeping their prices stable or even lowering them in an attempt to be competitive with British cloth, Languedoc manufacturers were forced to reduce the quality of the cloth produced, thus losing their credibility in the Levantine market. This in turn made French merchants reluctant to deal in cloth, when they could instead export specie to İzmir. In the last quarter of the eighteenth century, the chaotic monetary and financial situation in İzmir and its chronic lack of specie—which went hand in hand with a tremendous growth in its commercial activities, and in turn created opportunities for monetary speculation—prompted French merchants to engage in a systematic trade in specie and bills of exchange. Besides, by then, British, Dutch, German, and Swiss cloth were taking a substantial share in the cloth market of İzmir.

During the Napoleonic Wars, the absence of French cloth from the market of İzmir for two decades allowed competitors to establish themselves.[84] Once this had happened, it was difficult for the French to recapture the market. In the early nineteenth century, the Americans were the only major trading partner of İzmir who were not exporting to it large amounts of cloth, but rather sugar and tobacco.[85] By then, Greek merchants had also acquired a stronghold in the international cloth trade, importing British and German cloth into İzmir.

In 1820, most prosperous French merchants who had remained in İzmir or had reestablished commercial houses there, were trading with Egypt, not Marseilles. Those who were ostensibly exporting cotton and olive oil to the French port and importing cloth were in fact dealing in informal banking activities: lending at high interest rates and moving funds in and out of the market of İzmir according to the rate of exchange or money-changing.[86] Others were engaged in fraudulent practices, sending cloth to İzmir that was badly finished or bales of cloth that were not of the same quality throughout, in an effort to keep afloat. The result was an even bigger influx of British cloth. Part of the monetary surplus that İzmir got from its active balance of trade with a number of countries including France, was being sent to London, via Malta, to buy British cloth.[87] In the early nineteenth century the situation became worse for the French textile industry. Gold and silk stuffs made in Lyons, and popular in İzmir in the second half of the eighteenth century, were being supplanted not only by Venetian products but also by local products.[88]

In the early seventeenth century, the western Europeans could go to the local producers and purchase local goods, including cotton, directly from them in exchange for cloth and other goods.[89] In the eighteenth century, this was no longer the case. Non-Moslem merchants had become the intermediaries between local producers and the European merchants in all the major Ottoman ports, including İzmir. The former regime was still in force in the Aegean islands for the purchase of wheat and olive oil.[90] In the nineteenth century, western European merchants, having acquired the right to deal with local producers directly, used instead non-Moslem merchants as their agents, whom they sent to the interior of western Anatolia.

One reason for the intermediaries acquiring such a position in the eighteenth century, at least vis-à-vis the French, was the chronic lack of specie that the French economy suffered from throughout the eighteenth century. Pressed to buy cotton and other goods to fill a return cargo to the West and not always having the necessary cash to buy them with, the French merchant used an elaborate system of bartering made possible through the intervention of the non-Moslem Ottoman intermediary. It was credit in kind, in other words, instead of money; the intermediary advanced him goods. The advantage to the Ottoman dealer was that in this way he was creating a link that he could control through which trade had to pass. The Frenchman not only bought everything from him, but also sold his goods to Ottoman buyers and Armenian caravan merchants exclusively through him.[91]

One should not assume from the above that the Ottoman intermediaries were in a very strong position in the eighteenth century. The western Europeans held in their hands most of the external trade of İzmir for most of the eighteenth century. It was only in the final decades that the position of the European merchant began to be significantly eroded. This was due partly to economic and partly to political reasons. The social and political upheaval of the French Revolution and the period of continuous warfare that ensued between Great Britain and France during the Revolutionary and Napoleonic Wars broke the supremacy of France and left a relative gap in the international trade of the Levant, including İzmir, which the non-Moslem merchants filled. These events, accompanied by a sustained growth in the world-economy, forced France and Great Britain to open up their trade monopolies at a time when free trade was "in the air" but not yet an established state policy. Jewish and especially Greek merchants in İzmir took advantage of these conditions to increase their capital accumulation and enlarge their business activities in the international market at the cost of the European merchants in İzmir.[92]

For instance, by the end of the eighteenth century Greek merchants, who always had a share in the cloth trade, succeeded in ousting the Dutch merchants, who imported Dutch and other European-made cloth to İzmir. They did it in two stages. Greek merchants had established commercial houses in Amsterdam since the 1750s taking advantage of the liberal policies of the Dutch. They did well by sending Dutch cloth to their compatriots in İzmir, who then sold it. Greek merchants dominated both the wholesale and the retail market of cloth in the city. In the 1780s, with the international economic conditions favoring them, they created a monopoly of the buyers' market for Dutch cloth in İzmir and imposed their own prices and conditions of purchase. By the end of the Napoleonic Wars, the worst fears of the Dutch were to be realized. The Greek cloth dealers were fast taking over the entire Dutch cloth trade as they had already taken over the Dutch trade in silk stuffs. The Greeks had another advantage: they knew the internal Anatolian market well and could get their cloth distributed there through their agents.[93]

Greeks continued to expand their trading networks inside western Anatolia. Their success in this sector became apparent with the signing of the Treaty of 1838 between Great Britain and the Ottoman Empire, with which the British extended their trade ventures inland into western Anatolia. Here, they found that Greek and other non-Moslem Ottoman merchants were exporting the local produce, having obtained the monopoly of purchasing these goods from local Ottoman administrators.[94] Thus, the British, who remained in their commercial bases in İzmir, used Greeks and other intermediaries as agents, due to their contacts and expertise.[95] Sometimes they nominated a Greek merchant directly from Europe to represent them in İzmir and its hinterland.[96] As the nineteenth century progressed non-Moslem Ottoman merchants started to take a more active role in the process of production and consumption. Greek merchants, either working on their own or as agents of the British, speculated through advance purchases of crops much more extensively than earlier.[97]

Trade in cotton and cloth was an important factor in the economic growth of İzmir and also in the rise of the intermediaries who were actively involved. This trade does not, however, appear to have affected the relations of production in agriculture. The increase in the market orientation of İzmir's cotton production did lead to a relative strengthening of the position of the ayan. This strength, however, could not shelter them from the recentralization of the Ottoman state early in the the nineteenth century.

6

Migrant Labor in Western Anatolia, 1750–1850*

Reşat Kasaba

As a topic, migrant labor enters little into the discussion of the transformation of Ottoman agriculture in the eighteenth and nineteenth centuries. This is curious because sources originating in various regions of the empire contain many references to the presence of migrants, immigrants, temporary workers, seasonal migrants, and sojourners leaving little room to doubt that a sizable number of people moved periodically in and out and about various parts of the Empire, mostly in search of agricultural employment. For example, in 1860 the British consul estimated that out of 991,700 people living in Aydın province, 110,000 were "migratory."[1] In 1869, another consul put the number of seasonal wage laborers who were employed throughout the Asiatic provinces of the Ottoman empire at 200,000.[2] Examples can be multiplied both from this particular region and from other parts of the empire.

Sociological literature usually treats migration as a residual phenomenon where people move in order to fill in the disparity between the local supply and demand for workers. This is not the place to go into a detailed criticism of this literature. The perennial nature of circulation of labor in the entire historical development of the capitalist world-economy makes it imperative that we explain this phenomenon as an integral part of that development rather than as an *ex post* factor of adjustment.[3]

*I would like to thank Şevket Pamuk and Joel Migdal who read and commented on earlier draft of this paper.

In the specific case of Anatolian agriculture, the mechanical application of pull/push models would be particularly problematic because the sparseness of settlements and hence the relative scarcity of labor were not confined to any one region.[4] The corollary to this is that there was no readily available pool of laborers from which workers could be easily drawn into areas of high demand. Nevertheless, laborers did circulate in the Ottoman empire within and across many geographical regions. This paper seeks to delineate the source of this circulating work force and explain its place in the changing agricultural relations and processes in western Anatolia during the late eighteenth and the nineteenth centuries.

Most of the references to the growing number of seasonal migrants in western Anatolia date from the last decades of the eighteenth and the first three quarters of the nineteenth centuries. In Ottoman history this time period is better known for the rise of local notables (*ayan*), and the expansion of commercial agriculture that took place at the same time.

In western Anatolia, the best known of local notables was the Kara Osmanoğlu family. By the turn of the nineteenth century the members of this family had captured the important posts of both the deputy tax administrator (*mütesellim*) of Saruhan and that of the tax collector (*muhassıl*) of Aydın. Within this region, the lands over which they held some sort of private claim amounted to thousands of acres. At the time, Kara Osmanoğlu Hacı Ömer was reputed to be the sole power to be reckoned with within the area between the rivers of Gediz and Büyük Menderes.[5]

The commercial boom that western Anatolia experienced during this period is also well documented.[6] Here are the impressions of a traveler who visited İzmir in the closing years of the eighteenth century:

> In that trucking, trafficking city, peoples' ideas run upon nothing but merchandise: their discourse only varies between the exchanges and the markets: their heads are full of figs and raisins, and their whole hearts wrapped up in cotton and broad cloths. They suppose man created for nothing but to buy and sell; and whoever makes not these occupations the sole business of his life, seems to them to neglect the end of his existence. I verily believe that they marry for no other purpose but to keep up the race of merchants.[7]

It would be an attractive proposition to establish a relationship between these three developments. Then it would be possible to identify the migrants as landless peasants who were employed by the

local ayan who in turn could be shown to be engaged in large-scale
capitalist farming. However, it is not certain that the Kara Osmanoğlu
family or the other contending notables of western Anatolia had, in
fact, the means for affecting and overseeing directly the reorganization of the region's agriculture to support the flourishing commerce of
the region.

Like all ayans in the Ottoman Empire, those in western Anatolia
first became prominent in urban centers as a result of some useful
service they provided for the central government. But while the notables of Rumelia quickly extended their power into the countryside,
those in western Anatolia continued to rely on their allegiance to the
center as their primary source of power and influence in the region.[8]
(Kara) Osman Agha, the founder of the famous family, performed his
first significant service to the government in 1691 by confiscating the
crops of those sipahis who had failed to participate in the Vienna
campaign.[9] Then in 1743, the government turned to his son Mustafa
for help in getting rid of the bandits whose raids had caused extensive
damage in the countryside.[10] As late as the Ottoman–Russian war of
1786–92, Kara Osmanoğlu Hacı Mehmed and his brother Hacı Ömer
provided troops for and fought personally in the Ottoman army.[11]
Each one of these assignments resulted in the conferring of additional
titles on the members of the family, and these titles were usually
accompanied by various gifts and land grants in the form of life time
leases. In other words, for the families involved, performing these
services became a means of expanding their domains in western
Anatolia. Also, the successive titles they acquired made them the sole
assessors and collectors of taxes in their region and strengthened the
legitimacy of their claims over these lands and their products.

Given these circumstances, it was normal for these individuals
to have a vested interest in the expansion of commercial agriculture in
their localities since this would be likely to improve tax and other
revenues that would accrue to them. The problem, however, was that
for all their fame and fortune, the ayans failed to develop effective
means of translating their formal titles into instruments of pressure to
effect such a mobilization in the countryside. In this respect, their
relationship with İstanbul turned out to be more of a liability than an
asset. In the eyes of the peasants, the official nature of the ayans' titles
turned them into agents of the central government. As the difference
between the locally based families and the centrally appointed functionaries disappeared, the peasants availed themselves of various
means to actively resist the ayans' demands.

Patterns of land distribution and related conditions in western
Anatolia also favored the peasants over the ayans. At the time of the

rise of the ayan, the Anatolian countryside had come to be dominated by peasants who, having been freed from the supervision of the sipahis, owned or occupied small to medium size plots.[12] If the notables' claims were to go beyond the mere encircling of such plots, they would have to displace these peasants titularly, and sometimes physically as well.[13] Alternatively, they could establish big farms alongside the small holdings and compete with the latter.

In either case they would have to come up with net additions to the available labor force in the region since plague and other epidemics of the late eighteenth century had further depleted the already meager labor resources.[14] There were four potential sources of net addition to the labor force in western Anatolia. The first of these was the flow of people from the Aegean islands and Morea who for political and/or economic reasons regularly crossed over to Anatolia. The second was the nomads in and around the area who took part in settled agriculture, in addition to their main occupation of animal husbandry and dairy farming, especially during the times of harvest. The third source was the migrants from eastern Anatolia and the eastern coast of the Black Sea who came to work in western Anatolia where they would stay for a few years before returning to their homes. And finally there were the immigrants from the recently ceded territories in the Balkans, Crimea, and Circassia some of whom were settled in western Anatolia.

Ayans of western Anatolia were active in the recruitment of workers from the islands.[15] They also employed the nomads from around the area and the Kurds and Lazes from the east.[16] In fact, at one point, Kurds and Lazes were noted as the main group of hired laborers in western Anatolian agriculture.[17] As for the immigrants from outside the empire, some of these were skilled technicians who were employed in the construction of railways in western Anatolia. Another group came with capital and commercial expertise. They settled in coastal cities and became active in trade. The remaining group, which constituted the majority, were alloted land for settlement.[18]

Thus, for the most part, these immigrants should be seen as having expanded the scope of small peasant farming rather then providing another source of labor to the owners of large estates. In other words, the islanders, local nomadic tribes, and the migrants from the east were the only groups that provided a pool of agricultural workers that was accessible to the ayan. But since these people were only partially dispossessed, they entered western Anatolian agriculture only on their own terms and for wages that were quite high.[19]

For two of the three sources, the ayan had to depend on people who came or were recruited from considerable distances. Despite these difficulties, the owners of large estates managed to reserve part of their holdings for the cultivation of profitable crops that were destined for export markets.[20] They also contributed to the expansion of commercial agriculture by providing security and protection to villagers. But the uncertainty of labor supplies on the one hand, and their desire to remain closely affiliated with the imperial center on the other, prevented the ayan from becoming the primary force behind the expansion of commercial agriculture in western Anatolia. Instead, they concentrated their efforts on nurturing their political allegiance to İstanbul, and for the cultivation of the greater part of their estates, they came to depend on existing practices of sharecropping and other forms of tenancy that had devolved partly from the classical land system. Consequently, even at the apex of notable rule in western Anatolia, when the villages were being encircled and claimed *en masse*, and when increasingly onerous demands were being imposed on their occupants, peasants—as owners, tenants, and sharecroppers—maintained a substantial degree of freedom in the day-to-day management of their plots.

The limited involvement of the ayan in the direct management of commercial agriculture in western Anatolia can be further demonstrated by pointing to the fact that the commercial expansion in the area was not confined to the high point of the notables' tenure. In the case of the Kara Osmanoğlu family, their decline can be dated from 1813 when Mahmud II appointed an outsider as tax collector/deputy administrator upon Kara Osmanoğlu Hüseyin's death.[21] The subsequent generations of the Kara Osmanoğlu family continued to enjoy the fruits of their close relationship with the Porte, but their appointments became more conventional and veered further and further away from western Anatolia. For example, one of Hacı Hüseyin's sons served as the governor of Drama, and another died while he was the governor of Jerusalem.[22] But the easing of the ayan's hold in western Anatolia did not disturb the long-term expansion of commercial agriculture in the region; neither did it have a deleterious effect on the circulation of commodities or labor. On the contrary, both the production of commercial crops and their trade reached two further peaks in the 1850s and in the 1860s, that is, long after the grandeur of the local notables had lapsed.

Accordingly, another and more important source of circulating labor should be sought in the interactions among small peasant holdings. By themselves, peasants were not necessarily better equipped than the notables to deal with the formidable problems that had prevented the latter from leaving a long-lasting mark on the commercial-

ization of western Anatolian agriculture. But a number of developments that proceeded independently of the peasants themselves
ended up helping them overcome these constraints and facilitated the
commercial integration of the parcellized agrarian structure in the
countryside. Foremost among these was the rise of the local merchants to a new status of prominence in the area. Local traders took
advantage of the vacuum that was left in western Anatolia by the
forced withdrawal of the French from the eastern Mediterranean during the Napoleonic Wars. They installed themselves firmly in the
arteries of trade, and, in the absence of proper banking institutions,
they also became the bankers of the local populace—a position which
they utilized to inject money into western Anatolia. This in turn provided them with leverage with which they could pressure the peasants directly regarding the type and mode of cultivation on their
plots.

We are accustomed to seeing the activities of these merchants-
cum-bankers in a negative light. The high interest rates they charged
on loans, the practice of pre-emptive purchase at disadvantageous
prices, and the long-term burden of indebtedness which they imposed on the peasants are usually cited to demonstrate the adverse
impact on the local population of these new power relations. There is,
however, another side to this relationship. The establishment of a
direct contact between merchants and peasants meant that, under the
right circumstances, the latter could benefit from cultivating those
crops that were in high demand. Lacking the means to organize production directly, merchants had to transmit the favorable prices into
the countryside in order to ensure the steady supply of certain crops.
Contemporary records describe in detail the growing diversity of
goods found in local markets to show that the times of accelerated
commercial growth were often also the times of improvement in the
relative prosperity for the local population.[23]

The possibility of contacting the merchants directly facilitated a
relative intensification of farming activities and their concentration in
the immediate vicinity of towns. Peasants already had some labor-
saving methods which they employed as a means of improving the
efficiency of their activities in their own plots. For example, in Bursa,
mulberry trees were planted close to each other to prevent them from
growing to full size. They were thus made more easily harvestable
with limited labor.[24] Around İzmir, farmers would often intermix two
kinds of seeds on the same plot thereby doubling their chances in the
market.[25] Again in İzmir, in 1863 local producers refused to plant the
imported Egyptian cotton seed which was distributed to them free of
charge because it required more attention and hence more labor.[26] For

the most part, the peasants would use the time they would thus save to circulate in the area and do additional work on other plots of land that were either uncultivated or belonged to their neighbors. Also, harvesting time for the major cash crops of western Anatolia succeeded one another between the months of July and December. This timetable made it possible for an individual peasant or peasant household to finish the work on one plot or crop and move on to another.[27]

It should be emphasized that, like the nomads, the farmers who were taking part in the circulating labor force were not totally dispossessed. In fact, their continued access to land, livestock, and other sources of income enabled them to circulate and participate in reciprocal activities in a regular manner. In sum then, none of the main sources of migration can be shown to have generated a permanent flow of workers that would have altered the overall ratio of labor to resources in the area. Instead, they contributed to a circulating labor force which, for the most part, involved the redistribution and more intensive utilization of locally available labor.

In the Ottoman Empire, neither the circulation of people in the lowlands, nor the continuous interchange between the sedentary and nomadic forms of life was specific to the late eighteenth century. Those conceptions of classical empire as a strictly regimented and static formation usually overlook the considerable room that peasants enjoyed to maneuver around the complex maze of governmental regulations. Nevertheless, the circulation of labor in the post-eighteenth century period was substantively different from its historical antecedents. In earlier times, peasants moved primarily to protect themselves from the excessive demands of the government and its agents.[28] In the later period, however, the main impetus came from the perceived opportunities that could be derived from participating in commercial agriculture. Thus, it can be argued that in the earlier period the predominant impact of population movements (except for those that occurred as part of governmental policy of conquest and colonization) was to scatter peasant households further into the countryside, leading, ultimately, to a relative diminution in cultivation, whereas in the post-eighteenth century, the circulating labor force was a key factor that underlay the multiplication of crops and the expansion of cultivation.

Thus, the local intermediaries who injected large amounts of money into western Anatolia and the partially dispossessed labor force that was willing to circulate in a wide area interwove the small peasant holdings (both within and outside of the ayans' estates) into a commercial network. In this configuration nomads occupied a crucially important position not only as suppliers of livestock and purveyors of the main means of transportation in the area, but also as seasonal migrants and gatherers of Anatolian exports that grew in the wild such as madder and valonia.

To be sure, the interchange of labor and capital which served to mobilize western Anatolian agriculture was premised on a certain hierarchy of land holdings. The gradation in land size differentiated not so much the very large estates from subsistence plots but the medium size plots from small properties. The difference became increasingly marked as the nineteenth century wore on. By the 1850s there was a clear distinction between the gardens and farms that surrounded major towns and those that were dispersed in the countryside. While the high land/labor ratio continued to prevail as a general characteristic for the entire region, land came to be in relatively high demand, highly priced, and intensively cultivated in the vicinity of towns. It was primarily within this region and to this region that labor flowed. Consequently, more of the rewards from commercial agriculture concentrated in the hands of these better situated farmers.[29]

In the short run, the ability of the peasants to move in and out of certain areas and the concomitant ease with which the cultivation of certain crops could be expanded and cut back afforded them both an intermittent prosperity and valuable protection from the vagaries of the market place and from the onerous demands of the central government and of the local ayan. But these same factors also fettered the long-term growth of western Anatolian agriculture and were partly responsible for the halting manner in which the regions' exports grew in the eighteenth and nineteenth centuries.

In concluding, I would like to point out three broad areas where further research on migrant labor could be pursued. The first of these is comparative in nature. While our emphasis here was primarily on western Anatolia, similar flows of labor shaped an important part of commercial agriculture in other parts of the empire: most notably in the Balkans, southern Anatolia, and the eastern Mediterranean basin. A comparative evaluation of different forms of recruitment and integration of labor in such regions is one topic that awaits in-depth analysis.[30] It should be noted that in the frontier regions such as the Balkans, these interchanges had the further function of providing an organic link across borders, thus facilitating further the incorporation of these areas into the world–economy.

Secondly, the fact that the source of these flows included not only the nearby mountains but also more distant regions reveals an important but hitherto neglected aspect of the incorporation of the Ottoman Empire into the world-economy. The actual integration of the production processes to the world-economy proceeded in a discontinuous manner and through a limited number of areas in the Empire. But these linkages caused a series of displacements that affected the processes of production and social relations in a much wider area and opened channels between regions as far from each other as eastern and western Anatolia.

A third question relates to recruitment activities which, ultimately, paved the way for people to move. To be sure, part of the flow was spontaneous and derived from previous migrations and government policies. But beyond this, there was a wider and more sustained interchange. Since the ayans were not in a position to set up and maintain such a system, merchants were the only group likely to have acted as agents in such an enterprise. If true, this will add a further dimension to the already crucial role which these intermediaries played in the commercial integration of western Anatolia.

These are only some of the questions that are generated by an initial examination of the topic of migrant labor in Ottoman agriculture. Further thinking along these lines is bound to open up fertile ground that will help improve our understanding of the incorporation and peripheralization of the Ottoman Empire.

7

Property, Land, and Labor
in Nineteenth-Century Anatolia

Tosun Arıcanlı

Large-Scale Agriculture, Property, and Labor Relations

Whenever the question of large-scale agricultural operations is at issue in Ottoman history, or for that matter in the history of any other society, the nature of control that leads to large landholdings gains major importance. As it is argued in other papers in this volume, property is often implied to be the basis of large landholding. Yet this implication is made without adequate scrutiny. The way in which property makes its way into the argument is through an assumption derived from western experience.

There are many ways in which control can be maintained over agricultural production with varying degrees of property rights. Especially in the case of property in agricultural land, the usual assumption drawn from European experience does not explain the Ottoman reality. Here property remains an alien concept, often leading to confusion in understanding social and economic relations.

I shall discuss different forms of control of agricultural production in the Ottoman case and evaluate the role of property relations in order to demarcate the arena of economic interaction within which the Ottoman system makes sense.

What is Property?

Property is a bundle of rights that determines a set of relationships between people (and the state) with respect to relevant objects, in this case agricultural land. These rights are recognized by the society and the state alike. They are neither a logical derivation from a set of preconditions nor a requirement of social laws. The most important aspect characterizing property is its society-wide acceptance. It is a right originating from social interaction.[1]

The Weak Definition of Property. In the most general definition of property two sets of rights stand out: the right of ownership and the right of control. With respect to land, rights of ownership relate to the use of land to receive income in the form of rent, taxes, and commissions on taxes. The emphasis here is on the access to *income* from land which need not be an absolute right. It should also be noted that this excludes political control of a territory, say through military means, where the objective is other than direct agricultural management. Right to control, on the other hand, could derive from ownership, but it need not. Control can be delegated to an agent who does not have ownership rights.

Property rights can also be classified according to modes of acquisition, through exchange, gift, inheritance, assignment, or expropriation. On the other hand, classification can be made according to the conditionality of the property rights on the basis of whether they can be withdrawn or not. While these classifications are neither exclusive nor exhaustive, they provide a fair basis for a general understanding of property rights. The purpose of this discussion is to illustrate the wide scope of the notion of property, rather than to present an exhaustive taxonomy of its different forms.

Within the many possible configurations that the above scheme would yield, any claim on agrarian revenue in the Ottoman empire can be called "property." For example, the right to collect taxes, long-term *iltizam*, and sub-contracts in tax farming are forms of property with greatly varying privileges and protection. Yet, to define the forms of such property consisting of access to agrarian revenue, one must investigate the workings of the Ottoman system itself rather than borrow a concept from an alien social structure. Obviously, when property relations are central, the above weak forms are not of major interest due to the impossibility of drawing a causal relation between such forms of property and any form of social change.[2]

The Strong Definition of Property. The interesting aspect of property relations in social history, especially with respect to land, is the connection between their emergence and the radical transformation of European civilization. Existing relationships in European society and its economy were totally changed while property rights were being established in a process of long-lasting social struggle between the nobility, the state, and the peasantry.

The emergent form of property on land was much different from those forms found elsewhere, including the Ottoman empire and the Middle East. In the first place, the Western form of property meant solidification of rights as opposed to revokable privileges. This is the basis of capitalist property relations and it emphasizes two aspects. First, property is an absolute, and more importantly, its ownership is an "inalienable" right; secondly, it is transferable, ultimately transforming land into a "commodity" that is in principle indistinguishable from any other commodity.

The principle of inalienability establishes a strict limit on state encroachment on private property that almost resembles the containment of state influence through consolidation of local military strength, where central authority is checked by a local power. The difference, though, is that the nature of private property is not based on military strength but on continuity and general acceptability of the institution/right. At the same time this continuity is predicated on an institutionalization that maintains its inviolable nature indefinitely.

When the integrity of property is maintained through military protection, the issue of economic returns from land is basically a matter of distribution, or who gets the benefits. This is a redistribution problem between the local power, which could be the nobility, and the state. When the integrity of property is maintained by an "institution" that has gained currency, i.e., the "right" to private property itself, the distributional issue in terms of who holds absolute and continuous rights to the surplus disappears. There is no logical reason why a transformation of the economics of land use would follow the emergence of private property. On the other hand, the notion that private property appears with the consolidation of forces attempting to transform methods of land cultivation leads to a more plausible argument. In the case of British transformation, the fight between the state and the nobility was over the rights of agrarian taxation and peasant cultivation which the nobility, together with emergent capitalist farmers, were attempting to transform. However, one of the fundamental questions that must be dealt with once the field of study moves away from Great Britain to the Middle East is the nature of those forces that attempted to transform production relations on land. Outside the British example, it is often the state rather than local forces that maintains control. This sort of outcome has a direct bearing on the *nature* of property rights on land, which is often taken for granted.

In short, together with the emergence of strong property rights on land, methods of production underwent a revolutionary transformation in Europe. Here the definition and the practice of either property rights or their assumed derivative, production relations, could not be changed or reversed by the state. In other words, property was a defense against the infringement of the state, a basis of legitimacy inviolable by the state. This form of absolute, inviolable property is associated with social change and epoch-making transformations, and this is what the Ottoman form of property precisely is not.

To illustrate the point, on the basis of the strong definition of property (inviolableness) it should be impossible to argue that property existed in the eighteenth and twentieth centuries but disappeared through most of the nineteenth century. Yet such arguments are common, or at least implied by students of Middle Eastern social history.[3] If, on the other hand, property is there one day and gone the next, then it is essential to explain the comings and goings of this crucial institution. There have been attempts to explain the excursions of large landed property in and out of the game, but such explanations usually rely on exogenous variables and are usually wrong in terms of being internally inconsistent. If large landed property was there, it had to stay there in an institutionalized form. If it was not permanent, then the strong European notion should not be used. The indigenous forms of access to agrarian surplus need to be defined on their own terms for the important reason that distinct social processes can otherwise be confused due to indiscriminate use of inappropriate terminology. Following the demographers' analogy between death and being "ever-married," property is like death—it is either there or not. If this criterion is relaxed, then "property" becomes such a general concept that it is absolutely useless, for it can be applicable everywhere.[4]

Changes in Labor Relations and Property Rights
in Ottoman History: Is There a Causality Between the Two?

The observations presented above invite a turn to some examples from Ottoman history and the question of whether a simple causality between changing relations in cultivation methods dominated by local powers and the emergence of private property really existed. Three historical developments in the nineteenth and twentieth centuries should be considered: a) the development of commercial agriculture supported by the state; b) the emergence of what seemed to be capitalist property relations in the form of large-scale farming; and c) the impact of the abolishment of the state's claims on agricultural revenue. In each case one could infer the emergence of large landed property, yet that conclusion is unwarranted in the Ottoman context. Practically every major transformation can be explained by state action rather than private consolidation of landed property.[5] Each is a major transformation in methods of cultivation and production relations, but large landed property is not necessarily the result. On the other hand, the role of state action, in spite of powerful local forces, happens to be central to the transformation process.

Development of Commercial Agriculture in the Ottoman Empire in the Nineteenth Century

Anatolian agriculture was being commercialized at a rapid rate in the nineteenth century. Not only was there increased agricultural production, but a major increase in cash crops produced mainly for export as well. There was a conscious effort to improve and expand silk production and the cultivation of tobacco, as well as figs, raisins, olives, and cereals. The overwhelming consensus holds that these developments caused a major change in agrarian society in Anatolia.[6] Was there also a transformation in the patterns of land ownership? Did the drive for this transformation originate from among the future landowners of Anatolia?

Those responsible for this major transformation had the same goal: expansion of the base and yield of Ottoman state revenue. The two main actors in this process were the Ottoman state and, later, the Public Debt Administration, which collected a major part of the Ottoman revenue both for bondholders of the defaulted Ottoman debt and for the state itself. Before the Public Debt Administration actively took charge of agrarian transformation, the Ottoman state had undertaken major steps to contribute to an expanding revenue base through material action. Ottoman policy consisted not only of market-oriented moves directed to customs duties and trade incentives; indigenous moves towards pacification and resettlement of transhumant populations were even more effective policies.

With the spread of independence movements in the European provinces and the loss of Egyptian revenue, attention turned to alternative sources. Anatolia offered potential, because it had been continuously declining as a revenue base while the practice of animal husbandry (which escaped taxation much more easily) had been spreading at a rapid rate since the end of the sixteenth century. The

Ottoman state had been a land-revenue-based administration, and it was the enhancement of that revenue that the state had been working on. Interestingly enough, attention given to the enhancement of agricultural production followed a long and determined period of eradication of solidified claims on the revenue base. It was in the period of 1807–1839 that local powers who formed the basis of landed power in the Ottoman context were defeated.

Subsidies for the expansion of agricultural production, introduction of new crops, and the increase of cultivated areas all took place without any power struggle (or for that matter collusion) between the rival forces in the capital and the provinces. This was never an issue in the way that settlement policies had been. A major transformation in the expansion and diversification of agricultural production occurred without any major transformation in property relations.

Possible Forms of Emergent Landed Powers
Under the Tutelage of the State

Along with the nineteenth-century settlement policies of the Ottoman state, large expanses of land were granted to individuals with a title deed (*tapu*). Legislation to this effect is explicit in the Land Code of 1858.[7] This phenomenon at a time of expanding agricultural production may appear to be an indicator of emergent large private property; however, the two actually do not have anything in common. This development was restricted to unpopulated areas for the purpose of soliciting settlement on a voluntary basis through the intermediation of tribal leadership. Title deeds did not imply that inviolable private property was granted. They signified usufructuary rights contingent upon continuous cultivation.[8] This was nothing more than a policy for the purpose of expanding a revenue base for the state without any conflict or collusion between the central and local powers.

Nevertheless, large landed property eventually materialized as a result of this process in the twentieth century. However, areas in which such privatization occurred have been limited, confined mainly to Çukurova. Furthermore, legitimacy of such privatization has been actively checked by the central power and the judicial system.[9] Other forms of emergent large landed estates in eastern Anatolia can be seen as extensions of "feudal" relations due to the non-penetration of the state. This was a process of extension-fragmentation of political-military dominance. Again, in this latter case, large landed property was far from having established any legitimacy. Overall, solidification of power on land was not able to establish a norm, as it did in the

European or Latin American experience. Rather, the norm, in as much as inviolable rights are concerned, was small peasant property.

Whenever large landholdings emerged in Turkish history, the dynamic centered around the impetus of settlement by nomads without far-reaching conflict and consequent transformation of peasants' rights, and the role of the state was more pronounced than that of local powers.

The Significance of the Abolition of the Tithe (*Öşür*)

The nominal state property on arable land (*miri*) directly correlates with the state's claims on agricultural produce in the form of taxation. Agrarian revenue was the major source of revenue throughout the Ottoman Empire. Abolition of the agricultural tax in the early years of the Republic severed the relationship between agricultural land and the state. The formation of the Republic was based to a large extent on the support of local powers in Turkey. It seemed at the outset that a new base had been established for the emergence of large landed property through consolidation of local claims on the traditional revenue base. As a matter of fact, contemporary observers based their arguments on the social landscape with the assumption of a dominant form of large landed property in Anatolia.[10]

Agrarian relations, looked at from a longer historical perspective, were different from what is typically assumed. From the 1930s onward a monotonic state action was at work to break the consolidation of landed power. Historical continuity of this process was impressively consistent. By the 1960s, through distribution of pastures to the peasants and through taking individual local magnates to task, agriculture was overwhelmingly dominated by peasant property. Moreover, the nature of property at this time resembled the European form more than ever before—an outcome that was not the result of new legislation, but rather of a process of establishing central control, which had its roots in the Ottoman experience.

Of particular interest is the consistency of the mechanism that worked against the establishment of dominant property relations in Ottoman agriculture. Despite circumstances very conducive to their establishment, large property-based operations came and went without much staying power, eventually yielding to the dominance of peasant property. To understand the indigenous social system at work, it is essential to analyze mechanisms that impede the emergence of large landed property and to ignore non-existent property relations.

The force that thwarted consolidation of property on land has been the state. However, it is practically impossible to explain that force on its own terms without mentioning local representations of state power that worked against privatization. Otherwise, the state appears as a military force that dictates, without any integration with social factors. This was at least technically impossible over a long period. While, on the one hand, the main motives of the central power were revenue and control, local collaborators of state action were driven by redistributive considerations that militated against privatization. In a framework with constant surplus, such collaboration made sense, given appropriate power balances.

Landed Property and Agrarian Labor Relations

The issue of large-scale agriculture and the question of large landholdings have a special connection to agrarian labor relations. Analyzing land and labor together is crucial to the understanding of agrarian economy. The land-labor ratio was very high even in the most fertile Anatolian plains, which were conveniently located near sea routes. From a strictly mechanical perspective on the socioeconomic process, private property in land and the struggle for it did not make good economic sense when plenty of "free" agricultural land of prime quality was readily available. In the face of relative labor scarcity, it is in fact labor that needs to be monopolized to achieve large enterprises.

The conventional wisdom is simple: a high land-labor ratio leads to serfdom or slavery, and a low land-labor ratio results in wage labor (with private property in land).[11] Despite many supporting examples to illustrate this hypothesis, exceptions (noted by the author of the hypothesis himself) offer more puzzling and interesting outcomes. Ottoman experience is just such an exception where monopolization of neither factor of production has been institutionalized.

Evidence is insufficient to warrant the use of the concept of landed property in the Ottoman context, especially since European institutions had hardly penetrated social life by the middle of the nineteenth century. What then did state property (miri) stand for? I argue that it can only be understood in terms of access to revenue sources and its redistribution through a mechanism of taxation rather than the "property" of a demarcated area of soil.

What about labor? According to conventional wisdom, this is the factor that needs to be monopolized, as it was in serfdom, because it was scarce. Monopolization of either factor in turn would lead to the privatization of claims on the surplus.

The fact that neither factor had been controlled privately in the Ottoman system enhanced the institutional significance of the state in economic organization. The *revenue* and its distribution established the logic of the system, so any method of monopolization had to be prevented. While free peasants and the absence of widespread private property characterize Ottoman agricultural production, considerations of the continuity of the redistributive system need to be integrated into the analysis in order to complete the picture. Here state action has a greater explanatory power than the process of opening up the economy and the penetration of markets.

During the nineteenth century, production for the market became increasingly dominant in Anatolia, through a mechanism whereby peasant agriculture underwent an adaptation rather than being replaced by forms of large landownership.[12] The process involved mobilization of the labor force for peasant agriculture. With major transformations in the agrarian structure, as in the case of the settlement of transhumant population, came the creation of peasantry. Another example was the settlement of immigrants from the Balkans and Crimea as peasant households, a process that continued well into this century. The expansion of agricultural production depended predominantly on the nature of the labor supply rather than on the forms of property. As a matter of fact, it is difficult to pinpoint the emergence of private property on agricultural land in Turkey.[13]

The Ottoman state played a crucial role in most processes of transformation during the expansion of the world-economy. The periods of military reform and centralizing activities had a direct impact on agricultural production and enhanced the revenue base. It was not commercialization of agriculture that brought autonomous change, but the nature and effectiveness of state action itself. Commercialization not only increased the profits of merchants and the income of the producer, but also state revenue.

Çiftliks, Property, and Labor

Çiftlik ownership is frequently associated with private ownership of land. Historians also relate the prevalence of this phenomenon to the process of commercialization. If, on the other hand, labor was relatively scarce, what is the reason for accumulating land? Halil İnalcık's article in this volume provides the data for an adequate answer to this question. It lies in the *nature* of property, labor, and agricultural output on such establishments.

In terms of property, while there is no evidence that çiftliks were the harbingers of private property on land, there is plenty of data indicating that property on these enterprises mainly involved buildings, trees, and improvements—hardly a novel phenomenon in the Ottoman agricultural system. It was not a new kind of property, but probably an intensification of an already existing form during the expansion of commercialization.

If labor was scarce in Ottoman agriculture, the çiftlik owner had to provide his own laborers. İnalcık indicates that a common aspect of such farms was the existence of a small number of slaves—itself of limited importance in Ottoman agriculture. It is not at all clear that slave labor on an average çiftlik was sufficient for its operation. Labor from neighboring peasant farms served to compensate for the labor deficit.

The nature of agricultural production on such operations involved mainly tree crops, vineyards, and animals. The first two had high economic returns relative to labor input, and it is possible to engage in their cultivation with limited seasonal labor. The third required very small labor input. The adaptation to the existing agrarian formation was possible through high investment requiring activities with relatively low labor requirements. Furthermore, the greater part of the property on such operations was not land. Thus, it may be more appropriate to identify çiftliks by the nature of their output instead of implying property relations on land. Labor use appears to be limited and large-scale commercial operations on the basis of such establishments were unlikely.

İnalcık further indicates that subsistence-crop cultivation in the neighborhood of çiftliks, presumably farmed by independent peasants, may not have been a part of çiftliks themselves. This means that the size of the operation was even smaller.

Since cultivation of large tracts of land with wage labor was technically impossible in the Ottoman context, *reaya çiftliks* were the only other possible candidate for larger holdings. But these could be based on the existing redistributive system that worked through the state mechanism, and did not represent a novel phenomenon of commercialization.[14] They could also resemble sharecropping arrangements. The nature of property on such operations is still unclear. Too frequently, the existence of private property relations on land is incorrectly *inferred* from the observation of relations resembling sharecropping.

Concluding Remarks

The transformation of Turkish agriculture and the establishment of small peasant property can better be understood without using the alien notion of private property on land, as can the interaction between the state, trade, peasants and intermediaries, both public and private. The struggle for shares of the agrarian surplus between relevant classes better explains the phenomenon of Turkish transformation than a narrative based on emergent private property, which did not materialize until this century.

8

Agrarian Fluctuations and Modes of Labor Control in the Western Arc of the Fertile Crescent, c. 1700–1850

Faruk Tabak

This article addresses the issue of large-scale commercial agriculture from an angle slightly different than that presented in Part I. It does not trace the line of causality behind the advent of *çiftliks*. Nor does it depict their *modus operandi*. Rather, it investigates and reconsiders a relatively unexplored facet of commercialization of agriculture in the Ottoman East: namely, the changing anatomy of production within small holdings. Stated briefly, it argues that the consolidation during the eighteenth century of small-holding households is a key to understanding why plantation-type (*Gutsherrschaft*-type) holdings never took deep roots in the eastern Mediterranean. Conversely, it explains the omnipresence of rent-collecting (*Grundherrschaft*-type) holdings which inter-nested Levantine rural households into markets of input, output and credit.

The reasons for following this mode of enquiry are twofold. First, the literature on agrarian change in the Ottoman Empire during

* I would like to express my thanks to Terence K. Hopkins & Şevket Pamuk for their comments and criticisms. This work was made possible (in part) by grants made from the Ford Foundation/the Population Council MEAWards and the Institute of Turkish Studies, Washington, D.C. The statements made and the views expressed in this work are those of the author and do not represent the views of these institutions.

the eighteenth and nineteenth centuries hinges heavily upon discussions surrounding the genesis and structure of çiftlik agriculture. The
geographical distribution of these estates across the imperial domains
accordingly designates the Macedonian plain and the western Anatolian plateau as principal sites of change, with a conspicuous absence
of similar agrarian institutions in the western arc of the Fertile
Crescent—thus placing the region outside of the compass of changes
affecting the Ottoman countryside. The primacy assigned to the
çiftliks stems from the assumption that they represent a radical break
from patterns of production marking Ottoman countryside.

Further research, however, has cast doubt on this account
whereby çiftliks progressively came to embody practices and tech-
nologies not found elsewhere in Ottoman agriculture. In other
words, the line of demarcation separating çiftliks from other large
holdings tends to fade under close scrutiny.[1] This conclusion, tentative as it may be, demands new avenues of investigation. For one,
within the context of widespread petty commodity production, dispossession from land loses its analytical primacy. Against this back-
drop, what needs to be depicted are changes of a different order:
changes in modes of surplus extraction, cycles of production, and
regulation of work, which in the long-run had cumulative consequences for the organization of production and the use of labor.

Secondly, the strong central authority-independent small holders equation, advanced to explain the conditions of existence of petty
producers in the Ottoman East, was itself historically bound. The
state apparatus experienced systematic and episodic changes in military might and effectiveness, in administrative efficiency, and fiscal
strength and stability. These changes facilitated or hindered its ability
to keep inherent centrifugal tendencies under close control. Given
that this picture of a system in homeostatis is an ideal situation mostly
described in official documents, studies on Ottoman agrarian order
tend to take full stock of the "deviations" from the norm where this
equation is disturbed. In other words, it is mostly assumed that the
enfeeblement of the imperial center and/or the extension of market-
mediated relations would eventually erode the basis of petty production. Yet, given the weakening power of the imperial bureaucracy
during the eighteenth and early-nineteenth centuries to administer
and patrol the regions under its jurisdiction, the continuing predominance of petty producers—under strong satrap rule—can not be explained solely with reference to the ability of the central authority to
provide an environment that favored small producers. The dynamics
of this sector, that is, the mechanisms through which it reconstituted
itself in different fashions have yet to be fully explored.

From the vantage point of commercial agriculture, the predominance of small-holding rural households meant a greater role for rent-collecting agencies in extracting the rural surplus. In their absence each household/village had to make the decision to shift to the cultivation of export crops or alter their production patterns on an individual basis. That is, the networks linking peasant households/villages and large holdings within which these units were enveloped facilitated the extension of market-mediated relations and hence reconstituted the Levantine agrarian structure. Therefore, the role played by these loosely-knit units to tap effectively and to mobilize the rural surplus extracted from petty-producers needs to be accounted for in detail. Conversely, examining the workings of rural households, subject to an overarching rent-collecting practice, is of paramount importance. For this reason, an analysis of Grundherrschaft-type holdings in accounting for the dynamics of Ottoman agriculture allows greater latitude in depicting rural households not as pre-given and static entities, but as units reconstituted by historical trends.

Hence, in order to register fully the implications and ramifications of an agrarian transformation characterized by an overwhelming dominance of small-holding peasant households, what needs to be depicted are the conditions of the (co)existence of a plethora of large rent-collecting institutions such as *malikane*s, and *waqf*s. Unlike çiftliks, these institutions were not successful in carving out an enclave for themselves. Rather, they were grafted onto the existing agrarian fabric woven by small-holders.

As mentioned above, the Syrian provinces are customarily portrayed as a region ravaged by the heavy exactions of either insubordinate rulers or the bedouin—and not within the sway of agrarian changes manifest in the west Anatolian and Balkan provinces. Yet, since the absence of çiftlik-like estates is not necessarily an indication of the absence of agrarian change, these provinces provide an excellent geographical setting for pursuing the line of analysis outlined above, which privileges overarching rent-collecting practices.

Within this frame of reference, the repercussions of the process of incorporation into the world-economy which enhanced and reproduced the conditions of existence of rural household production will be spelled out in the first section of this paper. The complex web of relationships linking independent producers and Grundherrschaft-type holdings will be the object of analysis of the second section. Finally in the third section, the changing coordinates of, and strains within, the resultant agrarian structure, remolded during growing integration into the capitalist world-system, will be tentatively charted.

I.

That the eighteenth century in world-historical terms was an expansionary and inflationary period provides the contextual background against which the incorporation of the Ottoman Empire and its repercussions on the Levantine countryside will be depicted in this section. It will be argued that this renewed economic expansion proved to be favorable in reinforcing the status of small-holding rural households. An index of incorporation is responsiveness to price fluctuations constituted through cyclical temporalities of the world-economy. Tracing the repercussions of these fluctuations on the agrarian order necessitates a distinction between long-term price movements which span over, by and large, a century, and the A- and B-phases of Kondratieff cycles which are of a shorter duration.

Notwithstanding the up and downswings of the latter, the inflationary surge of the eighteenth century, which commenced in 1733, lasted till the end of the Napoleonic Wars. The prices of agricultural commodities in Europe, those of cereals most of all, soared sharply after 1750. Even though the general upswing in prices came to a halt in 1817, to be followed by a deflationary secular trend, the reversal in the movement of prices did not have any impact upon the course of agricultural terms of trade, since the prices of manufactured goods underwent a relatively sharper decline. As a result, the whole period bracketing the years from 1750 to 1850 was a time of agricultural boom.[2]

Flowing from and accompanying this inflationary surge was a similar rise in prices in the Ottoman dominions. Increasing prices throughout the eighteenth century were followed by a tripling of food prices between 1800 and the 1840s. The disruption of maritime trade along the shores of the eastern Mediterranean during the Napoleonic Wars and the Greek War of Independence, only to be followed by the Egyptian invasion of the Syrian provinces, were instrumental in keeping price levels high until the 1840s. The period of incorporation and peripheralization then was an inflationary period. Agricultural producers, more dependent on the market for marketing their surpluses than acquiring their means of production and consumption, benefited from the secular inflationary surge and terms of trade favorable for agriculture. This economic climate was conducive to the reproduction and consolidation of small-holders. Thereafter, except for the Crimean War boom, the prices in the imperial territories ferried along with the deflationary trend of the nineteenth century which persisted until the close of the 1890s.[3]

Within this context, the secular rise in prices was doubtless instrumental in drawing the Ottoman Empire into the expanding
world-economy. For one, soaring prices in Europe were transmitted
even to the most distant quarters of the globe through increasing
demand for goods originating from the periphery. The impact of this
secular inflation was felt from the Ottoman East to Mogul India *via*
Safavid Persia.[4] In the Levant, inflation of the *livre* alone led to price
increases of 25 percent to 100 percent.[5] With this upswing, in stark
contrast with price movements in the preceeding century, there was a
detectible inflationary trend visible in all spheres of Middle Eastern
economic life, and most conspicuously in the urban centers.

The price of bread, for instance, which had risen from 1/75 *guruş*
per *ratl* to 1/40 guruş throughout the seventeenth century, jumped
from 3 to 4 *paras* per ratl in 1748 to 10 paras in 1784. The annual rate of
increase in prices was 2 percent for the former, and 6 percent for the
latter period. In 1855, the price of bread was 1 4/40 guruş a ratl.[6]
Soaring grain prices were reflected in the attendant increase in expenditure on food. From the turn of the eighteenth century to the 1780s,
annual expenditure on food per person rose from 30 guruş to 130–150
guruş. In the 1840s, the figures remained around 300 to 500 guruş.[7]
The bleak panorama of the urban areas painted by the travelogues of
the period as well as complaints about recurrent food crises and gal-
loping grain prices accurately registered the state of things, though
this was but part of the picture. Detrimental as this rise was for the
townsmen, it signalled better financial conditions for those whose
incomes depended on agricultural prices, since the rise in prices of
manufactured goods was not as steep.

As the contemporary accounts amply illustrate, grain prices fluctuated markedly over the short term (especially at times of military
mobilization and war), and yet over the long term the secular trend
was a gradual increase. Of the members of the trinity of
wheat/flour/bread, for instance, the price of the former more than
tripled over a period of six decades between 1747 and 1810 from 8 to 15
guruş a *ghirara* to 50 guruş, reaching in times of scarcity 80 to 100
guruş. Setting violent fluctuations aside, this implies an annual average rate of over 3 percent. The rise was steeper during the first half of
the nineteenth century. Between 1810 and 1850, the price of wheat
increased from 14 guruş per *shunbul* to 50 guruş, an average annual
rate of 3.8 percent. Spiralling prices were more pronounced in the
case of barley, another bread grain, which was not directly subject to
the ebbs and flows of the world market. Its price galloped from 8
paras a *mudd* in 1741 to 2.5 guruş in 1771–72, and from 8 guruş a

shunbul to 35 guruş between 1811 and 1836—an annual average rate of 6 percent in each period. These high figures should not be surprising, for higher grain prices led to a greater demand for the cheapest product, as a result of which barley showed the greatest relative increase. The ratio between the prices of wheat and barley during the period under study attests to this rule: the ratio which stood at 2.1 in 1755 followed a downward trend until the 1840s, reaching 1.7 to 2 in 1811 and 1.4 to 1.6 during the Egyptian occupation. The "historical ratio" of 2 to 1 was eventually reached towards mid-century. On the other hand, the prices of raw cotton, silk, and cotton thread exported from the ports of the Levant, registered an annual increase of 2.7 percent to 3 percent during the eighteenth century.[8]

It goes without saying that, given the great and often unmanageable diversity of local weights and of monies in circulation, and the continual debasement of Ottoman currency, various qualifications need to be attached to the figures cited above. Yet these scanty if sporadic data attest to a secular trend of rising prices in the western arc of the Fertile Crescent, contemporaneous with the inflationary surge in, and emanating from, Europe. In the light of this assertion, note should be made of the fact that, although the blame for soaring prices was more often than not put on the monopolistic and monopsonistic practices of rebellious governors, as it was by European travellers in the region and indigenous contemporaries, the reasons of this surge were deeply rooted in the inflationary trend of the eighteenth century. In fact, the governors were able to use the spiralling prices as a pretext to extend their realms of governance at the expense of their local rivals.

The surge in prices accompanying growing integration into the global networks of production and commerce was supplemented by demographic trends in the region. That the urban population was increasing at a time when that of the countryside was being kept at bay by successive bedouin incursions also played a part in pushing prices up. Put differently, while land-under-cultivation contracted, the ratio between the number of consumers and producers underwent a notable change. Population figures for the Syrian provinces during the sixteenth century, the heyday of the Empire, range between 800,000 to 900,000 souls, 200,000 of which were urban (plus an additional 7 percent to 10 percent for nomads). This puts the ratio between producers and consumers at approximately 3.5 to 1. The population on the eve of the nineteenth century is estimated to be around 1.6 million, this time with an urban population of 250,000, if not more. Included in the population figures was a large number of pastoralists, in the neighborhood of 500,000. Assuming that at least

50 percent of this pastoral group relied on the sedentary producers for bread-grains, the number of people required to produce food for a non-agrarian person becomes 2 to 1.[9] Also, given that cereal was exported in amounts ranging from 6,000 to 10,000 tons per annum, either to the dominions of the Empire or to Europe,[10] and that the pilgrimage caravan was regularly provisioned, the decreasing producer/consumer proportion may indicate, among others, greater agricultural productivity.

In terms of the consumption of bread grains, the amounts consumed in the urban centers of the Levant were more or less in line with the average figures advanced in studies of European history. In Tripoli, for example, the daily consumption of bread grains was 40 to 45 shunbuls for a population of 15,000 at the turn of the nineteenth century, i.e., roughly 2.6 hectoliters per capita per annum. With a population of 10,000, Sidon consumed 8,300 ghiraras of corn, or 2.6 hectoliters per capita per annum. In European agrarian historiography, the estimates for eighteenth and nineteenth centuries range between 2 to 4 hectoliters for the annual consumption of bread grains per capita. Note should be taken of the fact that the figures given for Tripoli and Sidon do not include the consumption of lesser cereals which are not found in the records. At the turn of this century and in the aftermath of the presumably remarkable developments induced during the second half of the nineteenth century, the average stayed at a meager 2.75 hectoliters.[11]

Increases in the amount of tithes levied on the immediate producers can be considered as an additional index of the dynamism of agricultural production. One-to-one correspondance does not necessarily exist between the volume of production and that of tithes, but in the absence of reliable sets of data, tithe figures, despite their infrequent apperance, serve as a measure of the rhythm of agricultural production. A cadastral survey of the Syrian provinces shows significant increases in tithe revenues. In the provinces of northern Syria, tithe revenues increased from 2 million guruş in the 1780s to 5.6 million guruş in the 1830s, reaching an annual sum of 17.5 million between 1857–69. Within the same time-span, the revenues from tithe in the provinces of southern Syria rose from an annual average of 10.3 million guruş to 16 million guruş, and then jumped to over 30 million.[12] When set against the political background of the region at these historical cross-sections, the first set of figures might be regarded as too low, reflecting by and large the so-called chaotic character of the times due to incessant bedouin pressure, whereas the second set might be found too high due to the coercive measures set in effect by Egyptian authorities. Notwithstanding these qualifications, these figures do provide evidence of a change in the rhythm of agricultural production. Moreover, changes in the level of taxation provide further evidence. In Aleppo, for instance, taxes levied on each *faddan* increased from 4 *mekkuks* to 7 mekkuks between the mid-sixteenth and mid-eighteenth centuries.[13]

Moreover, both these tendencies, the growth in the amount of tithes collected and the decreasing producer/consumer ratio, are consistent with the increments in the amount of cereals produced by each household, even though they do not necessarily or automatically register it. The figures for the sixteenth century oscillate between 500 to 1,000 liters of grain produced per household, and reach 2,100 liters by the mid-eighteenth century. During the 1830s, an average of at least 2,000 liters of cereals was marketed by each household, attaining a level of over 4,000 litres in the case of well-to-do rural households, indicating an increase in the volume of marketed output.[14] The reduction of many agricultural producers to subsistence on lesser cereals must also have augmented the output of marketed bread grains.

Another factor increasing the amount of marketed cash crops was the wide range of crop rotation patterns in use in the region. The lack of beasts of burden and hence of manure, the chronic shortage of which was one of the structural characteristics of Mediterranean agriculture, was compensated by the application of various crop rotation patterns, which is also another indication of the set of changes set in train during the eighteenth century. Manure crops such as melons and cucumbers were planted so as not to exhaust the soil. Towards the end of the nineteenth century, vegetable marrows, potatoes, and tomatoes came to enrich the list of manure crops.[15] This, when coupled with widespread horticultural production, still another feature of Mediterranean agriculture, increased the supply and intake of non-grain products, and helped form the basis of a diversified agriculture, thereby increasing the amount of marketed cash crops.

Looked at in this way, the seemingly high yield ratios reported by travellers, which should be taken with a pinch of salt due to their impressionistic nature, are comprehensible. For the end of the eighteenth and the opening of the nineteenth centuries, estimates for wheat yields (return on seed) ranged between one to ten (for Hama) and one to twenty-five (for Hawran); barley yields were estimated to be higher. In the middle of the nineteenth century, yields in Hawran were put at seventeen to one for wheat and fourteen to one for barley. Estimates made by French savants at the turn of this century were lower, but not considerably. It was reckoned that wheat yielded nine- to seventeen-fold, and barley fifteen- to eighteen-fold. Again, yields in the northern parts of the region were relatively lower, eight times the amount of seed for wheat and ten times for barley. Even these lowest estimates of yield ratios were higher than the Anatolian averages of five- to six-fold return on seed.[16] The decrease in yield ratios during the ninetenth century may have stemmed from an actual decrease due to the rapid expansion of the area under cultivation; the latter option tacitly assumes that throughout the eighteenth century the land under cultivation was the most fertile as areas of lesser fertility were first abandoned under bedouin attacks.

These yield ratios which were high in comparison to those in Europe at the time, and corresponding levels of output have led some researchers to look for explanations for the "anomaly" between the high yields and presumed stagnation in agricultural production. One such explanation is that yields were low when measured in terms of the area planted, but not in terms of the seed sown. This however was not the case. From the sixteenth to the nineteenth century, there was an ostensible decrease in the amount of seed sown per hectare. During the sixteenth century, 10 mudds of seed (1/2 tons) was considered to be the average for sowing a *çift* of land. The amount of seed necessary to sow a hectare of arable land changed between 400 to 650 liters, depending on the quality of land. On the eve of the nineteenth century, this amount was approximately 250 to 375 liters per hectare, since six ghirara of seed was needed to sow each faddan of land. These figures are by and large in line with those of western Anatolian çiftliks where a field of one hectare was sown with 300 liters of seed. There was a further drop during the mid-century, the volume ranging from 150 to 200 liters per hectare. Yet, figures from the turn of this century show slightly higher amounts, 180–200 liters per hectare in the Biqa valley and 240 liters in Palestine.[17] This reduction meant that seed was sown more effectively in order to minimize the amount that could not be ploughed into the land properly.

The quantities mentioned above were by no means lower than those in Europe at that time, where a total of 100 to 200 liters of wheat were sown per hectare.[18] Consequently, as a ratio of the surface cultivated, the yield was definitely not poor. Nor was it poor in terms of the volume of the seed sown. Having said this, it should be noted that due to high yields, a low percentage of the harvest needed to be reserved for seed, adding to the amount of marketable cereals. Also, with increasing yields, an economic environment conducive to the existence of small holdings presumably dominated.

A further index of an unfolding change in the Levantine agrarian economy was the arrival of new crops and their cultivation in the region. Studies tracing the spread of çiftliks in the Balkan provinces during the eighteenth century concluded that the introduction and diffusion of maize cultivation made considerable headway basically due to its association with the çiftliks. Despite its advent in the Syrian provinces during the seventeenth century, maize cultivation did not receive as much attention as it did in the Balkan provinces, mainly because it was not transformed into a plantation crop and thus was less noticeable. That maize reached the shores of eastern Mediterranean sometime during the seventeenth century can be inferred from, among other evidence, its appearance as an entry in a dictionary of medicinal plants, published in İstanbul during the second half of that century. The fact that in this work it was referred to as *dhurra shami*, despite its arrival in the Serbian provinces in 1611, gives a clue as to its provenance and paths of diffusion.[19] (Later during the eighteenth century, this name gave way to "Egyptian corn.") Since it was primarily destined for consumption *in situ*, it does not appear very often in consular and commercial reports.

Though the extent of its cultivation and paths of diffusion are difficult to map, the scanty evidence we have reveals glimpses of its crucial role in the dietary régimes of the inhabitants of the region. According to French consular correspondance, the production of maize in the *sancak* of Tripoli was as important as that of customary staple foodstuffs, such as sorghum and barley. Towards mid-century, the balance in the province was definitively tipped towards maize production, which now constituted seven-eighths of the total *maïs* production, i.e., *maïs jaune* (maize) and *maïs blanc* (sorghum), and its quality was "superior to those imported from abroad." Towards the end of the century, maize crossing the Atlantic from the New World replaced the indigenous sorghum in certain localities, with the notable exceptions of Acre and Haifa.[20]

In a similar manner, other crops of the Columbian exchange, namely, potatoes and tomatoes, made their appearance in the region during the same period. Both seemed to have reached the Syrian littoral first, and Asia Minor therefrom. Reminiscent of the aforementioned oddysey of maize, the tomato which was brought to Anatolia both from Europe in 1659 and the Fertile Crescent, was given two names, acknowledging its differential sites of origin: *Frenk badıncanı* as well as *Arab badıncanı*. The potato never played as transformative a role as it did in Europe in terms of increasing the marketable surplus. Still, that the regions which specialized in export crops were also exporters of seed potatoes (i.e., Mount Lebanon) reflects the interdependence between the two. The geographical compass of its cultivation, along with that of the tomato, stretched from the northern to the southern fringes of the *bilad al-Sham*. The "Irish potato," as it was usually called, fared well. By mid-century, tomatoes and potatoes were found throughout the region and were also exported from Beirut and Tripoli to the southern Anatolian provinces. Unlike potatoes, however, tomatoes became part of the culinary repertoire in Anatolia much faster.[21]

The last crop to be mentioned in this family was the haricot bean which made its début in the region of Aleppo at the end of the eighteenth century. Under the name of *"lubiya ifranjiyya,"* denoting its path of transmission, it was sometimes cultivated in the region, though not in great quantity.[22] Not much needs to be said concerning the introduction of other new crops, such as the well-known case of tobacco, cochineal (introduced in Tripoli by İbrahim Pasha), and the re-introduction of sugarcane (planted in the vicinity of Saida and Beirut at the end of the eighteenth century),[23]—except that most of these newly introduced crops were summer crops and needed continuous irrigation. Correspondingly, it can be conjectured that some improvements must have been made to provide these summer crops with adequate supplies of water (though in the maritime plains the notoriously heavy dews served as an adequate supplement to rain). To recapitulate, the introduction of these new crops into the Syrian landscape bears testimony to changes in Levantine agriculture and rural household production.

In consonance with these developments, changes in the use of labor and in methods of cultivation accompanied or followed changes in cropping. To start with, the exorbitant prices of raw materials— silk, cotton—pushed up by the growing demand from Europe, rendered their processing in the rural areas less frequent. Subsequently, the processing of these raw materials came to be carried out primarily in larger towns and cities. In fact, a series of complaints by French merchants engaged in this trade arose from the lack of competence of the laborers located in the urban areas specialized in processing cotton and silk (these, in addition to the complaints arising from storing huge quantities of these products in not-so-convenient depôts).[24] Despite these complaints, with the transference of activities related to processing of raw materials, there was a new order in the countryside whereby immediate producers were forced to devote more time in agriculture, hence were employed in new tasks to more intensive cultivation. That lack of hands was a permanent phenomenon throughout the period under study mirrors the intensification in agricultural production.[25]

Along with these changes in cropping and the use of labor came changes in the agrarian cartography of the region. From this vantage point, one may distinguish, *grosso modo*, three zones: grain tillage dominated on the plateaus, arboriculture on the slopes, and both on the coastal plain. On the maritime plains, the crop rotation system was not heavily dependent on cereals. All too often, a two field system was practiced, since this allowed greater freedom in shaping the proportions of both winter and summer crops. (In three crop rotation systems employed in the interior regions, however, the areas of winter and summer crops had to be equal.) Heavy dews covering the whole southeastern end of the Mediterranean facilitated this mode of land exploitation, by rendering possible the insertion of a variety of summer crops into the production cycle. That these regions were more heavily populated and the land-under-plough was comparatively smaller must have compelled producers to persist on the biennal rotation system. This rotation pattern however forced cultivators to rotate between legumes and cereals every other year while keeping the cultivation of summer crops constant as export crops, thus rendering them dependent on imported cereals.

In the interior by contrast, variations of the three crop rotation system in which cereals predominated were put to work: in certain regions, a triennial crop rotation was followed, giving equal weight to cereals and legumes. Where it was possible, the land was not left for fallow, but was sown with manure crops. If agronomic and climatic conditions did not allow for this, a year of fallow was then inserted into the rotation system. Lands with better agronomic qualities and security measures against the bedouin were devoted to the culture of cereals and leguminuous crops. It should be noted that cultivable lands in the interior underwent a drastic change during the eighteenth century. Primarily because of the incursions from the desert, viticulture and arboriculture declined, the cultivation of lesser cereals became preferable, also forcing producers to migrate since dry grain cultivation was not as intensive as the former branches of production. What is remarkable in this divisioning was the gradual formation of a tripartite layering within which the southern and coastal provinces specialized in the cultivation of export crops, and the inland and northern provinces furnished the former with foodstuffs and labor.[26]

Hence, taking stock of the changes mentioned above, it can be argued that the period under study signalled the inauguration of a new era during which the consolidation of small-holding producers and the crystallization of a tripartite regional division of labour came to color the Levantine landscape.

II.

In a region dominated by large numbers of small holders, the institutional and organizational setting within which the process of incorporation was couched was of cardinal significance. Viewed from this perspective, Grundherrschaft-type holdings became instrumental in tapping and re-routing the rural surplus. As stated above, a wide array of rent-collecting rural holdings that had either fallen into abeyance or lost their constitutive role during the seventeenth century resurfaced in full force during the following centuries. My contention is that these loosely-knit units served to incorporate the region into the global division of labor.

The simultaneous resuscitation of these agrarian units was first and foremost linked with the aformentioned changes in agricultural production. As exemplified by the proliferation of malikanes and Christian religious orders, as well as the reincarnation of waqfs and a decelaration in the dismantlement of prebendal holdings, the agrarian restructuring was mostly but not exclusively imposed from above. The re-emergence of *musha'* and the new tribal configurations provided examples of restructurings from within. Despite the diversity in their internal properties, these were all organizational arrangements constituted around the establishment/consolidation of larger agrarian/pastoral units. In this rather roundabout way, the limitations inherent in the process of commercialization of an agrarian landscape dominated by small holdings was surmounted.

As the growing body of world-systems studies illustrates, the process of incorporation implies successive re-organizations within structures of production and polity. The inexorable growth in market–mediated relations and the subsequent divisioning of labor induced by the process of integration into the world-economy dictates that enterprises located in these localities operate on a plane defined by the vicissitudes of the world-economy. Accordingly, the creation of larger agrarian units provides greater flexibility in responding to constantly changing conditions in some markets by facilitating various combinations to meet the demands of contracting and expanding production. Within this context, the establishment of larger units can be located either within the sphere of production (e.g., the creation/consolidation of plantation-like units) or within the sphere of mercantile organization (e.g., the establishment of rent-collecting units to effectively tap and mobilize export crops).[27] Where petty-producing rural households dominate the scene, re-organization of the mercantile sphere takes precedence. It is against this background that the rise of Grundherrschaft-type units in the Fertile Crescent should be understood. Before sketching briefly the character of these holdings and the mechanisms of their domination over rural producers, I should point out that, in consonance with the tripartite regional division of labor, the general properties of these holdings also changed.

Geographically speaking, the shift in the cultivation of export crops (except for tobacco and dwindling amounts of silk) away from Aleppo and the northern provinces toward coastal and southern Syria brought about a corresponding economic efflorescence for the latter and altered considerably the agrarian cartography of the region. In the hinterlands of the port cities of the latter region, the cultivation of export crops such as silk and cotton increased steadily. In addition, the transfer of the command of pilgrimage to Damascus at the turn of the eighteenth century had by then given a considerable impetus to the economy of the Holy City and its environs. The collection of the *dawra* (the Damascus governor's contribution to the pilgrimage collected in his annual tour of the southern sancaks of his province), and the imposition of a regional division of labor to cater to the sacred journey (e.g., obligatory cultivation of barley for the livestock and grain for the caravan and the bedouin) furnished the Damascene notables with an exceptional command over the Syrian provinces. More or less coeval in historical time yet emanating from completely different historical developments, these two sets of events enhanced the economic status of the provinces of Saida and Damascus at the expense of Aleppo and its hinterland.

With southern Syria as the center of the new economic order due to its specialization in export crops, regions that were producing considerable amounts of grain gradually came under the control of Damascene notables. Not only did the pilgrimage command furnish them with the authority to acquire vast amounts of grain from south of Damascus, but also regions that were customarily within Aleppo's orbit, such as Hama, Homs and Ma'arrat al-Numan started catering to Damascus. The 'Azm family obtained the malikane of Hama and Homs which remained as one of the pillars of its economic power during most of the eighteenth century.

That is, the commercial expansion laid the basis of a new functional integration and areal specialization in the region. With the expansion of export crop agriculture in the southern and coastal regions, the inland and northern provinces started to furnish these regions with foodstuffs (and labor). Policing the continuous flow of export crops on the one hand, and securing the provisioning of these regions on the other were conducted under the aegis of strong rural notables. The emergence and centralization witnessed in the southern provinces, the hallmark of the eighteenth-century Fertile Crescent, stemmed from the necessity to establish tighter control over these networks. Consequently, the resultant effective command of these local lords in Mount Lebanon and Palestine, historically established long before incorporation started, found its full manifestation under the impact of growing commercialization. In these regions the countryside was effectively administered by families of notables who lived in the countryside, and whose position was hereditary. They were in *de facto* control of the agronomically attractive regions of the southern provinces. Concentration of malikanes in the southern provinces was another indication of this relatively tight control over the networks encompassing the countryside.[28]

Correspondingly, new political structures and institutional forms emerged in the periphery of southern Syria, geared towards extracting and re-routing rural surplus. Concentration of waqfs in and around Aleppo was indicative of changes in the northern provinces, since it signalled that the formation of larger unities kept apace with the regional trend at work. After a period of relative stagnation characterizing the seventeenth century, this new surge expressed and reinforced the dominant trends of the new era: a shift to local patronage in these newly-established waqfs made this expansion different from the sixteenth century boom. The number of waqfs established in Aleppo during the eighteenth century soared to new heights, reaching 596. There was a total of 61 newly-founded waqfs in Aleppo during the sixteenth century.[29]

Concomitant with this surge and changing patterns of patronage was a renewed interest by the imperial bureaucracy in the waqfs of the former era. Since these waqfs were mostly established by grandees from İstanbul, they were used to increase and consolidate the leverage of imperial rule in the face of extending indigenous rule. Hence, the resuscitation of the existing waqfs, as well as the foundation of new ones, gained momentum during the period under study. Consequently, though waqfs were not assarters on a grand scale, some lost ground must have been reclaimed in the due process.

To reiterate, even though the establishment of waqfs was a region–wide phenomenon, it was more heavily concentrated in and around Aleppo. An indication of this is that during the late eighteenth century (1777/1191), in the province of Aleppo, the revenues accruing from waqfs equalled nearly 40 percent of the total revenues, that of *tımar*s constituting a mere 12 percent, with the rest—47 percent—accruing from *miri* lands.[30]

On a micro-level, waqfs had in their possession items crucial for rural life. Most wheat mills, oil presses, and the like belonged in part or as a whole to waqfs, apart from their prominent role in the irrigation of gardens located in urban and rural areas.[31] Further still, most of these waqfs encompassed vineyards, orchards and vegetable gardens. The diversity in sources of income accruing to the waqfs provided a wider field of manoeuver for the direct producers in the region. As a result, the inland provinces specialized in an ensemble of horticulture and grain-production, amply documented in the *waqfiyyes* of the period, catered to the coastal and southern regions, specializing in the cultivation and procurement of export crops.

Along with the waqfs, the unit that was most prominent in the periphery of the Syrian desert was *musha'*, a unit built upon periodic redistribution of village land. In the countryside to the east, musha' appeared as the prevailing form of agrarian organization. Within this organization, the redistributive practice allowed a considerable degree of mobility for labor.[32] Parallel to this development, in the desert—the outer rim—crystallization of new tribal confederations got under way. These new configurations, overarching complex networks of commodity and labor flows, furthered the integration of sedentary and pastoral sectors of the economy. Both these new restructurings functioned both to supply labor to the eastern Mediterranean basin and to regulate production patterns in harmony with the migratory movements.[33] Accompanying, indeed underlying, this restructuring was the new spatial patterning of inter-regional flows. As the coastal and southern regions specialized in growing specific "export" cash crops, the inland and northern provinces had to begin to specialize in growing "local market" food crops, and still others in "crops" of migrant workers.[34]

Reflecting this new three-tiered spatial specialization, the vigor of the agricultural economy in the southern provinces retarded the erosion of the timar system. The prebendal units managed to hold out until the end of the eighteenth century. Also, the phenomenal growth of religious orders, controlling vast tracts of land, in and around Mount Lebanon, reflected this vigor in a different manner. In the northern parts, however, from about the middle of the seventeenth century the Janissaries' place as money lenders to the villagers was assumed by wealthy notables.[35]

In the countryside, spiralling debts were a telling index of the changes reshaping the Levantine landscape. Documents pertaining to the second half of the eighteenth century (1087–90/1676–79) testify to a level of indebtedness in the neighborhood of 2,000 to 3,000 guruş per village, the former figure being more or less average. Assuming that the villages comprised on average about 100 households, loans extended to villagers by the men-of-sword and urbanites were ordinarily within the range of 25 to 30 guruş per household. During the eighteenth century, the amounts extended to the immediate producers reached significant if not colossal proportions. With the tempo of lending reaching new levels, debts reaching nearly 55,000 guruş per village were registered, but figures generally ranged between

10,000 to 20,000 guruş per village. Of some 130 villages in the vicinity of Aleppo, the inhabitants of 40 villages contracted debts amounting to 10,000 guruş each, whereas the debts of 63 of them clustered around 15,000 guruş, the rest reaching 20,000 guruş. Again, assuming that during the eighteenth century villages were bigger, even the most cautious calculations will put the level of indebtedness per household somewhere between 75 to 100 guruş, if not more. Hence it can be argued that debts per household tripled over a century.[36]

This was hardly the case for the southern and coastal regions, which, as the center of a thriving economy, increasingly specialized in the cultivation of export crops and enjoyed a relative prosperity. Most probably, this relative opulence provided greater opportunity for the producers in this area in sharp contrast to the Aleppine peasantry who were principally engaged in cereal production and were more heavily indebted. To wit, a loan of 18,000 guruş, which was hardly exceptional in and around Aleppo, was hardly equalled at the time in the vicinity of Damascus.[37] The same tendency was more clearly visible in Mount Lebanon, the center of the lucrative silk trade. In contradistinction to Aleppo, both debts owed, and labour obligations to be provided, by the direct producers of the Mountain declined drastically, attaining modest, if not negligible, proportions.[38]

The sums extended to rural producers were quite substantial. In Aleppo, as mentioned, debts approaching 20,000 guruş were not uncommon, and people commanding between 200,000 and 600,000 guruş loaned considerable amounts to the inhabitants of the countryside. Even the modest sums of 60,000 to 90,000 guruş commanded by lesser notables were well above the sums held by the *ayans* of that age. Even notables of lesser rank, who established a network of loans, controlled sums that ayans in Anatolia hardly owned.[39] The injection of these significant sums into the countryside and the increase in their velocity of circulation were further signs of a vibrant economy.

Hence, in Mount Lebanon and southern Syria, where local notabilities reigned supreme and were strongly entrenched in the production and channelling of export crops, conditions favored the strengthening of such activities. Along with these mutations, new politial arrangements were established in the region to facilitate the changes induced by processes of incorporation. As to be expected, these political restructurings exhibited different characteristics in sympathy with the new cartography of the region. In southern Syria, a new political order was established under the aegis of local rulers: the rise and consolidation of the Shihab emirate in Mount Lebanon, the reign of the famous 'Azm family in Damascus, and that of Zahir al-'Umar and Ahmad Pasha al-Jazzar in Palestine established a stark contrast with the chaotic political climate persistent in the northern and eastern parts of the Fertile Crescent.

The successive waves of increasing scale flowed from the process of incorporation into the expanding world-economy, for, as mentioned at the outset, labor rather than land was the crucial factor of production, and units encapsulating larger demographic unities became the order of the day. The series of units extending from village level to that of the polity provided new possibilities in reorganizing production along new lines. The ups and downs of the world-economy found their echo in the organizational forms of labor mobilization.

III.

That the period under study usually does not receive the attention it deserves can be explained by a variety of reasons deeply anchored in assumptions inscribed in narrative structures of Ottoman historiography. First, the institutional and organizational edifice shaped during the eighteenth century is presumed to be mostly dismantled by the developments of the "revolutionary" nineteenth century. Despite the diametrically opposite character of their historical trajectories, western Anatolia, as the vanguard of commercialization, and the Fertile Crescent, as an agriculturally depressed region, are assumed to share a similar fate. The eventual eclipse of unruly governors in the Fertile Crescent and the relative inertia of çiftlik agriculture in reshaping the rural landscape in its own image are interpreted as indicators of this processual dismantlement. Herein lies the assumption governing most historical accounts: that the unprecedented dynamism generated by the Industrial Revolution inexorably re-shaped the global economic space in a radically new fashion. When set against the presumably profound transformations of the nineteenth century, those of the preceding century are generally characterized as ephemeral and transitory. Therefore, the establishment of *Pax Britannica*, the point of departure for most historical accounts, is seen as laying the groundwork for "discontinuous" change and "sustained" growth (to employ a present day lexicon) as opposed to the mercurial and sporadic character of those of the preceding era. Hence, the societal repercussions, and the solidity and longevity of changes of the eighteenth century do not often constitute themes of research.[40]

Secondly, the rise of large agricultural units and the enlargement of the boundaries of the existing ones are primarily taken as symptoms of a decline of the imperial order with the triumph of centrifugal forces as its corollary, and only tangentially as a result of mutations set in train by economic processes. Hence, these developments are principally examined to evaluate the relative strengths and weaknesses of holders of these estates or of insurgent rulers vis-à-vis the Sublime Porte. That the period under study was characterized by a growing tendency towards "self-assertion," at least until the recentralization efforts of the imperial bureaucracy during the mid-nineteenth century, facilitates a political reading of these developments, and devalorizes the constitutive force, and the the unfolding, of economic processes at work. In this imagery, the growing command of the local notables is perceived to have been reinforced by the Land Code of 1858, which provided a stable framework for the exercise of a strict control over the producers. To recapitulate, the argument is that a chain of events over the period under study enfeebled the viability and the survival of immediate producers to the benefit of rural/urban notables.

Yet, the social weight of small holders was never seriously threatened during the period under question. On the contrary, the hegemony of local families in the southern and coastal regions over immediate producers throughout the eighteenth century was unrivalled. Their continuing dominance and the establishment of centralized political structures in the southern provinces facilitated the new patterning in flows of goods and labor across and beyond regional boundaries. Eventually, however, it was precisely in the same geographical setting that the peasant insurrections in Mount Lebanon, culminating in the events of Kisrawan, and decades of civil strife in the Judean Hills and Jabal Heights signalled the demise of the grip of local notables, thereby consolidating the sphere of the small peasantry within the social map. The augmentation in the numbers of commoners at the expense of tax-farmers in controlling land in the former and the mushrooming of new families contending for power in the latter set in motion a new dynamics in the region. That is, it was only during the first half of the following century that large estates and the hold of rural notables over direct producers in the southern and coastal regions lost their initial impetus, thereby consolidating the hold of the *fallah* over the means and organization of production. That is, in the long-run, the presumed hegemony of the rural/urban notables was considerably undermined.

Recent studies charting the course of the Ottoman economy have raised doubts about the applicability of the theory of peripheralization to this province of the globe arguing that large-scale commercial farming, with the notable exception of *izbas* in Egypt, never dominated the Ottoman countryside.[41] Equating peripheralization with the emergence of large estates, however, does injustice to the theory in question. As depicted above, world-systems perspective postulates that the process of incorporation entails concomitant processes of formation/consolidation of larger decision-making units (and not necessarily plantation-like units), with its attendant forms of labor control.

The argument advanced in this paper is that the creation of large agricultural holdings and the reign of centrifugal forces administering and patrolling agronomically attractive areas throughout the eighteenth century signalled incorporation into the expanding world-economy. The institutional and organizational rearrangements, as discussed above, allowed for the increased coercion of labor and the effective mobilization of export crops. The decline of these arrangements, however, did not denote a breakdown of the eighteenth century ones. Agricultural producers were by then inter-nested within the global networks of commerce and production, shifting easily within the parameters set by the continuously changing axial division of labor. The dwindling cotton production was reignited by the American Civil War, and the volume of cereal produced skyrocketed during the Crimean War boom. That is, ebbs and flows of the world market came to determine the background for the continuous restructuring of the agrarian order in the region.

9

The Introduction of Commercial Agriculture in the Province of Mosul and its Effects on the Peasantry, 1750–1850

Dina Rizk Khoury

In the historiography of Ottoman Arab lands, it has generally been accepted that major changes in the rural economy of the area took place in the nineteenth century under the impact of the capitalist world market.[1] This paper attempts to locate changes in the rural sector in the eighteenth century before the Ottoman Empire was fully integrated into the world market. More specifically, it seeks to demonstrate that a number of trends in the rural economy of Iraq, usually attributed to the impact of capitalist Europe on a precapitalist economy,[2] can be detected in northern Iraq as early as the last decades of the eighteenth century. Among the most important of these trends was a gradual *de facto* privatization of land accompanied by the introduction of commercial agricultural production.[3] Moreover, the "prime mover" behind such developments appears to have been an internal and regional dynamic rather than an exogeneous one.

It is important to stress at this point that commercial agriculture was not predominant in Mosul's hinterland and that it coexisted with semi-feudal relations. It was mainly practiced in villages where urban notables could control the peasantry either through coercive methods or through relations of increased dependence. Furthermore, growth in agricultural production remained erratic and dependent on rain, frequency of natural disasters, and security from wars. Therefore it is

155

all the more remarkable that given all these obstacles, land-lords/officials thought it lucrative to invest in Mosuli villages. Thus, accumulation must have been large enough in periods of prosperity to warrant such investments.

There were three major catalysts for the development of commercial agriculture in the province of Mosul: the change in the land-tenure system; the emergence on Mosul's political scene of one local family that intermittently ruled Mosul for 108 years (1726–1834); and the increase in the regional trade of the areas surrounding Mosul.

The changes in the land-tenure system that took place during the seventeenth and eighteenth centuries throughout the Ottoman Empire have been discussed by various scholars.[4] The introduction of the *iltizam* system, coupled with the transformation of the *malikane* form of land grant into semi-hereditary ownership of land, led to the privatization of land and to the commodification of both land and its products. While these developments did not lead to any changes in the relations and methods of production in the countryside, they did involve major changes in the distribution of surplus among various sectors of the ruling class and among producers and non-producers.[5] Under these arrangements, the peasant surrendered a large part of his surplus to urban-based *mutasarrıfs* (in fact, landlords) under the guise of taxes. By the eighteenth century, these taxes had become more like rents accruing to urban officials who became grain merchants. Local Mosuli historiographers of the eighteenth century invariably mention the word *malaka* (owned) in relation to villages the taxes of which accrued to certain officials.[6] By the end of the eighteenth century, most of the villages of the Mosuli hinterland that were registered as *has* in the sixteenth-century *defter*s had become malikanes of the governors (*valis*) and various Mosuli officials.[7]

Furthermore, the *tasarruf* rights to villages in Mosul's hinterland were often held in shares by city notables who felt free to sell and buy these rights without the permission of the central government or its representatives in the city. In 1834, for instance, an individual from the *sadah* (descendents of the Prophet), sold half of his share of a village for 400 *guruş*.[8] In addition, notables in partnership often held shares in the *miri* taxes of certain villages, especially those in which they owned lands and groves as private property.[9] The rents of these villages were collected in kind (usually grains) and were sold or hoarded by officials who became speculators on the grain market.[10] Bruce McGowan has aptly called these officials "fiscal entrepreneurs."[11] They regarded their offices and their benefits as commodities. In Mosul, it was these fiscal entrepreneurs and not the owners of merchant capital who controlled access to agricultural goods and who undertook the introduction of small scale agricultural enterprises in some villages.

The gradual transformation of state-owned lands into a form of private ownership was accelerated in Mosul by the hegemony of a family of local origin that ruled Mosul between the years 1726 and 1834. In their position as governors (valis) the Jalilis were able to transform many of the villages in the province from has to malikane, and the fifteen households of the family owned the most productive villages in Mosul's hinterland.[12] Furthermore, in their effort to maintain economic and political hegemony, they found it necessary to appease a number of potential contenders for supremacy in the city, either by granting tax-farming privileges or by overlooking the transfer of state and provincial revenues to private coffers.

The concentration of land in the hands of the Jalilis allowed them to spearhead the movement towards commercialized agricultural production. Their access to the products of the land coupled with the large size of their rural surplus enabled them to invest in the countryside. They were also better able to sustain the frequent losses incurred by epidemics and wars. Other landlords/officials preferred the safer route of depending on the extraction of the surplus through tax/rent and then its sale through agents.

Finally, there appears to have been an increase in the regional trade of the area that acted as an impetus for landlords/officials to invest in Mosul's hinterland. The province of Mosul lies at the intersection of numerous trade routes. The city and its environs were traversed by caravans carrying Indian goods from Basra through Baghdad, Diyarbakır, İstanbul, and Aleppo. Furthermore, Mosul was a center for the Kurdish areas around it.[13] The increase of British and Indian trade through Basra led to a revival of the transit trade through Mosul which had experienced a slump during the Ottoman–Persian hostilities of the mid-eighteenth century.[14] Goods such as Indian cotton, coffee, spices, and sugar went to Mosul for local consumption as well as for re-export to other parts of the Empire.[15] At the same time, trade with Europe through Aleppo, basically in gallnuts and wool, remained important to Mosuli merchants.[16] Writing in 1835, John Bowring lists twenty-five Mosuli merchants trading with Aleppo with a capital of 170,000 to 200,000 dollars.[17]

Mosul's other trading partner was Baghdad. It gradually became a major recipient of Mosuli agricultural products, such as grains, dried fruits, galls, and other items destined for the consumption of Baghdadis. Baghdad's hinterland could not provide it with enough to feed itself. The unrest in the countryside, where tribal confederations refused to submit any of their agricultural surplus in taxes, coupled with the continuous confrontation with Persia, turned Baghdad, especially in the second half of the eighteenth century, into a major consumer of Mosuli agricultural goods.[18] Furthermore, as the territorial and political influence of Baghdad grew, it became essential for the governors of Mosul to maintain a constant supply of grains in the event that the governors of Baghdad demanded it.[19] In the 1830s, the provisions of the armies of Dawud Pasha of Baghdad were often provided by the governors of Mosul.[20] By mid-nineteenth century Mosuli grains were exported as far south as the Hijaz.[21]

In addition to Aleppo and Baghdad, Mosul had close trading ties with the regions surrounding it, that is, Shahrizur, Amadiya, the Kurdish mountains, and Diyarbakır. There is nothing available to document the increase in this regional trade. However, among these various regions, there had always existed a strong exchange based on a degree of regional specialization. The Kurdish mountains provided gallnuts and wood; Sulaymaniya and its environs provided some staples, while Diyarbakır furnished the copper used by coppersmiths. The sources do not document an increase in this trade; they merely mention that it existed and that it was essential to Mosul.[22] Therefore, there will be a certain degree of speculation in any discussion of the importance of this trade in the eighteenth century. John Bowring mentioned the existence of such a strong regional network of trade, carried out by local merchants, but admitted that it was very difficult to quantify its volume.[23] No doubt, the rule of the Jalili family in Mosul (1726–1834) provided stability in the area and encouraged trade. Their construction of numerous *hans* and *qaysariyyas* (enclosed structure with shops) as well as *suqs* is sufficient evidence for a tremendous increase in trade.[24] However, what might have been of equal importance was the gradual incorporation of the areas surrounding Mosul into the city's political and economic orbit as urban-based landlords acquired *iltizam* and other rights over hitherto independent communities. This point will be discussed in more detail below. It is sufficient to say at this point that as city notables became involved in various forms of agricultural pursuits, either in sheep-herding on a large scale or in renting camels (both functions of pastoralists in the area), they subjugated and brought into settled city life a sector of the rural population that had previously avoided it. More communities found it necessary to become part of an urban and rural market economy in order to survive. Again this trend can not be quantified, nor are there any consistent references to it in contemporary sources. One can deduce it from the increase in the size of the city of Mosul where there were tribal communities settled outside its walls and where a number of mosques and *mascids* were erected in the course of the eighteenth century. There are also some incidents of brigandage directed against herders of city notables' sheep and camels.[25]

The Introduction of Commercial Agriculture

The issue of the form of land usage in commercial enterprise has been a point of contention among Ottomanists. While most agree on the emergence of the *çiftlik* as a form of commercial agricultural enterprise, it remains difficult to specify what exactly is meant by a çiftlik.[26] The most common feature ascribed to it has been the disenfranchisement of the peasantry who become laborers living on the estate and produce for the market. This phenomenon appears to have been limited to eastern Europe, and to estates on main waterways that produced for an international market.[27] At the same time, the owners of çiftliks in certain areas were merely "receivers of rents" rather than entrepreneurs who became involved in the production process itself. These çiftliks were small in size and in many cases they catered to regional rather than international markets.[28]

In the case of eighteenth and nineteenth-century Mosul, commercial agricultural enterprises did not take the çiftlik form. They produced primarily for the local and regional market. Surplus extraction through rent remained a favorite method of acquiring agricultural products and selling them on the market. They involved very little capital outlay and no change in the methods of production. What was involved was an increase in accumulation by the village proprietors, and a gradual encroachment on the peasant's rights to the product of the land, as the owner became the moneylender, tax collector, and the primary power holder in the village. At the same time, in villages where horticulture had been a traditional agricultural pursuit undertaken by independent peasants on small plots of land, city notables acquired outright legal ownership (*mülk*) over extensive groves and lands. It was in these areas that a commercial form of agricultural production developed involving total disenfranchisement of the peasantry, enclosures of groves, and outright ownership of previously communally owned water rights. It is this form of land usage that is of interest to us at this point.

By the mid-eighteenth century, the main form of extraction of the rural surplus was tax/rent. The landlord/official tried to squeeze as much rent as he could from the peasantry. However, by the mid-eighteenth century much village land began to be converted into groves (sing. *bustan*) and farms (sing. *mazra'a*) planted with specific commercial crops under the supervision of urban notables. This process, for reasons mentioned above, was spearheaded by the Jalilis. From the various *waqfiyyes* of Mosuli mosques, often built by the Jalilis, it is clear that they started their active investment in Mosul's hinterland by at least mid-century after establishing themselves firmly at the helm of political life in the city.

At first these investments were in rural real estate, such as hans and grocery stores (*baqqals*).[29] However throughout the eighteenth century, more and more city notables began investing in watermills. These watermills were considered major investments on the part of the urban notables and were often held in partnerships.[30] They entailed quite a large capital outlay. For instance, a mill was sold for 18,000 guruş in 1859, a substantial amount at the time.[31] The watermill also required major investment in terms of its upkeep, and it presupposed a strong foothold in village life since the urban notables needed to ensure that the mills had their share of water rights held in common by the villagers. As in eastern Europe, these watermills were a major excuse for the urban landlords to acquire control of land in their vicinity. Many of these watermills were found in the vicinity of villages with a heavy concentration of urban-held groves, or in villages which were held as malikane.[32] The Jalilis, for instance, owned the mill of Tarjala village, but also ended up having access to the rents of the peasants of that village.[33]

Urban-owned mills represent one form of investment in Mosul's hinterland; the other was the establishment by urban notables of groves and farms. These seem to have been differentiated by what was cultivated in them rather than by the difference in the methods of exploitation of the peasantry. Groves, which were not uncommon in the seventeenth and early eighteenth centuries, had been located mainly around the city itself, much like the Ghuta of Damascus.[34] By the end of the eighteenth century, groves spread to various Mosuli villages, and it seems that they did so at the expense either of peasant-held land or at the expense of village commons. The groves were usually planted with some kind of tree such as olive, grape, or fruit trees. They varied in scale, and there is no evidence as to their size and how much they produced. The 1850s court records show that the value of groves varied from 13,000 guruş to as little as 1,500 guruş.[35] It would be safe to assume that while the average grove may not have been a large one, it generally was of a size big enough to generate quite a beneficial commercial surplus for its holder. When Claudius James Rich, East India Company resident in Baghdad, visited Ba'shiqa and Bahzani in 1820, he said that almost all the olives, olive oil, and soap of Mosul was produced by these two villages.[36]

The groves were usually not subject to any prebendal tax as they were regarded as absolute mülk that could be sold at a hefty profit. They were mainly irrigated by the waters of the rivers and rivulets that abound in Mosul's hinterland. The Jalili groves of Ba'shiqa and Bahzani were irrigated by the waters of the Khawsar river on which the Jalilis owned a number of watermills. Their investments in these two villages was so extensive that they thought it lucrative to install their own centrally owned and located olive press and the only grocery store in the village of Bahzani.[37] The press allowed them some form of control over the major cottage industry of these two villages, soap production.

Another form of outright mülk in the villages was simply called "land" (*ard*). As in the case of a grove, it was not unusual for urban notables to own land in the vicinity of Mosul in the seventeenth and eighteenth centuries. The founder of the 'Umari family, Qasim al-'Umari, owned a small piece of land in the vicinity of one of the villages,[38] but this was not a common occurrence. By the mid-eighteenth century, there was a trend towards acquiring land as mülk in the villages of Mosul. One document shows that Nu'man Pasha al-Jalili owned land in the village of Bahzani that amounted to a *faddan*. He had bought some of it from the family of Qara Mustafa.[39] In another example, another Jalili owned three pieces of land in and around Ba'shiqa where he also possessed a total of twelve groves.[40] These parcels were often scattered around the village and never found in large pieces. The faddan, according to Haidar, was an amount of land that can be hoed by one ox using a scratch hoe in one day.[41] Nu'man Pasha's faddan yielded only 40 *tughar* of grain, not a very large amount.

The fragmentation of land implies that its acquisition may have been the result of the disenfranchisement of the peasantry, since most of it was interspersed with land that had been cultivated by villagers for a long time.[42] Unlike groves, which seem to have been constituted of large blocks of land and to have been instituted along very commercial lines, the size of privately owned plots of land remained small. Their main products were grains destined for private consumption or for sale in the local market. In a document dated 1853, a certain 'Aisha Khatun sold 40 tughar worth of land for 1,400 guruş. The amount is quite small compared to the value of smaller-sized groves.[43] At any rate, the outright mülk acquisition and registration of village land by legal means remained very limited, and the acquisition of surplus grains took other legal forms.

The third form of mülk land in the countryside was the farm (mazra'a). The farm was not a new form of land ownership. The defters of the sixteenth century record a number of farms that were granted to *sipahis*.[44] Yet they were not held as mülk, nor could they be made into waqf. They were granted to supplement the income of a sipahi. By the end of the eighteenth century, the meaning of the word "mazra'a" had changed. It became mülk, to be sold and bought at will. It is not clear from the sources available what was cultivated on a farm, how it was cultivated, or by whom. We are told, for instance, that the products (*mahsul*), of the farm of the village of Tahrawa and that of another farm were made *waqf* by Ahmad Pasha al-Jalili in 1816 endowing the mosque of Nabi Shit.[45] Obviously, the produce was agricultural, but of what kind is not clear. There seems to have been a number of farms in Mosuli villages, although none were made waqf except these two, an indication of the illegal means by which they became mülk.

The Rural Social Structure of Mosul: 1750–1850

The impact of the introduction of the "mercantile domain" [46] into Mosul's rural social structure was by no means uniform. It did not lead to the wholesale pauperization of the peasantry nor to their reduction to mere sharecroppers who depended for their subsistence needs on their landlord. This latter development took place only towards the end of the nineteenth century. The changes brought about by the commercialization of land and its products resulted in an increase in social differentiation within the village community and to the break-up of the self-sufficient household economy among certain sectors of the peasantry.

This process of rural transformation was closely bound with three factors. The first was the degree of urban penetration into the village or tribal community. What Talal Asad has observed in relation to systems of pastoral production holds true for systems of agricultural production. He wrote, "[i]t is misleading to isolate systems of production from systems of power. There is always a connection between exercise of coercive power and modes of generating surplus."[47] The degree and method by which the city notables and their various governors encroached on the traditional rights of rural communities, whether they were sedentary or semi-sedentary, determined how these communities were transformed. In other words, the way that rural surplus was generated in Mosul was closely connected with the way the surplus was extracted: the tax/rent method, or through direct appropriation of the product under the guise of new property relations, or finally, through direct coercion.

The second determinant in the rural transformation of Mosul involved the geographic location of the villages. In villages lying directly on the various trade routes that traversed Mosul's hinterland, there developed a specialization in certain cash crops and increasing differentiation among the peasantry. This differentation was not merely in terms of access to land and implements, but also in terms of the development of a sector of the village population that engaged in providing services.[48] Thus we have a shopkeeper (baqqal), dyeing shop (*masbagha*), a man who rents beasts of burden, a man who rents boats, etc.

Thirdly, the way that the rural population reacted to the incursion of the dominant urban forces determined the extent to which it was exploited. In the case of Mosul, the reaction of the settled community varied from increasing production to finding new economic roles, indebtedness, and finally increasing dependence on city landlords. In semi-sedentary areas the reaction was in many cases outright rebellion.

It has already been stated that commercial agricultural production was not predominant in Mosul's hinterland. Up to the mid-nineteenth century the tax/rent method of extracting the surplus remained very important. However, this does not mean that there were no changes caused by the intensification of exploitation of the rural community by the urban fiscal entrepreneurs. Unfortunately, the sources are not very informative when it comes to delineating these changes. The inheritance records available tend to record the belongings of middle and rich peasantry. A totally disenfranchised peasant does not go to court to divide up what few, if any, possessions he has. Furthermore, the cases available to the researcher give no clear indication of the land-tenure arrangements in the village to which a specific peasant belonged. Nevertheless, it is possible to arrive at some tentative conclusions regarding the rural social structure in general.

In communities where some kind of iltizam arrangements were made, the *mültezim* seems to have increased his demands on the peasantry without attempting any kind of change in methods of production. This was the case of a Kurdish mültezim who told Rich in the 1820s: "I allow the peasants to cultivate my estate as they may find convenient, and I take from them my due, which is *zakat* and as much as I can squeeze out of them by any means and under any pretext."[49]

The peasant's response seems to have been either to increase his indebtedness to the landlord/official, or to attempt to meet the new demands by working his own land and that of others as well. In cases like these intensification of exploitation meant that the family plot was no longer sufficient to maintain a peasants' subsistence needs. Of the twenty-seven cases reviewed of peasants who left less than 1,500 guruş in belongings to their wives and children, there were two who had incurred debts. One of these peasants owed approximately eight times the value of his possessions, while the other owed more than one-third.[50] Furthermore the first peasant appears to have been a sharecropper owning only his implements and a cow. He left behind no grains or seeds. The second peasant may have worked his land and that of others since he left behind two sets of implements and some seeds, but no draught animals.

About one third of the cases reviewed of peasants leaving less than 1,500 guruş appear to have been sharecroppers who might have lost their usufruct rights to their land. In almost all of the instances they did not own implements, but left behind grains sufficient for consumption and a draught animal or beasts of burden. The ownership of the latter allowed the peasant to engage in the transport of goods for a share in the grain. The more prosperous among this first group cultivated their own land and supplemented their income by renting out draught animals for transport. A few owned a number of sheep which were easy to maintain in seasons when land lay fallow.[51]

Hence it can not be argued with any degree of assurance that the majority of the peasantry in Mosul's villages became sharecroppers or lost control of the products of their land to city notables. On the contrary, the inheritance records show that some elements in the peasant community were able to retain their traditional rights to land and to augment their holdings in the wake of an increase in the demand for grains and other agricultural products. This was usually the case in communities where agricultural production was combined with animal husbandry either in sheep, draught animals, transport animals, or horses. Invariably, the middle or rich peasant owned more than one draught animal, two sets of implements, several sheep, copper, and grains (wheat and barley) in quantities exceeding his consumption needs. In most cases, the peasant did not leave behind a family large enough to take care of the household resources as a unit, which indicates that he must have employed outside labor using sharecropping arrangements. In almost all the recorded cases of middle and rich peasants the major staple of cultivation was grain, in addition to a substantial amount of animals that were obviously raised and bred for commercial reasons.

All this does not explain how the middle peasant was able to acquire access to more land and to accumulate surpluses beyond his needs as head of a household, as a member of the village commune, and as a payer of tax/rent to a landlord, to the provincial government, or to a local powerholder. The peasant might have been able to acquire rights to cultivation of land that had been abandoned or neglected, through special arrangements with the *malikaneci* or mutasarrif of the village. This is indicated by a decree or *buyuruldu* issued in 1826, which grants the right of tasarruf (nearly as private ownership) to a Jalili of the village of Bahzani. The mutasarrıf's only obligations were to pay the *öşür* tax and to cultivate the land that fell to him. The decree (buyuruldu) states:

> Conflicting laws being in existence and interfering with bringing lands back into cultivation the following declaration is made in response to the requests of landowners. For the last three years disasters have caused lands to remain fallow. The law is the following: if the land is cultivated after having lain fallow for three years on account of disasters, and it is some outsider who farms that land while not holding a deed or permission from the legal owner, a debt is owed to the legal owner. This latter ruling is made to protect resident landholders from outside interference and is in agreement with the wishes of the central government, in spite of conflicting laws about bringing land back into cultivation.[52]

The decree (buyuruldu) not only indicates how the peasant might have been able to increase the area of cultivable land available to him, but also points to the confusion about land rights in periods of rural unrest. This confusion must have provided both the city notable and the peasant with opportunities to increase their access to rural surplus.

Although there is no documentary evidence of contractual agreements between peasants and proprietors in eighteenth and nineteenth-century Mosul, there are some examples available for Baghdad that may shed some light on how the rich and the middle peasantry was able to extend its control of cultivable land. In a document dated 1798, a number of peasants reached a rental agreement (*mugharasa*) with the son of the governor of Baghdad to cultivate some land that had lain fallow near Hilla. Under one agreement, the agent of Sa'id Pasha sold the right to cultivate some groves to a peasant for a certain amount of money. Sa'id Pasha forfeited his right to the rent on the condition that the peasant invest it in reclaiming and enclosing the land. In exchange, Sa'id Pasha acquired three-fifths of the expected produce, and the peasant retained the rest. The duration of the agreement was twenty years, in effect giving both the peasant and the proprietor secure tenure.[53] In another document, the duration of the agreement was ninety years, and the ratio of the division of produce was similar to that in first agreement.[54] It is obvious from the examples mentioned above that although the middle peasantry did acquire a semblance of security of tenure over uncultivated and unreclaimed land, their position was highly dependent on the needs and benevolence of urban officials.

In villages where the landlord acquired direct access to the products of the land through his ownership of it as mülk, there seems to have been a total disenfranchisement of a sector of the peasantry, especially those who worked on land transformed into groves. There is no evidence about how these peasants survived, or whether they became wage laborers or sharecroppers. Some of them might have become totally dependent on the market economy of the village to fulfill their basic needs. However, it was common in villages where mülk was instituted to find peasants cultivating their own small plots of land and working for a wage or as sharecroppers on the groves of city notables. This is supported by the fact that Bahzani, an olive and fruit-growing village, continued to pay its miri tax in grains up until the third decade of the nineteenth century.[55] While some peasants cultivated grains on their own plots and worked in the groves to supplement their income, there seems to have been a middle peasantry even in villages where city notables were an economic force. In a case recorded in 1853, a peasant owned 19 olive trees worth 570 guruş as well as a flock of sheep and a substantial amount of wheat.[56]

It is difficult to draw definite conclusions about the effects of the imposition of new property relations (mülk) on the peasantry. There is no doubt that part of the peasantry lost their rights to their lands. However, it would be wrong to conclude that this was widespread. It was far cheaper and safer for the owner of a grove to ensure that the peasants were not totally disenfranchised and could maintain themselves independently of him through the cultivation of small parcels of land.

In other villages where the city notables were not able to acquire mülk rights directly, the peasants engaged in some form of commercial agricultural production (in cotton and grains or horticulture) and were able to extend the area of cultivable land. This was the case in the Christian villages of Tall 'Uskuf and Tall Kayf both on trade routes from Baghdad to Diyarbakır. The sources do not offer an explanation of how and why these peasants were able to reclaim hitherto deserted villages. There might have been an increase in the population of these villages due to migration from other Christian areas because of the demands of local notables. At the same time, the increase in surplus available to these villagers may have been caused by their direct contact with traders interested in agricultural products. In any case, it is clear that there was a definite increase in the population of these two rural districts that led their inhabitants to cultivate a number of deserted villages in the surrounding areas.[57] Although the urban notables, primarily the Jalilis, may have had a direct hand in controlling part of the surplus through their ownership of a seed shop, it is also possible that the peasants were able to accumulate some surplus. In the case of the village of Tall Kayf, the city notables could not acquire direct access to land because the village was a waqf of the Nabi Jiryis Mosque in Mosul.[58]

By the first decades of the nineteenth century, there existed a fairly large group of Christian middle peasantry which prospered from the increase in the demand for agricultural goods. In a *cizye ferman* issued in 1835, by far the largest group was the middle peasantry which numbered 2,454 of the adult male population, while the poorest numbered 972 and the richest 396.[59] Allowing for inflation in these figures (especially the first and the last) in order to increase the amount of *cizye*, the middle peasantry were still large in number compared to the poor ones. While there are no figures for the preceding years that would allow us to see any increase in the number of middle peasants, it is safe to assume that such an increase existed given the general economic trend in the area at that period. Furthermore, this is supported by the fact that by the third decade of the nineteenth century, the Christian villages, specifically Tall 'Uskuf and Tall Kayf, were paying the highest amounts in provincial taxes.[60]

The geographic position of the villages vis-à-vis the trade routes that traversed Mosul's hinterland led to a degree of specialization within the village community itself. In villages such as Qara Qush, Bartilla, Karamlis, Tall 'Uskuf, and Tall Kayf, there existed a healthy cash economy as well as a sector of the peasant population that seems to have been exclusively engaged in offering services to other peasants and traders. These villages developed into small market towns and drawing areas for neighboring hamlets, as peasants began to sell their surpluses directly to other villagers and to caravans for cash. As early as the third decade of the eighteenth century a priest in the village of Qara Qush, which was a major stop for traders going to Baghdad and to the Kurdish regions, alludes to peasants who were able to do so.[61] Two decades later a document lamented the damages incurred by Nadir Shah's invasion of two other Christian villages, Karamlis and Bartilla. It stated that a great deal of crops and money were stolen. In all of these instances, money was a common medium of exchange, and the priest recorded the value of various agricultural goods and animals in cash.[62]

In most of these villages, the presence of city notables was strongly felt either through their ownership of land as in the case of Bartilla, Qara Qush, and Karamlis,[63] or through their establishment of mills, presses, seed shops, grocery shops, and even a tannery. There is no doubt that these landlords/officials encouraged the cultivation of cash crops and the development of a certain degree of specialization among the peasant population. The inheritance records indicate at least two examples of villagers who owned nothing but very expensive pieces of village property (in one case, it was worth 1,400 guruş),[64] which was to be held in shares by their descendants. In other cases there are examples of villagers leaving rafts (*kallak*), which were used to transport goods and people down the Tigris, as well as a modest amount of grains probably sufficient for household consumption. However, the most lucrative specialization for peasants in these villages seems to have been the renting of draught and transport animals since these constituted their biggest investments.[65] It is clear in the case of these peasants that the family plot had ceased to be the main source of livelihood, and that they were able to accumulate a surplus by catering to an increasingly complex village economy that was being transformed by the demands of a widening regional market and by the incursions of the city into the countryside.

One last issue must be addressed: the reaction of Mosul's rural population to the incursion of the city into the countryside. In settled communities, it is very hard to delineate the reactions of the middle peasantry as opposed to the poor peasantry. In all probability, their reactions were not widely divergent. The middle peasant led a precarious existence in which whatever surplus he was able to accumulate could easily by lost by war, natural disaster, and the demands of the more powerful city notables. In the year 1786 for instance, there was a drought that led to a rise in the price of agricultural goods and to a decline in the price of animals. We are told that the price of oxen and cows went down to such an extent that it was no more than the price of the skin.[66] This was because these animals were expensive to maintain in times of scarcity, and it was easier to get rid of them.

Since the middle and rich peasantry of Mosul depended for their surpluses on animal husbandry, the price increases caused by droughts, cold, or floods threatened their existence and must have reduced them to subsistence levels. Their reaction to this might have been the abandonment of their villages and migration to the city or the curtailment of their consumption during the years of the drought. There is every reason to believe that if they were forced to curtail consumption they became more dependent on city notables and their village representatives to carry them through the bad years.[67] There is no indication that this middle peasantry ever attempted any independent political action. On the contrary, it appears that they, along with the landlords/officials, exploited the poor peasantry whom they employed on their plots and to whom they rented animals.

In the settled villages where the peasants had witnessed the gradual infiltration of city notables into their communities, there appears to have developed over a period of time relations of patronage with these notables at the expense of older alliances with village *shaykhs* and Christian priests. Previously, the shaykhs and priests had been the intermediaries between the rural population and whoever held coercive power over them. This point is extremely tentative and needs further research based on new sources concerning peasant subculture. However, we have some information on four Christian villages, all "owned" by city notables, namely Merki, Ba'shiqa, Bartilla, and finally Qara Qush. In a letter addressed to Muhammad Pasha al-Jalili, the Patriarch of the Jacobites stationed in Diyarbakır and responsible for the Christians in Mosul, complained to the governor of the conversion of Christians of the villages of Bartilla and Ba'shiqa to Catholicism. He ostracized a certain clergyman called "Bishara" who had converted half the inhabitants of the village of Ba'shiqa into *ifranj* (Catholics).[68]

Ba'shiqa primarily consisted of olive and fruit groves owned by the Jalilis, and the new local priest must have been closely allied with them. This is supported by the fact that throughout their rule, the Jalilis encouraged and fostered the spread of Catholicism partly in an effort to assert their independence from the Diyarbakır diocese and to acquire more political control of Mosul's rich Christian villages.[69] In the aftermath of Nadir Shah's invasion for instance, Husayn Pasha al-Jalili rebuilt the church of Qara Qush.[70] Towards the end of the eighteenth century 'Uthman Pasha al-Jalili renovated the shrine in the village of Merki.[71] For the peasant, conversion to Catholicism meant two things: increased reliance on the city notable who now directly became the sponsor of the new religion, and freedom from the dues he had to pay to his old church in the form of cizye.[72] It is impossible to say whether similar developments took place in Muslim and Yazidi villages.

In semi-sedentary communities, where both pastoralism and agriculture were practiced, the reaction to the new demands of landlords/officials was often outright rebellion. In the Sinjar region, where the Jalilis undertook punitive expeditions solely for the purpose of acquiring herds, there was often rebellion, brigandage on caravans, and retaliation. In the aftermath of the plague of 1772, Sulayman Pasha al-Jalili undertook an expedition against Sinjar and acquired a large number of sheep as well as horses.[73] Three years later the Sinjaris attacked the shepherds in the Mosul area and acquired the herds of Mosul.[74] In the villages of Jabal Maqlub, where the Shaykhan Yazidi tribes lived, and where the notables of Mosul owned rights to the products of a number of villages, the reaction of the community was more varied. In at least one recorded instance, the rents accruing to city notables had to be forcibly extracted from these villages. In the year 1799 for example, the *kahya* of Mosul, Bakr Efendi, invaded the Shaykhan and took the products of 15 villages, most of which belonged to the people of Mosul.[75] In other cases, the shaykhs of the villages chose to ally themselves with one political faction against another. During the political infighting that took place between Fattah Pasha al-Jalili and Husayn Pasha's sons in the year 1762, the former used the Shaykhan to fight against his enemies.[76]

The situation was slightly different in the case of tribes that engaged solely in pastoral production or in renting out beasts of burden to caravans. In one recorded case, the tribe of Tayy, allies of the Jalilis during their early years as governors, attacked Mosul and were able to get some of Sulayman Pasha's camels that he rented out to traders. In other cases, tribes responded with acts of brigandage against Mosuli villages or against caravans, as happened in 1807 when the Arab al-Jubur attacked the villages of Mosul and took about 30,000 sheep.[77]

However, not all tribes were able to resist the incursions of city notables or stronger tribal confederations, such as Tayy, who were closely allied to the governors of Mosul. Some tribes were forced either to settle in Mosul proper and become small-time renters of camels,[78] or to settle on the outskirts of Mosul, and provide seasonal labor to its notables. This latter was the case for the 'Arab al-'Ukaydat, who settled outside the city walls at the beginning of the eighteenth century.[79] They lived in wooden shacks, cultivated small patches of land in order to feed themselves, and raised a cow or a donkey to transport goods in the city. By the end of the eighteenth century the southeastern flank of the city had become the permanent home for a number of pastoralists.

Conclusion

The development of commercial agriculture in the province of Mosul did not develop into agrarian capitalism because of the precarious position of the owners of land whose fortunes remained closely tied to their political position. Hence, much of the surplus they accumulated was spent on maintaining their political and social position rather than on changing methods of production. Only the Jalilis, whose position remained more or less stable for a long time, were able to reinvest some of the surplus in agriculture. However, they were not consistent in doing so, as there were years when they had to spend much of their surplus on fighting and appeasing enemies and potential clients.

Secondly, commercial agriculture did not lead to the development of wage labor in the countryside. Although the peasant often became dependent, there were institutional limits to this dependency that he could have recourse to in defending himself. The ideological instance always remained predominant in the extraction of surplus, and this allowed for the prevalence of non-economic relations of patronage between the peasant and the landlord. Furthermore, it remained much less costly for the landlord/official to maintain sharecropping arrangements since he could always appropriate some of the peasant's share in bad years.

Lastly, the limited development of the village division of labor put a constraint on the evolution of a middle peasantry. Accumulation by the middle peasant was threatened by the major landholder(s) of the village and by natural and man-made disasters. His affluence was basically due to his connection to city notables and to his ability to exploit the labor power of other peasants, as well as of other members of his household, rather than to an improvement in methods of agricultural production.

10

The Grain Economy of Late Ottoman Syria and the Issue of Large-Scale Commercialization

Linda Schilcher

Increases in agricultural production in the Syrian provinces of the Ottoman Empire during the nineteenth century were substantial, marking a clear break with the production pattern of at least two centuries. Greater Syrian grain production grew from an estimated 500,000 tons in the 1830s to an estimated 1,300,000 tons on the eve of World War I.[1] Significant growth is also evidenced by large increases in the amount of land under cultivation, the population engaged in settled agriculture, and the extent of surpluses for non-farm consumption and for export.[2]

Though the influence of the European industrializing world began to significantly alter local economic relationships already in the late eighteenth century, not until the 1870s and 1880s was there any sustained, direct economic intervention and colonization. European intervention therefore can not be proposed as the principal factor in early agricultural development. Nor can technological change or development of infrastructure be held responsible. Mechanization or the building of roads, communications networks and railways did not affect grain production until several decades after production increases began to appear. To explain production increases we will have to consider many facets of the local grain economy and especially the situation of the peasants who produced the surpluses. What were the

173

economic, social, and political conditions of increased agricultural production? Was this growth linked to the *local* emergence of large-scale commercial agriculture?

Clarification of historical problems in Syria's grain economy will be rewarding also because grain was at the heart of the economy of greater Syria. First of all, grain was the chief source of food, always constituting at least 50 percent of average daily food consumption and as much as 90 percent of personal food intake for the majority of the population.[3] Unlike Egypt, which in the nineteenth century had substituted cotton for grain as the chief agricultural commodity— eventually driving up the price of Egyptian wheat and obliging the population to turn either to imported wheat or to less expensive secondary grain crops such as millet—Syrians continued to eat locally produced wheat and barley. These were the primary staples around which the entire diet was built.[4]

Secondly, the cultivation of grain took up the largest cropped area and occupied the largest segment of the productive population.[5] It also revealed much about the labor force, the division of labor, the level of technology, and the productive contribution not only of rural men but also of urban workers producing agricultural implements and of workers in the domestic setting, especially rural women and children who performed much of the work of harvesting, sorting the seed, storing it, cleaning it, and preparing it for consumption.[6]

Grain was the chief commodity in both the formal and informal internal market. It was the basic wage good and the commodity upon which urban–rural economic relationships pivoted and which consequently determined the fluctuations in seasonal economic patterns such as cash flows and employment cycles.[7] It thus reflected the patterns of economic dependency among the region's urban, mountain, and desert populations.[8]

Finally, as the chief source of profit, grain was also the most common item of local investment, speculation, and risk.[9] It was also the chief source of revenue for the Ottoman government either directly through the tithes or, later, indirectly through the land tax. There is an old expression in Syria which runs: *"Fi al-Sham, kulli shai'in min al-qamh"* (in Syria, everything comes from wheat).[10] Wheat was, as it were, the locomotive of the economy.

While the importance of grain in the pre-industrial political economy of the region has long been recognized, there are few studies on the grain economy of the region of greater Syria as a whole or on any particular grain-producing region.[11]

On the whole, the study of the Syrian countryside in the pre-industrial era is far more difficult than the study of its cities. First of all, there is the problem of sources. In the cities we have records kept by the city dwellers themselves. We have the court records, the written chronicles, the biographical dictionaries, the observations of visitors, and, later in the century, even newspapers. The sources in the countryside are far less comprehensive, and those that exist were often written by travellers and other city dwellers rather than by the rural inhabitants themselves.[12] The historian, therefore, has to rely on indirect indicators and circumstantial evidence such as both general and specific economic trends, demographic patterns, and the influences of the natural environment, to gain some rural perspective that is not colored by the interpretations of urbanites. Secondly, the few studies on the rural areas of Syria generally deal in social and political categories defined by ethnicity, overlooking or distorting socioeconomic differentiation within the rural population that cross cut these ethnic boundaries.

But, precisely because of the pivotal position of grain cultivation in the total Syrian economy and its penetration of the social matrix, a third difficulty arises. It is difficult to isolate and characterize the critical functions of, for example, advance purchasing, wholesaling, milling, and trading, and to differentiate these from land ownership, money lending, and grain trading. It is also difficult to discover when such functions were performed within the sphere of local producers, be they large landowners, tenants, share-croppers, self-sufficient peasants, or farm laborers, and when within the sphere of consumers, be they local non-producing populations in the urban, desert, or mountain areas, or buyers abroad. Without this detailed information it will be very difficult to judge, when, where, and by whom economic decisions were made in response to internal or external forces and/or developments. These developments include the emergence and transformation of economic and national status—a process that was not necessarily linear.[13]

Finally, one must try to integrate into the whole picture the specific events that occurred during the period for their relevance to the process under study. To go beyond human geography, legal studies, ethnography, and economic surveys is the task of the historian who hopes to understand a process, its interactions, and its relationship to processes of yet a broader context. What follows is an attempt to contribute to an understanding of the relationship between the Syrian grain economy and socio-political developments in greater Syria at this time. It will focus on the issue of large-scale commercialization, the special area of concern of this volume.

Pre-Nineteenth Century Agrarian Patterns

We can distinguish an inner and an outer ring in the economy of greater Syria in the later seventeenth through nineteenth centuries— a period when central Ottoman control had become more tenuous, and localist forces had successfully challenged this control. The cities had their immediate supply rings, mostly irrigated regions, which were closely controlled and usually exploited by urban merchants and *ulama* (who were often one and the same). On the other hand, there existed a more remote, dry-farming supply ring.

The outer ring was the locus of increases in grain production during the nineteenth century. Remoteness, inaccessibility, and danger were often crucial for the persistence of certain land tenure systems.[14] Land *control* was far more economically and politically important than outright land *ownership*, not only for legal reasons—the outer ring being formally inalienable from the state[15]—but for economic reasons having to do with the particular situation in Syria. The outer ring was controlled only precariously by a hardy crowd of rural strongmen called *aghas* and *beys*. In the early part of the nineteenth century, the first were locally based chieftains with links, sometimes only alleged, to the Ottoman janissary corps. The second were similar to the aghas but sustained vague and historically tenuous ties to the pre-Ottoman Mamluks, the Mamluks of Egypt and/or the families of Ottoman pashas who had established roots in the province.[16]

Though active in the rural areas, the aghas and beys usually maintained households in the peripheral quarters of provincial capitals where they constituted an active urban political force.[17] The only rural chieftains in Ottoman Syria whose land exploitation system came anywhere near European manorialism or feudalism were the *iqtajis*, who lived on their estates on the terraced mountainsides of Lebanon and Palestine, rather than functioning in an urban environment.[18]

Considerable evidence indicates that the concept of large-scale agricultural holdings was not unknown to late Ottoman–Syrian land controllers. In the eighteenth century the state itself initiated, encouraged, or condoned the creation of large-scale holdings under the control of private individuals. These were usually persons who farmed the state's revenue-collection apparatus in particular districts and were given lifetime leases (*malikane*) in recognition of their services.[19] There were also a few examples of large land grants to leading ulama in recognition of their piety or perhaps of the legitimizing functions they performed vis-à-vis the state.[20] The state also condoned the large-scale agricultural undertakings of some local secular notables who had ties to the artisan guilds or other quasi-municipal institutions.[21] At about the same time, the 'Azms, a locally based family whose members repeatedly held provincial and district governorships and developed dynastic tendencies, also consolidated their holdings in Syria, transforming much of this land into religiously sanctioned family endowments (*waqf dhurri*).[22]

The Ottoman Empire was a vast area of economic and cultural exchange, and there was enough interaction of the Syrian elite with others from all over the Muslim world and especially from Anatolia and Egypt, for some in Syria to have recognized the potential of different agrarian models. The Anatolian model of *çiftlik* or that of the *mazra'a* of the Egyptian Mamluk households was there to be emulated.

On top of these general developments, however, the grain economy received a strong added impetus in the late eighteenth and early nineteenth centuries. External demand for dry farming commodities increased dramatically as a result of the French Revolutionary wars in Europe and especially the Napoleonic campaigns in the Mediterranean.[23] Some provincial officials who came close to or actually did usurp Ottoman authority in the coastal districts adopted mercantilistic and monopolistic practices in order to profit from the commodities trade. The economic practices of the Egyptian Mamluk beys and of Ahmad al-Jazzar, the Pasha of Acre in Palestine, challenged the traditional patterns of grain trading which had generally channelled surpluses to provision the large cities of the interior and the Ottoman armed forces based there, and the pilgrimage to Mecca.[24] The reports of profits made in coastal trade must have come as both a shock and a revelation to Syrian grain traders of the interior. Not much later Muhammad 'Ali Pasha of Egypt attempted to boost agricultural commodity production under monopolistic quasi-government control and was to attempt an extension of this type of land exploitation system to Syria during the Egyptian occupation of the 1830s.[25]

The redefinition of agrarian patterns that followed was to disrupt and transform both the economy and the socio-political balances in Syria far into the nineteenth century. Though there were some exceptionally expansive personalities—for example, Muhammad 'Ali of Egypt or 'Abd al-Qadir al-Jaza'iri, who settled in Syria as an exile from French-occupied Algeria—most of the aghas (*aghawat*) and beys who attempted to set up and exploit commodity monopolies were not persons with broad political ambitions. On the whole, a political vision, around which a new social and political consensus could be formed, was lacking.

It seems fair to add that judging by its role in the events of this period, the Ottoman state was also confused, participating as only one of the many contenders in the struggle of economic interests which would eventually determine political and ideological developments.

The New Role of Dry Farming
in the Nineteenth-Century Urban Political Economy

In another study, I have described political developments in the eighteenth and nineteenth centuries that led to factionalism, replacing a more broadly based and vertically stratified "estates" system in Syrian urban politics.[26] The following discussion reviews some of these developments that are relevant to the topic under study here. Syrian urban factionalism had been perfected into a political system in conjunction with the rise to power and influence of the 'Azms as provincial officials. The factional structures that emerged rested on a multitude of crosscutting social, economic and political factors. The 'Azm faction's own economic base was in the exploitation of lands of the inner rings around the towns they controlled, and also in the trade in luxury goods and the business of the markets at the center of the towns. Their rivals' base was in the artisanal industry of the peripheral quarters and dry-farming agriculture of the outer ring. If the grain controllers of the Damascene outer ring were politically "uncooperative," the 'Azms could supply their own faction's food needs from lands they controlled in the vicinity of Hama, a town north of the provincial capital.

The nineteenth century economic opportunities in the grain trade provided the out-faction Damascene notables—and particularly, those of the southern quarter of Maydan—with the bargaining chip they needed to renegotiate the power relationship in the province and its capital.

There were several attempts to unseat the 'Azm faction and to disrupt the terms of their collaboration with the Ottoman state as the century progressed. The out-faction notables were greatly aided in this effort by European merchants and their protégés in the process of "opening up" Ottoman Syria to European and American economic penetration. By the middle of the nineteenth century the out-faction commodity traders had established extensive ties with Westerners (and their local protégés) in the export of grain and livestock. From the 1850s onwards, and with the new boom in the external grain trade brought about by the Crimean War, the more profitable field of investment in greater Syria had shifted away from the production of local manufactures—now locked in withering competition with European imports—to the transit trade of European manufactures and the exploitation of the outer ring.

The factional struggles enmeshed with these economic developments led to serious breakdowns in civil order such as the rebellion of 1831 and the riots of 1860, both in Damascus. The Ottomans intervened directly and effectively in the affairs of Syria from the year 1860 onwards, imposing a new compromise on the Syrian factions and linking their cooperation with new patterns of agrarian exploitation through both public and private sector development. Order was restored but under a new political arrangement greatly favoring the notables of the outer ring. By 1875 an uneasy coalition of the eighteenth century urban, inner-ring merchants and ulama of the old 'Azm faction and the new nineteenth century agricultural commodity traders had come into being. Their collaboration was promoted by the Ottoman state.

To a large extent, this is what the period of the Ottoman Tanzimat meant in terms of economic change and the political economy of elite formation in late nineteenth-century Syria: many old family names, but very different economic bases and functions. It was exceptionally rare for an eighteenth-century agha, ulama, sufi, or *ashraf* family of either faction to remain represented in the late nineteenth-century elite if they did not find some way of participating in the dry farming agricultural boom.

Throughout, the state granted farming rights to tracts of land to appease and co-opt notables. This was done in the case of entire ethnic groups such as the Druzes in southern Syria and the Ismailis in central Syria.[27] That was nothing new in Ottoman provincial practice though the scale of these grants was formidable. In the nineteenth century, moreover, the state also granted land to aid the resettlement of groups of refugees who entered Syria from territories lost by the Ottomans in the imperial struggles of the time. For example, the defeated leader of Algerian resistance, 'Abd al-Qadir al-Jaza'iri, was granted control over tracts of land southwest of Damascus immediately upon his arrival there in 1855.[28] Another example is that of the Circassians who fled Russian occupation of their lands and were granted tracts of land in southern Syria by the Sultan where they were repeatedly used as frontier and buffer groups against recalcitrant rural elements.[29] All these migrants and settlers contributed significantly to the rural work force and to extending the outer ring of cultivation into unoccupied or nomadic lands.

The rural struggles that ensued revealed the Ottoman state to be a far more resolute force in deciding the future of Syria's outer ring than it had been in the eighteenth century.[30] The state seemed determined to win this land for settled agriculture, for the production and export of agricultural surpluses, and for monetarization and capitalization of the rural economy.

The state condoned and tolerated the predominance of external trade over local exchange for reasons that are not difficult to fathom. There were the obvious fiscal advantages, and these were magnified by the Ottoman Empire's balance-of-payments difficulties and its increasing level of private and public indebtedness to European financiers. The Empire's desire to open up new economic opportunities to provincial elites in order to win their support and sustain their loyalty constituted added impetus to increased grain production and exports. It seems clear, however, that at least sometimes individual men of state promoted the interests of Syrian exporters in order not only to keep a hand in the province through patronage of the most aggressive economic elements but also to share personally in the profits. Some of the largest farms in Syria were the personal property of the Sultan himself.

Were the rights and needs of the rural peasants and nomads "conveniently" assumed to be identical with those of the state and the exporters? Historians have not yet reported a single contemporary voice raised in skepticism or calling for concern or restraint in this respect. The export bans in times of shortages that were often imposed by the Ottoman authorities were clearly in response to urban not rural needs. If the government intervened in the countryside with seed distribution in times of shortages, this was motivated by the desire to re-establish cultivation, not as a relief effort for starving peasants.

The Issue of Privatization

With the gradual enforcement of the Land Code of 1858 the role of the state in promoting *de facto* privatization of state lands became systemic and was understandably viewed by Europeans as part of a necessary modernization process for the *mise en valeur* of the Empire's resources. We have evidence of considerable acquisition and consolidation of land rights under private individuals. The consolidation of the most productive Damascene oasis villages in the hands of foreign protégés in the late 1850s and early 1860s is well documented in the European consular reports.[31] It was also reported that subsequent to the riots of 1860 in Damascus the state confiscated tracts of land in the inner-ring—even though some of them were *waqf*s and supposedly immune from confiscation—and put them up for auction. At the end of the 1860s the government sold large quantities of land along the Palestinian coastal plain to urban interests in Beirut and Haifa.[32]

We must, however, be wary of exaggerating the extent of this trend within the land system as a whole. We must be candid, for example, about the lack of quantitative data concerning the relative extent of these developments. Even greater caution is called for in relation to the lands of the outer ring where we have only scattered evidence for the alteration of land tenure patterns in the direction of privatization in the 1860s and 1870s.[33] If in those decades many individuals were permitted to buy and/or create extensive private holdings, this may have been important for their role in urban politics; but the extent of privatization in the outer ring may just as likely have remained relatively limited. An exaggerated interpretation of the impact of privatization generally derives from historians' urban myopia, for in the context of urban politics the privatization of even some land could greatly inflate the fortunes of a particular family and/or tip the urban political balance in favor of one or the other faction. It might also create a new form of urban economic power or even lead to new class formations in the city. But none of this proves much about trends in the outer ring of grain farming lands, where the majority of the Syrian population lived.

But if the new and massive expansion of dry-farming did not proceed through the privatization of land, how can the nineteenth-century grain production increases be explained.

Market Forces in Nineteenth-Century Grain Production

The descriptions of production and exporting difficulties in the 1870s–90s available in the European consular records help us to formulate a pattern of demand and supply influences on the nineteenth century grain economy. These factors could be classified into a number of categories. On the demand side:

a) There was external demand: markets beyond the immediate local exchange economy sought new sources of supply, not just to cover temporary shortfalls but on a regular and sustained basis. Price differentials between the world market and prices paid to cultivators demonstrate the movement of external demand and their impact on exports.

b) There was also an increasing internal demand due to increases in population or its restructuring in the process of urbanization, or the transformation of diets as new tastes were made affordable by new levels of income. The population of Syria grew in the nineteenth century from roughly 1 or 1.5 million to 2.7 millions.[34] Cities were especially pronounced growth areas.

c) Internal demand could be further broken down into a sub–category best termed environmental. It would be activated when, for example, a sustained period of drought prodded cultivators to restructure production to meet needs of the first priority, usually their own food supply. Conversely, favorable environmental factors could generate demand for diversification and the extension of agriculture into previously uncultivated areas or diversification into additional crops such as sesame and legumes. Environmental demand could also be generated externally when droughts elsewhere created a demand for exports beyond the bounds of the local exchange market.

d) A fourth type of demand could be termed governmental. The state could, for example, create demand for increased production through its fiscal or conscription policies. The state might raise demand directly by collecting agricultural production in kind or indirectly by raising the level of monetary demands made on the producers, manipulating the currency so that those demands required an increase in resources with which monetary demands could be met, or by conscripting manpower to the army which could only be avoided by payments in produce or money earned through the marketing of produce.

e) A fifth kind of demand could be termed "political" when groups competing for political or economic power manipulated the agricultural commodities' supply lines (especially food staples) on a sustained basis as part of a strategy of political negotiation.[35] This happened, for example, in Damascus during the 1831 revolt, prior to the events of 1860, and again during World War I.[36]

f) This political demand is sometimes referred to as artificial demand. To avoid confusion, however, it would be best to add speculative demand as similar but not identical to political demand, though motives here were often difficult to disentangle. Speculative demand was built into the very nature of the entire Syrian grain economy. It was manifested in its crassest form during the devastating famine of 1915–18.[37]

g) Finally, demand could be termed aspirational when, e.g., expected increases in agricultural production became the collateral upon which the feasibility of other plans—for example, the floating of the state's currency by foreign creditors or the funding of developmental projects such as the construction of railways, or the availability and productivity of land envisaged for settlement—depended.[38] This kind of demand would often result in specific pressure on particular agricultural zones under consideration. It also led to inflated reports of production capabilities.

On the supply side, the following elements seem to have been operative in the Syrian grain economy:

a) the most important factor necessary for increasing agricultural output was an adequate supply of good land. In principle, unsettled land belonged to the state. Falling into the legal category of *miri*, it could theoretically be claimed by anyone who managed to cultivate it on a regular basis, as long as the tithe was paid. Though there was a considerable amount of land on the fringes of the cultivated area of each village and on the fringes of the entire cultivated zone which could be settled, much of this land was the grazing land of the nomadic populations who would not necessarily tolerate the extension of agriculture at their expense. Though the Ottoman state was not particularly friendly to the nomads, it could not risk alienating them totally and tried a number of measures to win or force their cooperation.[39]

b) The weather was clearly a visible supply-side factor. In conditions of an arid zone a minimum of 30 cm. of rainfall, but also appropriate timing of the rainfall, combined with the right temperatures and winds, were all crucial factors. Linked to these were seasonal plagues of insects and mice, which periodically infested crops, storage bins and threshing floors, and disease among ploughing and transport animals. Drought, plague, and infestation seemed to come in cycles.[40]

c) Since sufficient land was available for cultivation, at least at the outset of production increases, an adequate supply of laborers, willing to devote their efforts to particular crops, to divert their efforts from other activities, to migrate and settle uncultivated lands, etc. was one of the most critical production factors on the supply side. It was necessary to have an adequate labor force, versed in the agricultural practices best suited to the region, and able to survive its adversity. The export reports and the reports of rural rebellions address these issues.

d) Capital inputs affecting supply fell largely into four categories: an adequate supply of draught and transport animals; a sufficient quantity of quality seed; rudimentary agricultural implements such as plows, sickles, threshing forks, sieves and sacks, money to pay taxes and meet other production-tied obligations. The supply of mules, oxen, donkeys, and camels had to be adequate to meet the needs of thousands of plowmen and harvesters, all in their respective seasons. The animals had to be fed through the winter and again be available for threshing and transporting throughout the summer months. For the most part, the nomadic populations bred and grazed animals necessary for the peasants' production, tending them through the growing season until they were again needed for harvesting. Seed could be supplied from the surplus of the previous year, but if there was no surplus, the planting seed was often consumed by the peasants. Implements were few and rudimentary. They were produced both in the villages and in the towns where an elaborate network of markets existed in the peripheral quarters for marketing these implements.[41]

e) The farming of lands which were too remote for effective governmental control allowed the intrusion of factors opposed to the cultivation of new lands and/or the diversion of labor and surpluses to new markets. New cultivation patterns constituted threats to the previous forms of agricultural exchange between cultivators and nomads, plainsfolk and mountaineers. If production was to increase in the dryfarming regions bordering on the desert, it would do so at the expense of the pasturage of nomads' livestock, and threaten their wealth and survival. Providing security for cultivators and their activities therefore played an important role. Reports of disruptions of cultivation caused by recalcitrant rural groups, are often found in the sources.[42]

f) At the outset when profit margins were large, the exporters of grain could afford expensive overland transport. As profit margins shrank, however, cheaper means of transport had to be found. A number of roads were improved, and from the 1890s onwards railways were built, not only displacing camels but reducing the need for the construction of roads.[43]

g) A final supply–side factor was the mode of organization of production. The sources provide only sparse indications regarding this factor. The aim here is to focus on the mode(s) of production in which large production increases occurred. Was increased grain production a result of the extension of already functioning production forms to a larger territory or was it linked to the development of entirely new forms?

Defining Large-Scale Commercial Agriculture

At this point it seems important to define large-scale commercial agriculture as something qualitatively different from just the extension of thousands of rather small subsistence production units into surplus-producing units. To address this question we are going to raise a more fundamental issue and then project a model of large-scale commercialized agriculture appropriate to Syria in the late Ottoman period.

The definition of large-scale commercial agriculture must clearly include structural features. But need these structural features necessarily be related to the size of the *production* unit? Could the size of the investment, marketing or overall *managerial* unit also be taken into consideration? It is our hypothesis that in the case of late-Ottoman Syrian grain agriculture, an increase in the size of the managerial unit was the key to large production increases.

We would like to suggest that the mode of production responsible for large production increases in Syria is directly analogous to a mode of production that emerged in late sixteenth-century central Europe. In German it has been called the *Verlagssystem*[44]; in English, the "putting-out" system. The incidence of this mode in the agrarian structure of the Middle East has been studied by Bobek in the case of Iran, under the designation *Rentenkapitalismus*.[45] Its use was extended to the case of modern Syria by the German geographer Eugen Wirth, who also found the term Rentenkapitalismus appropriate.[46] Neither Bobek nor Wirth likened Rentenkapitalismus to the Verlagssystem of European proto-industry.

Though this concept has become accepted in European history by those interested in the prehistory of industrial capitalism, western historians have not generally acknowledged that this mode of production already existed in the manufacturing industries and cash crop oasis agriculture of Middle Eastern cities. Rather than an innovation in the case of late Ottoman Syria, the Verlagssystem was simply the transferral of a well-established mode of production, from artisanal manufacturing, vineyard, garden, and orchard agriculture to remote and extensive dry-farming agriculture.

In the context of pre-industrial Europe, the paradigm of the putting-out system centered in the activities of a single entrepreneur who was himself the managing coordinator of production in what was not yet formally a "factory." He did not need to own property in order to work the system but had to have command of capital resources in order to coordinate the flow of production at a number of different locations and through a number of steps between the acquisition of the raw material and the marketing of the finished product in response to a multitude of supply and demand factors. The system involved an intricate division of labor among workers and the dependency of the workers on the entrepreneur for capital inputs and remuneration. It did not, however, require the outright ownership of, or concentration of workers in a factory.

The classical (i.e., sixteenth century) Ottoman land system included large-scale holdings. The land was not owned outright but supervised on behalf of the state; nor was the peasantry concentrated into large-scale plantations under, as it were, one "roof." The rights to the *control* of entire villages might be granted to a single supervisor by the state,[47] but the village itself continued to be divided into smaller production units, isolated from each other but connected to the market through their parallel relationships with this supervisor or his agents. In Syrian agriculture of the sixteenth century the person in this supervisory position was called a *shad*,[48] a term that survived into the late Ottoman period and beyond.

In 1842–45, the terms used for pieces of agricultural land were *hanut*, çiftlik, mazra'a, and malikane. Rafeq's study of court records from this period show that the words çiftlik and hanut were used interchangeably, though the hanut appears to have been an integral part of a village and the çiftlik something distinct from it. The hanut could, moreover, be a religiously-sanctioned endowment (waqf) as well as state-owned land (miri).[49] Rafeq suggests that the really valid distinction between these land-holding types had to do with the crops grown. The çiftliks and mazra'as were devoted to cereals; the hanuts to orchards and vegetables.[50]

The çiftliks and mazra'as were leased by the state on a yearly basis for the payment of a fixed sum or a sum decided by auction. On top of these arrangements, some entire districts were auctioned off as tax-farms (*muqata'a*) by the state. These districts could be grain-growing areas (like the Hawran) and could include the smaller units of çiftliks and mazra'as.[51] The malikane was similar to a çiftlik, mazra'a, or hanut in that it was granted on state-owned lands for the purposes of tax farming, but the rights were granted for a person's lifetime and were heritable.[52] Rafeq's findings show that state-owned lands were at this time divided for exploitation by tax-farmers (*multezims*) and *muhassils* rather than by the state's military supporters as in the classical period, though a few of the latter still survived.[53]

The key to the economy of the whole system was the twin concept of usufruct (*tasarruf*) and exploitation (*mashadd maska*).[54] The first was the right that the state granted in exchange for revenue collection; the second was the mode by means of which the land-controller could make a profit. Whereas Rafeq translates *shaddad* as "cultivator",[55] he also notes that the term was often extended into *shaddad sahib al-hanut*, and that this latter term was often used interchangeably with the simpler *sahib al-hanut*.[56] The term *sahib* clearly implies something closer to ownership than supervision and certainly something more supervisory than cultivatory. In one example cited by Rafeq this is clarified: a village near Damascus was "divided into four *hanut*s held individually and exclusively by Damascene cultivators, *shaddada Shawam*. There were no local cultivators."[57]

By the end of the nineteenth century, similar terms implying control over land for purposes of exploitation were reported and described by the encyclopedist al-Qasimi. In his dictionary of the crafts and occupations of Damascus, he described the terms *shaddad* (now, "land owner"), *waqqaf* ("supervisor of an endowed plantation"), *musta'jir* ("lessee"), *muzari'* ("farmer"), and *zurra'* ("share-cropper").[58] At this time it was also possible to give a title to the supplier of capital for agricultural undertakings who was called a *murabi*.[59]

The shaddads were clearly the entrepreneurs in the process of land exploitation. They might find themselves in the countryside as land owners and/or merchants and/or tax farmers/collectors and/or money-lenders and/or supervisory "cultivators." They could make agreements with the peasants, provide the seed and other capital goods, and/or lend them money. They could also provide for the temporary and/or seasonal hirings of ploughmen, harvesters, threshers, transporters, and day laborers if these were lacking. (This division of labor is described by al-Qasimi in great detail).[60]

The shaddad did not need to own the land in order to exploit it. Exploitation of the land was called mashadd maska reflecting the entrepreneurial role of the shaddad. Especially in the dry-farming belt ownership rights were not the critical factor of exploitation. Given both the economic and political insecurity of outright investment in land located far from the seat of government and population concentrations, the indirect "putting-out" mode of production was far better suited to the task than the consolidation of large-scale private holdings.

The arrangement with the peasant who could still hold the usufruct rights to the land vis-à-vis the state and/or the other peasants of the village (in which case the system was called *musha'*) might be legitimized through the instrument of a "partnership" (*sharika*) contract, something seen in the West as a form of sharecropping or sharetenure, which is generally correct if one keeps in mind that no ownership was involved.[61]

The critical position of the shaddad in the production process may have made him the crucial link in increasing Syrian grain production in the nineteenth century as demand from the coast and growing cities increased dramatically. It is essential to understand that he approached his work in the countryside as a commercial venture, and as an entrepreneurial undertaking in the most literal sense of the word. His relationship with the peasantry had nothing to do with feudalism, and was not based on any of the precepts of a "moral" economy, being entirely commercial.[62] Even later, when deeds to land exploitation rights (*tapu sanad*) were introduced (selling, as it were, the rights that had until then only been leased by the state), the "owning" partner was still functioning as an entrepreneur.

The shaddad had a number or urban collaborators. He could work closely with a grain wholesaler in the city (*buwaiki*) or with a Damascene "commercial" miller (*tahhan al-suqi*), either of whom could—given the extent of the profits they were reported to be making—[63] double as a banker or money-lender (murabi). At the outset of the grain boom several thousand tons of grain grown at a great distance from Damascus were diverted there and expedited from there annually through grain and flour merchants.[64]

Another Damascus-based contender for the grain surplus with whom the shaddad could negotiate was the government itself, either as a revenue collector or as a procurer of supplies for the locally based troops or the needs of the Meccan pilgrimage caravan.

Alternatively, the shaddad could deal directly with ship captains in the coastal harbors or their consignment agents called *negociants* in the French reports, who could, presumably, also double as bankers and money-lenders.

Can we see in the functions of the shaddad the emergence of large-scale commercialized agriculture? Did his control over all the "strategic points in the commodity trade" between production and market mark a fundamental restructuring of the relations of production, and was this the key to large-scale commercial agriculture? Did the shaddad play as pivotal a role in the history of agriculture in Ottoman Syria as did the entrepreneur of the pre-industrial "putting-out" mode of production in Europe? I think we have to answer all these questions in the affirmative.

The Urban Reaction to Commercialization
in the Dry-Farming Regions

Some aspects of the shaddad's work were not universally appreciated, not even in the cities. The Damascene commentator al-Qasimi, a pious jurisconsult and encyclopedist of the 1890s, tells us that his business associates, the buwaiki, and tahhan al-suqi were generally reprehensible from an ethical point of view. Their profits might be ample, but they were "bitter."[65] On the whole, there is very little evidence to indicate that anyone in Damascus rejected commercialization.[66] The late nineteenth century establishment ulama of Damascus who had survived the Tanzimat and the aftermath of the events of 1860 were certainly not averse to commercial activities or to the accumulation of wealth. That struggle of conscience, if it ever existed, probably took place in the process of factionalization and the breakdown of the eighteenth century estates system. al-Qasimi praised the functions and the profits of the shaddad and all the agricultural entrepreneurs he described. If there was any complaint, it seems more in the nature of carping. al-Qasimi, whose family would have fallen into the old 'Azm faction, may just as well have been rankled by the economic and political influence gained by the wealthy Maydani faction families who dominated among the numbers of buwaiki and tahhan al-suqi and whose nineteenth century careers were launched through connections with exporters and foreign protégés benefiting from the dry-farming trade, with whom he was unlikely to have much contact or affinity.[67]

This was the situation in urban Syria of the 1850s through the 1880s: a whole generation of newcomers to wealth came into being in this period as a result of the boom in commercial agriculture.[68] Alongside some larger-scale farms, the growth in the grain economy had also been facilitated through an intricate system of entrepreneurial networks of urban-based shaddad. The extent of Syrian grain production had increased dramatically, and the ties to the city, the state, and the world market of the most remote peasantries had become a fact of life. For an ever-increasing segment of the population, coastal urbanization and the further intrusion of monetarized market relationships were driving a wedge between production and consumption. With the externalization of the grain trade, the wedge now pressed further, transforming the country's most basic informal economic sector—food—into a formal monetarized sector.

The Rural Impact of Large-Scale Commercialization

The Syrian countryside did not undergo any of these transformations without considerable upheaval. In fact it was the dry-farming countryside which was the scene of the most major and sustained conflicts of late Ottoman times in Syria. I have elsewhere analyzed the violent clashes of the 1860s in the Hawran of southern Syria,[69] and those results support the arguments pursued here. Urban and foreign commercial interests as well as the Ottoman state all vied for control and attempted to penetrate the countryside, but they were resisted by local coalitions of peasants, mountaineers and bedouin.

A number of counter trends appeared beginning in the late 1870s. First of all, there were extreme hardships for the peasantry stemming from conscription, droughts, and pestilence. Secondly, the demand for Syrian grain in the world market began to flag.[70] As discussed above, internal prices for wheat came heavily under the influence of these world market trends. Questions: Did the peasants ever benefit from high prices as tax-payers and consumers? Did they reject commercialization or did they object to the prices they were getting? Because of the complexity of the commercial parameters and differentiation within the peasantry these questions are difficult to answer, even on the level of theory, as is the case with other regions of the world economy. The lack of information from the peasants themselves is, of course, the greatest handicap.

Rural protest and peasant conflict in southern Syria of the 1880s and 1890s can, however, be linked to socioeconomic change. Though not always a continuous and visible phenomenon (due to intervening local supply-side factors) the decline of prices in world markets set in motion a trend that reduced profit margins and increased competition among those who had prospered as entrepreneurs and intermediaries in the grain trade. This competition signaled the disintegration of the 1860s informal cartel through which entrepreneurial interests had restructured urban politics and administration in the province of Damascus for more than a generation.

As the scissors of falling world prices and increased internal subsistence demand closed, these intermediaries began to feel the squeeze between what they had to pay to the peasants and the price on the world market. The Ottoman government attempted to maintain its interests by exploiting the discord of others from above. The peasants did the same from below. Caught in the middle were the layers of economic brokers and political intermediaries.

The reports indicate that tax farmers sustained losses in 1884; tax farming collapsed altogether in 1887.[71] The expensive efforts made by the Ottoman state to collect taxes without these intermediaries formed yet another important element in the ferocity of its campaigns against the peasantry in the Hawran in the 1880s and 1890s.

Though there is not conclusive evidence, it is fair to say that a considerable amount of capital investment moved out of grain farming in Syria in the course of the 1880s. Since capital was not actually sunk in land but only invested on a year-to-year basis in the activities of the cultivators, it could be shifted without great loss into more profitable fields in Syria or outside Syria, in Egypt or even in Europe, America, and Australia—all areas to which Syrians migrated at this time. This fact alone is important evidence of the nature of agricultural investment at this time.

For investors who commanded only limited or more immovable capital resources, however, options were more limited. If their "capital" were of a more political nature, being tied to rural offices or leadership of rural factions, for example, they had the option of pressuring the government to act in their interests against the peasantry on the justification that it would be in the interests of the fisc. We see a number of high local officials leading the Ottoman campaigns into zones where they themselves held farms.

The peasants had become subject to fluctuations in the world market and their situation, after more than thirty years of market-oriented production, was very different than it was before the process had taken hold in the countryside. Had the world market first encouraged and now disappointed their aspirations? Would they attempt to go it alone without intermediaries?

By the end of the 1890s and the early 1900s the market had recovered somewhat. An industrial flour mill was opened in the port city of Haifa, and a railroad was extended from the Hawran to Haifa in 1907. But, this development was more likely to strengthen the producers in that range of the spectrum between small-scale commercialization and large-scale plantation agriculture and may have threatened the local subsistence exchange economy.

Conclusion

I have attempted to review some developments in the dry-farming belt of Syria in the late Ottoman period, specifically the impact of the market, land tenure, forms and modes of production, in order to answer these questions: Was there large-scale commercial agriculture in late Ottoman Syria? Did it explain the impressive production increases? Was there a transformation in this central economic sector that influenced social change and the development of political events?

In the absence of adequate detailed land tenure documentation the research has attempted to suggest answers to a complex series of problems by utilizing alternative sources of information and comparative analyses. In the main, five types of information have been utilized: data on grain production, pricing, and trade; data on land settlement; material from the court records of Damascus; material concerning urban politics; and material on peasant movements and rebellions. The results may be summarized as follows:

In the late eighteenth century, the majority of the land of the Syrian dry-farming belt was state land (miri), cultivated by tax-obligated peasants who escaped taxation due to remoteness and to the success of rural political resistance. The demand for grain on the world market was to affect the Syrian countryside from the end of the eighteenth century onwards. Beginning at that point, a struggle was unleashed to gain influence over the peasants by entrepreneurs, rural chieftains, and state officials, which continued for the remainder of the Ottoman period and beyond. In many instances the state officials supported the interests of the entrepreneurs. On some occasions, the representatives of the state were themselves the entrepreneurs.

The pressures that motivated the changes beginning in the eighteenth century accelerated under the influence of the Mediterranean grain trade boom of the mid-nineteenth century. Constraints in supply promoted large-scale commercialization through managerial networks rather than through the creation of large-scale production units. Commercial investors found it more profitable to invest in the peasants' labor rather than directly in the land.

The initial large-scale increases in Syrian grain production in the nineteenth century can therefore be attributed to the extension of previously (basically) urban modes of production to the dry-farming belt. A flexible definition of large-scale commercial agriculture would have to include the activities of the likes of the shaddads who worked through extensive managerial networks rather than privatizing the land or concentrating their efforts on plantations.

The social and political changes accompanying these develop-ments contributed significantly to the important rural political crises of nineteenth-century Syria. A new ordering of relationships among the various urban, coastal, state, and rural participants emerged out of a series of revolts in the 1860s. Coming at a time when external demand for Syrian wheat was strong, the order of the 1860s was most successful in promoting urban-based interests and remained for them an attrac-tive model. But hardships stemming from natural disasters and war-time conscription in the 1870s reduced the bargaining position of the peasantry vis-à-vis both the commercial entrepreneurs and the state.

At that juncture a limited number of investors attempted to consolidate large estates and more plantation-like units of produc-tion. They utilized the advantages of new land legislation to acquire ownership rights, converting the land under their influence to private holdings (mülk) or into perpetual family endowment (waqf dhurri). The land might then be exploited as a plantation or might continue to be exploited according to "putting-out" production modes. But this trend remained limited in scale in Ottoman times.

Rural developments carried in them the seeds of economic transformation in the direction of socio-economic differentiation within the peasantry along a much broader spectrum than had pre-viously existed. At one extreme was the trend toward consolidation on the part of capitalists and entrepreneurs which would end in the creation of large-scale holdings and a more plantation-like mode of production. At the other end of the spectrum was the reinforced trend toward local subsistence agriculture. Somewhere in the middle was the trend toward commercialization of small holdings by the peasants themselves.

The indications are that, though the creation of plantations may have been important in the transformation of the economic bases and perceptions of the urban elites, this trend was not extensive enough in the dry-farming countryside to represent a major shift in the overall pattern of land tenure. The profitability of plantations was contingent upon sustained external demand for Syrian dry-farming com-modities. With the stagnation of grain prices on world markets from the mid–1870s and their radical decline by the 1890s, this trend proba-bly did not become generalized. Peasant resistance was also an impor-tant inhibitor.

In the dry-farming regions, the late-nineteenth century market trend resulted in a scramble for survival among the entrepreneurs and middlemen who had previously prospered from the trade. There was also an attempt to squeeze the peasants to sustain the profit margins of the middlemen. This seems to be the best explanation for the conflicts in the dry-farming regions of the 1880s and 1890s.

The Ottoman yearbooks of 1892 through 1908 give some indication of the existence of some large farms (mazra'a) listing 110 in the whole province of Syria, of which 51 were in the dry-farming region of Qunaitra (in southern Syria) alone.[72] A gap in our data prevents us from knowing exactly when these large farms appeared. If similar privileges were extended by the state to these plantations as had been done in the eighteenth and early nineteenth centuries to large-scale holdings in the inner ring, they would have benefited from very special advantages such as release from taxation and government-guaranteed inviolability.

But the existence of a few large-scale, plantation-like farms can not explain the large production increases of the nineteenth century. There is, therefore, a puzzle. To solve this puzzle, I have suggested that, first of all, the emergence of large-scale commercial agriculture in the dry-farming zones of late Ottoman Syria resulted from an increase in the amount of state control in the countryside and from an increased maneuvering ability of middlemen who extended the "putting-out" mode of production to newly-settled areas. Secondly, once the extension of agriculture into new areas had occurred, it was economic *contraction* rather than expansion that encouraged consolidation of a limited number of larger estates. Thirdly, the phenomenon of large-scale plantation agriculture nevertheless remained of limited extent in the dry-farming regions chiefly because of market conditions and the resistance of the peasantry. Besides these few large farms, the majority of grain-producing units were small. Investors and entrepreneurs were obliged to recognize that plantation agriculture was not going to be profitable or even feasible in Syria.

In other words, though exploited by sharecropping and money-lending arrangements, the peasants had for the most part succeeded in retaining a land-tenure system and a mode of production that conformed to their view of things. Syria's grain-producing peasants could retain something of a bargaining position regardless of world market developments and the pressures of entrepreneurs and the state. A number of factors of special significance to the Syrian situation played a role in their success:

1) The peasants never entirely broke their ties with other rural groups (such as the bedouin and mountaineers) who could support them in times of revolt.

2) The peasantry was differentiated in the process of commercialization along a spectrum ranging from near slaves on plantations to autonomous farmers with some direct access to the market. When the grain trade was expanding there were opportunities for some peasants to become supervisors and entrepreneurs themselves.

3) Once the export value of the crop had dwindled, and because the rural population had grown, grain could return to its previous position as sustainer of local self-sufficiency. In this way, grain could be at the heart of struggles in the rural political economy.

4) In that their crop was also their chief source of food, the peasants had the option of cutting their ties to the market and the state and retaining their crop for their own sustenance during a revolt, even disappearing with it into the desert at times.

5) After three decades of producing for the world market, the peasantry had also undergone an educational process. The various adjustments that had to be negotiated and renegotiated between entrepreneur and rural producers involved a level of market comprehension which could not have totally escaped the peasant's consciousness. It is not surprising that some peasants took advantage of the dwindling ground on which the shaddad and other entrepreneurs stood to assume commercial control over their own surpluses.

6) The fact that Syria's peasantry continued to rebel, generation after generation, is perhaps the strongest indication that something in their local social, economic, and political arrangements sustained them and gave them the aspiration and motivation to continue the struggle. How else can we explain the fact that the Syrian peasantry of the late Ottoman period retained a stronger bargaining position vis-à-vis the government and vis-à-vis interlopers than was retained by peasantries of peripheralized economies elsewhere in the region, or, for that matter, in many parts of the world?

Notes

Introduction

1. See Wallerstein 1989, chapter 3; Richards 1979.

2. The classical statement is in Wallerstein 1974.

3. Weber 1906. These issues have been addressed in the debate occasioned by Robert Brenner's 1976 paper "Agrarian Class Structure and Economic Development in Pre-Industrial Europe." For this article and others responding to it, see Aston and Philpin 1985.

4. Anderson 1974.

5. In addition to his contribution to this volume where Veinstein cites McGowan as calculating that such çiftliks employed an average of 3.5 (three and one-half) persons, also see Veinstein 1984.

6. Stoianovich 1953.

7. McGowan 1981.

8. Pamuk 1987a.

9. World trade between 1800 and 1914 increased fifty-fold, while trade of the Ottoman realms (excluding Egypt) only ten times. See Issawi 1980, 76.

10. İnalcık 1977.

11. Bloch 1966, 129.

12. Gerber 1987.

13. For a recent account of the vagaries of the life of a bureaucrat, living in an earlier and more stable period, see Fleischer 1986.

14. Gould 1976.

15. Compare the attempts to build a theory of estates in eastern Europe, of which Kula's (1976) is only the best known.

Chapter 1

1. For a comprehensive description of land tenure in the Ottoman miri regime see Barkan 1937–38; Barkan 1940, 321–421; and my s.v. "Çiftlik" in *EI (2)*.

2. Usually a formal contract between peasant and sipahi acting in the name of the state was concluded, for example see, *Belgeler*, 1980–81, 52–53, document no. 157.

3. A çiftlik is defined in the kanunnames as follows:

(Arable Land in dönüm; 1 dönüm equals 920 sq. meters)

	Fertile	Medium	Poor	Source
Aydın (1528)	60	80	130	Barkan 1943, 8–13
Erzurum (1540)	80	100	130	Barkan 1943, 6–66
Musul (Murad III)	80	100	150	Barkan 1943, 308
Sirem (Murad III)	70–80 80–90	100–110	120–130	Barkan 1943, 307–08
Morea (1711)	80	100–120	150	Barkan 1943, 322–26

4. On the tımar system in general, see İnalcık 1973a, 104–18; and Ö. L. Barkan's s.v. "Tımar" in *İslam Ansiklopedisi*, 286–333.

5. The Ottoman kanunnames put at the beginning of each survey book are designed to regulate and secure the smooth functioning of the tax and land tenure system within the framework of the tımar; for kanunnames see *EI (2)*, 562–66.

6. No study exists examining Islamic *iqta*, Byzantine *pronoia*, and Ottoman tımar as part of one traditional system in the Middle Eastern history; the tradition can be traced back to the ancient Persian Empire in which the basic features of the system appear to have their definite form and continue through the successive empires in the region.

7. The Ottoman writers on the causes of the decline at the end of the sixteenth and seventeenth centuries focus on the widespread practice of granting the miri lands as private property; see Ayn-i Ali 1872–73/1289; *Kitab-ı Müstetab* 1974; Röhrborn 1973, 29–34; the author gives a partial list of sources on the Ottoman decline, 163–64; Murphey 1979, 547–72.

8. İnalcık 1982, 69–141; also see my s.v. "Mā'" in *EI (2)*.

9. For an example of sınırname see İnalcık 1954, 219–23.

10. See İnalcık 1980, 283–337; 1977, 27–52.

11. İnalcık 1979, 25–52; and 1982. The researchers who focused on the Ottoman agrarian system have not given due attention to reclamation activities and its relevance to the formation of big çiftliks. A Marxist interpretation of the

formation of big çiftliks in the classical period of Ottoman history is introduced by Vera P. Moutavcieva 1962, which provides some insightful analyses.

12. The text in Barkan 1942, 364–65. Here, A. Feridun is the famous author of the *Münşeat al-Salatin* and Sokollu Mehmed, Grand Vizier, 1566–79.

13. Akdağ 1963, 37–44; Adanır 1979, 35–41.

14. İnalcık 1967, 126–27.

15. Examples in the registres of kadı courts: see, Faroqhi 1980, 87–99.

16. İnalcık 1977, 27–52.

17. Keyder 1976; İslamoğlu and Keyder 1977. Wallerstein's capitalist world economy and peripheralization theory had a strong impact on interpretations on dynamics of Ottoman social change, see note 18.

18. In his recent work, McGowan (1981, 1–44) examined these points in detail on the basis of Ottoman archival materials. There, he tried to show what particular areas were affected by the "commercial revolution" of the eighteenth century; cf. Wallerstein 1980, 117–22.

19. Stahl 1980.

20. İnalcık 1977.

21. Cvijić 1918; Busch-Zantner 1938; Stoianovich 1953, 398–411; 1960, 234–313.

22. Stoianovich 1953, 401–02.

23. Now see McGowan 1981, 121–70.

24. Soysal 1976, 38–90; Kotschy 1958; Baer 1962; Abdul Rahman and Nagata 1977, 169–94.

25. Nagata 1976b.

26. For mütesellim see İnalcık 1977; Nagata 1976a, 1979.

27. Gandev 1960.

28. İnalcık 1969.

29. Nagata 1976b, 5–11.

30. İnalcık 1979–80, 13–16.

31. Nagata 1976b, 18–23.

32. İnalcık 1943, 90–92.

33. The expansion of the market coincided with the extension of the capitulary privileges to western nations, see my s.v. "İmtiyāzāt" in *EI (2);* see also McGowan 1981, 1–44.

34. İnalcık 1943, 95.

35. See İnalcık 1973b.

36. İnalcık 1943, 98.

37. Gandev 1960, 207–20.

38. Veinstein 1975, 136.

39. Nagata 1976b.

40. See Veinstein's review of it, 1979.

41. Veinstein 1975, 138.

42. Veinstein 1975, 137, n. 28.

43. Veinstein 1975, 136–37.

44. For cotton, see İnalcık 1979–80.

45. Veinstein 1975, 138–42.

46. For substantial profits accrued from muqata´a-malikane, see Genç, 1975; for various dues which the aghas were taking from the tenant-peasants, see İnalcık, 1943, chapter on "Gospodarlık Rejimi."

Chapter 2

1. On the various uses of the terms "çift" and "çiftlik" in the Ottoman terminology, see Barkan 1943, 392–97; and İnalcık 1967, 32–33.

2. Gandev 1960, 207–20.

3. Busch-Zantner 1938. See also Cvijić 1918; and Ancel 1930.

4. Stoianovich 1953; Braudel 1972–73; and Sadat 1969, 1972.

5. Braudel 1973, II: 725.

6. Wallerstein 1980; Keyder 1976; İslamoğlu and Keyder 1977; and Sunar 1980.

7. On this rich literature of Ottoman "pamphlets" and advice books, see Tahir 1907–08/1325; 1911–12/1330; Babinger 1927; Röhrborn 1973, 163–65; and İnalcık 1980, 283, n.1, 287, n. 11. Some of these works have been published: Koçi Bey 1939; Wright 1935; and Ayn-i Ali 1872–73/1289.

8. See Cvetkova's work, 1960.

9. İnalcık 1983, 108–11.

10. The document was published in Barkan 1942, 364–65.

11. Veinstein 1984.

12. İnalcık 1943; 1983, 119–24.

13. İnalcık 1983, 108.

14. McGowan 1981, 141–42.

15. McGowan 1981, 54, 69, 141.

16. Faroqhi 1980, 88.

17. Veinstein 1987a, 793–94.

18. McGowan 1981, 137.

19. Faroqhi 1984, 263–66. While the existence of mülk-tarla created the possibility for the further constitution of çiftliks, Faroqhi does not see any obvious connection between the two phenomena. On the contrary, she emphasizes that it "does not mean that the emergence of freehold property was necessarily accompanied by çiftlik formation." (1984, 263–66)

20. On the special land regulations of Crete, see Barkan 1943, 352–54; 1983, 21–22; and Veinstein and Triantafyllidou-Baladié 1980, 201.

21. Veinstein 1987a, 794.

22. Veinstein 1987b.

23. Stoiavonich 1979, 186.

24. McGowan 1981, 145–46.

25. McGowan 1981, 62–67.

26. İnalcık 1967, 126; *Kitab-ı Müstetab* 1974, 34.

27. İnalcık 1980, 287.

28. İnalcık 1980, 297; Akdağ 1963, 250–54.

29. Gandev 1960, 215.

30. Stoianovich 1979, 185

31. McGowan 1981, 60–61.

32. Cvetkova 1960, 203.

33. Kunt 1983, 85–88.

34. İnalcık 1980, 330–31.

35. Genç 1975; 1979.

202   *Notes*

36. İnalcık 1980, 329.

37. İnalcık 1980, 329.

38. İnalcık 1983, 107–08, 114.

39. Uluçay 1955, 16–36; Veinstein 1976, 74–76, n. 17, 18, 23, 27, 28. I shall deal below with the obstacles to the constitution of çiftliks by local notables.

40. McGowan 1981, 72, 171.

41. Kiroski 1973, 115–20, quoted by McGowan 1981, 165.

42. McGowan 1981, 164.

43. Nagata 1976b, 30, 55; İnalcık 1983, 117.

44. Stoianovich 1979, 186.

45. Veinstein 1976, 74–75.

46. McGowan 1981, 79.

47. Cezar 1977, 59.

48. İnalcık 1983, 117–19.

49. İnalcık 1983, 115.

50. McGowan 1981, 74–78.

51. McGowan 1981, 135–36.

52. Aymard 1966; and Braudel 1966, I: 535–38; see also Veinstein 1986, 15–36.

53. Aymard 1966, 50–51.

54. Veinstein 1976, 76.

55. Stoianovich 1953, 404.

56. Veinstein 1976, 76.

57. Nagata 1976b, 37, 56.

58. Archives Nationales de France, Paris (hereafter AN), Affaires Etrangères B[i] 1053: Dispatches of Peysonnel, le 13 avril 1752.

59. Uluçay, 1944, 123–26. The Court registers (sicils) of Manisa contain a number of documents pertaining to Kara Osmanoğlu Mustafa's attempts to change the limits of his farmed-out lands, as well as the complaints of the population against these practices; see Gökçen 1950, 6.

60. Veinstein 1981, 125–29; Röhrborn 1978.

61. Gökçen 1950, II: 82; Uluçay 1946, 58.

62. Cezar 1977.

63. Faroqhi 1981, 61–62.

64. AN, Affaires Etrangères B^i 1053: Dispatches of Peysonnel, le 27 août 1752.

65. Olivier 1801, 186–190.

66. Cezar 1977, 58–59.

Chapter 3

1. İnalcık 1983; McGowan 1981.

2. For a detailed empirical study of this region based on Ottoman fiscal surveys (tahrirs) and court records (kadı sicils) see İslamoğlu-İnan 1987.

3. For a recent debate on the political economy of agrarian change in the Middle East and North Africa, closely related to the issues discussed here, see Glavanis and Glavanis 1983; Keyder 1983b; Seddon 1986.

4. For an example of such a view of the Ottoman state, İslamoğlu and Keyder 1977.

5. For a treatment of this concept see Thompson 1971.

6. For a discussion of this world-view, see İnalcık 1969.

7. For a general discussion of the Ottoman institutions see İnalcık 1973a.

8. For örf, see *EI (2)*, s.v. "'Urf" by H. İnalcık.

9. İnalcık 1967.

10. See, for instance, McGowan 1981; Pamuk 1987b; and Kasaba (in this volume).

11. İnalcık 1943.

12. Barkan 1940.

13. Richards 1977.

14. The understanding of state power presented here owes a great deal to Gramsci's ideas (1980, 206–69), and those of Mouffe 1979.

15. İnalcık 1969, 1967, as well as his s.v. "'Urf" in *EI (2)*.

16. For an excellent treatment of the role of the ulama in the production of "culture" and changes in that role during the late eighteenth and nineteenth

centuries, see Gran 1979, esp. 178–88. Gran also explores the relationship between the ulama and the mystical orders—the convergence and divergence of their interests.

17. For the adoption of new modes of administrative organization and of new regulations during the Tanzimat era, see Davison 1963; and Lewis 1968.

18. Berkes 1964.

19. For changes in the modes of taxation and therefore the role of the state, see Owen 1981, 59, 292.

20. For this hybrid legal structure, see Quataert 1987.

21. This was the case, for instance, with the appropriation of waqf lands and the establishment of a regular police force. See Mardin 1962.

22. For a formulation of the approach that stresses the centrality of local cultures in political expressions of peasants, see Scott 1977.

23. İnalcık 1983.

24. İnalcık 1982.

25. For a masterful application of the Malthusian view, see Le Roy Ladurie 1977.

26. Chayanov 1956.

27. For a dynamic treatment of the population factor, see Bois 1978.

28. For an application of a similar approach to pre-industrial European societies, see Brenner 1976.

29. Such a view of the demographic factor largely borrows from Boserup 1965. For a detailed discussion of Boserup's views in relation to the Ottoman peasant economy see İslamoğlu-İnan 1987.

30. For the distribution of the divani and malikane shares in the 1520–30 and 1574–76 period, see tables 5.1 and 5.2 in İslamoğlu-İnan 1987, 135–36. A detailed description of this system is in Barkan 1939. The system is also described in various kanuns (state legal codes); see Barkan 1943, 73–74, 77, 115–16, 182, 299–300.

31. In the fifteenth century, malikane-owners who were assigned administrative duties were required to deliver a specified number of *eşkincis* or mounted soldiers to the imperial army. See s.v."Eshkindji" by Halil İnalcık in *EI (2)*.

32. For political and military histories of individual areas studied here, see s.v. "Tokat" by Tayyib Gökbilgin in *İslam Ansiklopedisi;* s.v. "Çorum" by Franz Taeschner in *EI (2);* s.v. "Niksar" by Besim Darkot in *İslam Ansiklopedisi.* For a description of general conditions in the province of Rum which included the districts studied here also Hüsameddin 1927–35.

33. For a detailed description of how the figures in the tables are arrived at see İslamoğlu-İnan 1987, 406, n. 14.

34. The category of "unspecified" shares that appear in tables 5.1 and 5.2 (İslamoğlu-İnan 1987, 135–36) refer to those shares that directly accrued to the central treasury. Hence, it is assumed that revenues from these shares were collected by *emins* (state officials) who were responsible for the sale of the product tax on markets and who sent the cash returns to the treasury. In the later sixteenth century, the proportion of "unspecified" shares in the total number of shares declined significantly—in the case of divani shares this proportion dropped from 41.6 percent in 1520 to 27.9 percent in 1574. These revenues were assigned to waqfs of mosque-medrese complexes and to tımars.

35. For a discussion of resm-i çift taxes see İnalcık 1959.

36. İslamoğlu-İnan 1987, 137–138.

37. Cook 1972, 11–29. For conversion of mazra'as into villages during the sixteenth century see İslamoğlu-İnan 1987, Table 5.21.

38. For changes in crop patterns and introduction of legumes in the sixteenth century İslamoğlu-İnan 1987: 142–43.

39. For a description of these entries, called *balta yeri* in the Ottoman registers, see Cook 1972, 79–80. For a general discussion of forest assarts, see Boserup 1965, 24–31.

40. For a discussion of the causes of population growth in this region, see İslamoğlu-İnan 1987, 112–115; and for figures on cabas see İslamoğlu-İnan 1987, 137, 140: Tables 5.4 and 5.7.

41. For indices of population and production of wheat and barley, see İslamoğlu-İnan 1987, 141: Table 5.9.

42. For increased production of non-grain crops, see İslamoğlu-İnan 1987, 154–58: Tables 5.18, 5.19, 5.20.

43. For population growth in the three towns located in the region under study, see İslamoğlu-İnan 1987, 139–40: Tables 5.6, 5.8.

44. Cook 1972, 22–25, 37–39.

45. Cook 1972, 74–75.

46. For a detailed discussion of these levies, see Güçer 1964.

47. Exemptions from *avarız-ı divaniye* and *tekalif-i örfiye* as these extraordinary levies were called, were granted to entire village populations in return for their work in maintaining roads, bridges, passes (*derbents*). See, for instance Tapu Kadastro Genel Müdürlüğü Arşivi, Ankara, *Kuyudu Kadime* (hereafter *KK*), (Volume) 14 (1547): 183a; *KK*, 38 (1576): 233a; *KK*, 14 (1574): 222b. For similar exemptions granted to rice growers in Niksar, see Başbakanlık Arşivi, İstanbul (hereafter BA), *Tapu Tahrir* (*TT*), (Volume) 54 (1528): 103.

48. For changes in grain yields throughout the sixteenth century, see İslamoğlu-İnan 1987, 143–48: Tables 5.14, 5.15.

49. İnalcık 1978b, 89.

50. For increases in the production of these crops and sheep raising, see İslamoğlu-İnan 1987, 149–50: Table 5.15, 157–59: Table 5.20.

51. İslamoğlu-İnan 1987, 157–58: Table 5.20.

52. İslamoğlu-İnan 1987, 151–52: Table 5.16.

53. For such government regulations see Barkan 1943, 113, 200–05.

54. For rice cultivation and its organization in the Ottoman empire, see İnalcık 1982.

55. For changes in sheep production, see İslamoğlu-İnan 1987, 149–50: Table 5.15.

56. On rural craft production, see the discussion in section 4.

57. The number of *çayır, otlak, kışlak,* and *yaylak* entries recorded for each district under study in the later surveys are as follows: 8 in Yıldız (with a total tax of 255 akçes); none in Cincife; 3 in Venk (total tax of 120 *akçes*); 1 in Kafirni (total tax of 72 akçes); none in Çorumlu; 2 in Karahisar-ı Demirli (total tax of 1280 akçes). For a detailed description of these entries in the surveys, see Abdulfattah and Hütteroth 1977, 71.

58. İnalcık 1983.

59. For destination of revenues from waqf lands, see İslamoğlu-İnan 1987, 134, Map 3.

60. For commercial and manufacturing taxes in rural areas, see İslamoğlu-İnan 1987, 151: Table 5.16. These taxes represent the amounts paid annually to the treasury by the people to whom the revenues from these installations were farmed out. As such, they are not always accurate indicators of the amount of business carried out at dye houses, because those franchises were often granted for a fixed sum; actual receipts accruing to tax farmers could be in excess or below that sum. At the same time, while presence of a dye house in a given region may point to textile production in that region, the converse may not always be the case. Evidence for other parts of Anatolia suggests that villagers often did their own dyeing in their houses or cattlesheds. There is, of course, no way to assess the extent of such activities, thereby to determine the extent of rural production of fibers and cloths in areas where there were no dye houses. Nevertheless, where there was a dye house, it is probably not too inaccurate to suppose that tax-farmers exerted considerable pressure on rural craftsmen to have their dyeing done at the dye house. Thus, for instance, one encounters complaints by villagers to the effect that the dye house administrators sought to prevent them from doing their own dyeing. See BA, *Mühimme Defterleri (MD),* 74: 38.

61. For the role of production of non-agricultural goods in the economic development of peasant household economy see Hymer and Resnick 1969; Jan DeVries, in his critique of Boserup, also emphasizes this aspect of the peasant economy, 1972.

62. e.g., McGowan 1981; Pamuk 1987b; Kasaba (in this volume).

Chapter 4

1. See Faroqhi 1986a, 1986b, 1987b.

2. Compare among others Veinstein 1976; Özkaya 1977; İnalcık 1983; and Schilcher 1985; Akarlı n.d.

3. On Tunisia see Chater 1984, 73-136; Pascual 1984; and Rafeq 1984.

4. Levi 1985.

5. İnalcık 1980; McGowan 1981.

6. Compare Tapu ve Kadastro Genel Müdürlüğü Arşivi, Ankara, *Kuyudu Kadime* (*KK*) (Volume) 152, fol. 213b ff (981/1573-73) which mentions a *"Cami-i kebir"* and a *"Cami-i evsat."* The modern inventory *Türkiye'de Vakıf Abideler ve Eski Eserler* 1977, 40 ff. also mentions but two mosques, one of them fairly recent.

7. Göknil 1943, 338-57. I thank Mr. Adnan Akçay for providing me with a copy of this article.

8. Masson 1911; Paris 1957.

9. de Planhol 1958.

10. On the institution of müsadere compare Cezar 1977, and for the general background, Cezar 1986. Both these very important studies constitute the starting points for the analysis undertaken here.

11. The document examined here is found in Osmanlı Arşivi (Başbakanlık Arşivi), İstanbul (hereafter BA), *Maliyeden Müdevver* (hereafter *MM*) 19759: 441-451 (dated 23 Rebi ül-âhir 1239/28 Nov. 1823). On page 443, where the sum total of the debts owed to Müridoğlu is recorded as *zimemat-i mezkure*, 10 percent of this sum has been subtracted from the total, with no other explanations than the word *"ondalık"* (one-tenth). Thus the treasury apparently expected to collect only 90 percent of the recorded debt. What happened to the remaining 10 percent is unclear.

12. BA, *MM* 19759: 450-451.

13. Nagata 1976b.

14. BA, *MM* 19759: 441.

15. Cezar 1986, 215. In 1827, the *bedeliye* payable for every one of 13,829 *kalyoncus* had been raised to 500 guruş, see Cezar 1986, 231.

16. İnalcık 1980, 321.

17. Cezar 1986, 174 ff.

18. Cf. Faroqhi 1986a.

19. BA, *MM* 19759: 441.

20. The register records a total of 298,817 guruş; it is not quite clear whether the discrepancy is due only to a mechanical error or whether certain debts were consciously excluded by the scribe.

21. BA, *MM* 19759: 441, 444.

22. I thank Nüket Sirman Eralp for pointing out this reference.

23. Gökalp 1980, 158.

24. In BA, *MM* 19759: 444 the scribe arrives at a total of 3,830 jugs.

25. Cezar explains why the officials compiling inventories of goods to be confiscated generally had an interest in showing the monetary value of recorded items higher than it actually was. But his discussion does not bear upon cases where guarantors (*kefil*) were involved (1977, 52).

26. BA, *MM* 19759: 447 ff.

27. Gökalp 1980, 161.

28. Göknil 1943, 350.

29. On this matter compare Barkan 1940.

30. Compare for instance the inventories published by Barkan, especially the discussion on çiftliks in the hands of sixteenth–seventeenth century *askeri* (1966, 53–56).

31. However given the fact that the inventory was prepared in the fall of 1823, it is possible that seed for the crop of 1824 had also been removed before the compilation of the document under investigation.

32. For the use of court records in seventeenth-century Kayseri dwellings, compare Faroqhi 1987a, 101–03.

33. For the probable décor of these dwellings compare Arık 1976.

34. Other documents of the times call these dwellings *aylakçı hanesi*.

35. While the inventory contains a sizeable number of references to vineyards (*bağ*), there are no data on their size, value, or manner of exploita-

tion. Nor is there any information on the possible commercialization of raisins, grape syrup, or vinegar.

36. Issawi 1980, 13.

37. This total includes not only the grain produced on Müridoğlu's own lands, but also the taxes in kind which he had collected as voyvoda of Mihaliç (Karacabey).

38. Cezar 1986, 214.

39. Cezar 1977, 43. From a sales record concerning part of Müridoğlu's property (BA, *MM* 19759: 455 ff), we can gather that the mills and probably the çiftlik of Kazdağlı were among the more valuable of the agha's properties. However since the documents record only the down-payment (muaccele) and not the final sale price, these figures have not been used for the estimation of Müridoğlu's fortune. But one can assume that Müridoğlu's real estate and animals were worth something between 150,000–200,000 guruş.

40. Wolf 1982, 85–86.

41. Cezar 1977, 44ff.

42. Cezar 1977, 56.

43. To a certain extent, the perpetuation of ayan power in the provinces was furthered by the central administration's practice of selling off property of deceased ayan in large lots. Thus on p. 455 ff of BA, *MM* 19759, we find a list of the Müridoğlu properties sold to a certain Mehmed Esad Agha, consisting of over sixty items and worth 139,250 guruş.

Chapter 5

1. Frangakis 1985a, 162.

2. Each bale is calculated at 300 lbs. Public Record Office, London (hereafter PRO), Foreign Office (hereafter FO), 78/1760, Consul Werry, İzmir, 23 January 1863 to Foreign Office in London.

3. Archives de la Chambre de Commerce de Marseille, Marseille (hereafter ACCM), I: 26–28.

4. ACCM, I: 26–28.

5. Archives du Ministère des Affaires Etrangères, Paris (hereafter AE), Correspondance Consulaire et Commerciale (hereafter CCC), Smyrne 50, Consul Bentivolgio, İzmir, le 26 Mars 1863, to Minister, Paris.

6. Archives Nationales de France, Paris (AN), Séries Affaires Etrangères (AE) B[iii], 242, Consul Fourcade, Mémoire, İzmir, 1820.

7. Along with cotton, plague was also transmitted to İzmir from these centers. When an attack of plague was particularly heavy, such as the epidemic brought to İzmir from Aydın and Manisa in 1835, there were not only population losses but a temporary paralysis of all economic activities too. Panzac 1985b, 156.

8. AN, Marine B7/452, "Etats des cotons en laines et filés du Levant entrés à Marseilles par le lazareth pendant 1782–1785."

9. AE, CCC, Smyrne 43, "Importation et Exportation de Smyrne," 1832.

10. Hecksher 1922, 146–47.

11. Farley 1862, 94–95.

12. AN, AE Bⁱⁱⁱ 415, "Importation et Exportation de Smyrne," 1858; AN, AE Bⁱ 1054, "Etat des draps arrivés à Smyrne, janvier à juin 1755" included in letter of Consul Peyssonel, İzmir, le 24 août 1755, to Minister, Paris.

13. AN, Marine B7/446, Castagny, le 18 août 1782 in "Commerce des ports de L'Europe avec ceux du Levant," le 1 fevrier 1783.

14. AN, F12/1850A, Consul Fourcade to French Minister, İzmir, le 12 juillet 1812, to Minister, Paris.

15. Williams 1972, 372.

17. Echinard 1973, 65

18. ACCM, MQ, 5.1, Deputation of French Merchants, İzmir, le 23 juillet 1820, to French Consul.

19. AN, AE Bⁱⁱⁱ 242, Consul Fourcade, "Mémoire," İzmir, 1812.

20. AN, Marine B7/446, Bertrand, 19 octobre 1782 in "Commerce des ports de l'Europe avec ceux du Levant," le 1 fevrier 1783.

21. Syrett 1985b, 38–40.

22. Nanninga 1966, 1468–1513.

23. Cunningham 1983, 44.

24. PRO, State Papers (hereafter SP) 105/337, Consul Hayes, İzmir, 15 May 1789 to Levant Company, London.

25. Cunningham 1983, 44.

26. AN, AE Bⁱ 1053, Consul Peyssonnel, "Mémoire," İzmir, le 22 novembre 1751.

27. ACCM, I: 26–28.

28. AN, AE Bⁱⁱⁱ 242, Consul Fourcade, "Mémoire," İzmir, 1812.

29. PRO, FO 195/177, Consul Brant, İzmir, 17 September 1840 to British Ambassador, İstanbul.

30. Erder 1976, 41.

31. Veinstein 1976; Nagata 1976b; İnalcık 1983.

32. PRO, SP 105/129, Consul Werry, İzmir, 31 January 1803 to Levant Company, London.

33. AN, AE B^i 1054, Consul Peyssonnel, İzmir, le 7 juillet 1754, to Minister, Paris.

34. AN, AE B^i 1054, translation of letter of İsmail Agha Araboğlu, Governor of Bergama to Peyssonnel, included in letter of Consul Peyssonnel, İzmir, le 9 mai 1754, to Minister, Paris.

35. AN, AE B^i 1054, Consul Peyssonnel, İzmir, le 7 juillet 1754, to Minister, Paris.

36. AN, AE B^i 1052, Consul Peyssonnel, İzmir, le 16 décembre 1749, to Minister, Paris.

37. PRO, SP 105/128, Consul Werry, İzmir, 16 May 1801 to Levant Company, London.

38. Cunningham 1983, 43.

39. PRO, FO 195/241, Consul Brant, İzmir, 25 August 1845 to Levant Company, London.

40. Veinstein 1976; Sadat 1973; Stoianovich 1976.

41. Habesci 1792, I: 205; II: 21–22

42. Veinstein 1976, 137.

43. PRO, FO 105/128, Consul Werry, İzmir, 17 September 1801 to Levant Company, London.

44. PRO, FO 105/337, Consul Hayes, İzmir, 15 May 1789 to Levant Company, London.

45. Erder 1976, 41.

46. PRO, FO 105/129, Consul Werry, İzmir, 31 January 1803 to Levant Company, London.

47. AN, AE B^i 1061, Consul Peyssonnel, İzmir, le 5 janvier 1773 to Minister, Paris; see also Algemeen Rijkarschief (hereafter ARA), 164, European Consuls, İzmir, 15 mars 1773 to their Ambassadors, İstanbul in Nanninga 1966, 178–80.

48. PRO, SP 105/337, Consul Hayes, İzmir, 15 May 1789 to Levant Company, London.

49. PRO, SP 105/128, Consul Werry, İzmir, 17 August 1801 to Levant Company, London; see also, SP 105/130, Consul Werry, İzmir, 2 August 1805 to Levant Company, London; FO 78/868, Consul Brant, İzmir, 1 August 1851 to Foreign Office, London; and ACCM, I: 26–28, for increase in the prices of the exports of İzmir in the second half of the eighteenth century.

50. Nagata 1987, 323–25.

51. PRO, SP 105/337, Consul Hayes, İzmir, 15 May 1789 to Levant Company, London.

52. Hasselquist 1766, 30.

53. PRO, SP 105/126, Consul Werry, İzmir, 17 May 1797 to Levant Company, London; other ayans also fulfilled this function; see, e.g., PRO, SP 105/338, Consul Werry, İzmir, 10 July 1810 to Levant Company, London.

54. AN, AE B[iii] 242, "Commerce du Levant," le 16 decembre 1812.

55. PRO, SP 105/338, Consul Werry, İzmir, 7 June 1809 to Levant Company, London.

56. AN, AE B[i] 1053, Consul Peyssonnel, İzmir, le 8 juillet 1751, to Minister, Paris; see also AE B[i] 1062, Consul Peysonnel, İzmir, le 22 juillet 1775, to Minister, Paris.

57. Veinstein 1976, 136.

58. PRO, FO 78/1760, Consul Blunt, İzmir, 23 May 1863 to Foreign Office, London; see also Kasaba 1988, 61–65.

59. PRO, FO 78/1760, Consul Blunt, İzmir, 23 May 1863 to Foreign Office, London.

60. PRO, FO 78/442, Consul Brant, İzmir, 6 December 1841 to Foreign Office, London.

61. PRO, FO 78/1760, Consul Blunt, İzmir, 23 June 1863 to Foreign Office, London.

62. *Accounts & Papers*. Vol. XCV, 5247, 24.

63. AN, AE B[i] 1054–1055, "Draps venus à Smyrne et distingués par qualités," Consul Peyssonnel, İzmir, le 2 avril 1753 - le 20 août 1756, to Minister, Paris.

64. AN, AE B[i] 1054, Consul Peyssonnel, İzmir, le 7 juillet 1754, to Minister, Paris.

65. ACCM, MQ, 5.1, "Memorandum from Deputies of western European and Greek Cloth Importers to the Union of Greek and Armenian Shopkeepers and to the Jewish Nation," İzmir, 5 september 1820.

66. AN, AE B[iii] 283, "Etats des draps expédiés de Marseille pour les échelles du Levant, İzmir, 1756–1788;" and AE B[i] 1052, "Draps français importés à Smyrne," İzmir, 1750.

67. AE, CCC, Smyrne 8, Consul David, Mémoire, Chios, 1823.

68. AN, AE B^i 1054–55, "Draps venus à Smyrne et distingués par qualités," included in dispatches of Consul Peyssonnel, İzmir, le 2 avril 1753 - le 20 août 1756, to Minister, Paris.

69. AN, AE B^i 1054, Consul Peyssonnel, İzmir, le 29 novembre 1751, to Minister, Paris.

70. AN, AE B^i 1053, Consul Peyssonnel, "Mémoire," İzmir, le 22 novembre 1751.

71. AN, AE B^i 1053, Consul Peyssonnel, "Mémoire," İzmir, le 29 novembre 1751.

72. AN, AE B^i 1058, "Eclaircissements sur la supputation qui a été faite du prix des londrins seconds de Carcassonne à Smyrne," Consul Peyssonnel, İzmir, le 20 novembre 1767.

73. AE, CCC, Smyrne 36, Consul David, İzmir, le 3 janvier 1821, to Minister, Paris.

74. This holds both for the Archives of the Chamber of Commerce of Marseilles and for the consular correspondence.

75. E.g., ACCM, I, 19 and AN, AE B^i 105f3, 1056.

76. See Svoronos 1956, 329–31, for prices of cloth in Salonica, see also. e.g., ACCM, I: 20 and AN, AE B^i 1062–63; AE B^{iii} 273–74, 276.

77. AN, AE B^{iii}, "Etat du nombre des draps de 16 aunes de long, destinés pur le commerce du Levant, admis à l'inspection de Marseille, depuis l'année 1749 jusqu'en 1788 avec leur évaluation."

78. E.g., ACCM, I: 19 and AN, AE B^i 1053, 1056; AE B^{iii} 273.

79. E.g., ACCM, I: 20 and AN, AE B^i 1062–63, AE B^{iii} 274, 276.

80. AN, AE B^i 1066 for British trade figures for the 1770s and 1780s. See also AN, F12/1850A, Consul Fourcade, İzmir, le 10 octobre 1812, to Minister, Paris.

81. AN, AE B^i 1066; see also Frangakis 1985c, 173, 177–78.

82. AN, AE B^i 1054, Consul Peyssonnel, İzmir, le 9 mai 1754, to Minister, Paris.

83. AN, AE B^i 1069, Consul Amoureux, İzmir, le 6 & 13 décembre 1790, to Minister, Paris; see also Eldem 1986.

84. ACCM, MQ, 5.1, Deputation of French merchants, İzmir, le 22 juillet 1820, to French Consul, İzmir.

85. AE, CCC, Smyrne 43, "Exportation et Importation de Smyrne," 1832; see also New York Historical Society, Bradish Papers, Bradish, İstanbul, 20 December 1820 to John Quincy Adams, Washington, D.C.

86. AN, AE B[iii] 415, Maruscheau Elève, "Réflexions sur la situation politique et commerciale de la France dans les états du Grand Seigneur," 1820.

87. ANF, AE B[iii] 243, Felix de Beaujour, "Inspection générale," le 5 janvier 1817.

88. AN, AE B[iii] 242, Consul Fourcade, "Mémoire," İzmir, 1812.

89. Goffman 1985, 230–32.

90. AN, AE B[iii] 242, Jumelin, "Commerce de Levant," le 16 décembre 1812.

91. AN, AE B[i] 1052, Consul Peyssonnel, İzmir, le 29 janvier 1749, to Minister, Paris.

92. Frangakis 1985b, 38–39.

93. Nanninga 1966, 950–51.

94. PRO, FO 195/128, J.A. Werry İzmir, 10 September 1839 to Vice Consul Charnand.

95. PRO, FO 78/442, Valsamachi to Muhassil of Adramit, 1 January 1841, included in Consul Brant, İzmir, 21 January 1841 to Foreign Office, London.

96. PRO, FO 78/1020, Consul Brant, İzmir, 5 May, 1854 to Foreign Office, London.

97. Nanninga 1966, 480–81; PRO, FO 195/128, Vice–Consul Charnaud, İzmir, 18 May 1839 to British Ambassador, Istanbul.

Chapter 6

1. Public Records Office (hereafter PRO), Foreign Office (hereafter FO), London, 78/1533: 277–78.

2. Cited in Pamuk 1987a, 93.

3. For a critical review of pertinent literature, see Portes and Bach 1985, ch. 1, and Chapman and Prothero 1983.

4. Issawi 1977, 157.

5. Uluçay and Gökçen 1939, 56.

6. Between 1775 and 1877 the current value of exports from İzmir expanded by about ten times. For the growth of İzmir in the eighteenth century see Frangakis 1985c; for the nineteenth century, see Kurmuş 1974; and Kasaba 1988.

7. Hope 1820, 1.

8. For ayans in general see İnalcık 1977; for those in Rumeli, see Sadat 1972.

9. Uluçay 1942, 199.

10. Uluçay 1942, 302.

11. Uluçay and Gökçen 1939, 56.

12. See Gerber 1987, 22–31; Pamuk 1987a, 90–95, 99–102.

13. This is the route that was taken in the Balkans. See McGowan 1981, 65–67.

14. Panzac 1973.

15. Yannoulopolos 1981, 31; Baykara 1980, 280–81.

16. PRO, FO 78/868: 94–103; PRO, FO 78/1450: 72.

17. PRO, FO 78/1609: 35.

18. Later, their descendents complained that that was the only thing government did for them: Hütteroth 1974, 23; Karpat 1985, 60–77.

19. See Issawi 1980, 114–19.

20. See İnalcık 1983, 114–19.

21. Uluçay and Gökçen 1939, 57.

22. Uluçay and Gökçen 1939, 57.

23. PRO, FO 78/1302: 313–325.

24. PRO, FO 78/1534: 30–39.

25. Issawi 1980, 248.

26. PRO, FO 78/1760: 121–128.

27. Georgiades 1885, 382; Barkan 1942, 356.

28. For example, see Rafeq 1984, 382; Barkan 1942, 356.

29. Georgiades 1885, 28.

30. Different types of communal ownership (*musha'*) that existed in the Middle Eastern provinces of the Empire promises to be a particularly fertile area of comparison. For an overview see Owen 1981, 256–59.

Chapter 7

1. For an analysis of property rights in the African case and their non-correspondence to European forms, see Berry 1987.

2. Cuno provides an excellent example utilizing this weak definition of property, see 1980.

3. Cuno (1980) offers the weak definition of property on land which actually is a set of claims on surplus. Later he argues that in the nineteenth century the "strong state" revoked those claims, which were to reappear later on in the shape of property. Although Cuno's cause in making his argument against modernization theorists is commendable, his acceptance of the argument that the institution of the property itself explains social change (that property in land existed earlier than the "modern" times seems to be his main emphasis) causes a methodological confusion that can not be reconciled with similar work that has been done in other regions. An alternative argument, which seems to be more powerful and universal, is that "property" does not explain what the modernization theorists claim that it does. Furthermore, property as understood by the modernization theorists is an extremely narrow concept which does not carry the universality that is was claimed to carry.

4. For another example of confusion on landed property, see Keyder 1983a, 131–45. After arguing extensively for the prevalence of small peasant ownership in Turkish agriculture, Keyder *assumes* the existence of large landlords. Part of his argument is based on the property of different qualities of land according to class despite "land abundance." While the same story could be told in terms of a process of sharing agricultural surplus, landed property seems to get in the picture with neither any substantiation, nor explanatory power.

5. This conclusion is not at all surprising especially in light of so many parastatal organizations in Africa based on peasant ownership.

6. Akarlı 1976; Quataert 1973.

7. See 1858 Ottoman Land Code, Article 130.

8. Arıcanlı 1986.

9. Arıcanlı 1986.

10. Arıcanlı 1986; Arıcanlı, Bademli and Uğurel 1974; Tezel 1982, 306–78.

11. Domar 1970.

12. Kasaba (in this volume).

13. Arıcanlı 1986.

14. McGowan 1981.

Chapter 8

1. Vergopoulos 1978.

2. This periodization is borrowed from Slicher Van Bath 1966. Of course, the secular inflation in agricultural prices, more emphasized during periods of expansion (1730–1770 and 1789–1817), was accompanied by relatively calm Kondratieff downswings (1770–1790 and 1817–1850). On the impact of secular decline in prices on agrarian structures during the nineteenth century, see Friedmann 1978; and of Kondratieff waves on rural transformation, see Keyder 1983a.

3. Issawi 1984, 187.

4. For an account of the impact of this expansion on the prices of agricultural goods, see Le Roy Ladurie and Goy 1982; and on its impact on Asian empires and Russia, see Athar Ali 1975, 385–91; and Mironov 1986.

5. Paris 1957, 583.

6. The figures are taken from Abdel Nour 1982, 116–17; Ibn Jum´a in Laoust 1952, 233; Volney 1825, 252; and Archives du Ministère des Affaires Etrangers (hereafter AE), Correspondances commerciales (hereafter CC), Alep (Volume) 13, le 16 juillet 1855.

7. The estimates are compiled from Rabbath 1905, I: 117; Volney 1825, II: 88; Burckhardt 1812, 327; & Carne 1842, II: 43.

8. The conversions are made following Hinz 1955. The following sources are used: al-Dimashqi 1912; al-Budayri 1957, 4–5, 25, 35–36, 106, 108, 151–52, 155; Abdel Nour 1981, 395; Bowring 1840, 123; and *Accounts and Papers*, Commercial Reports from Aleppo for the years 1850 & 1855; and for export prices, see Posthumus 1946; and Romano 1956.

9. The production and population figures are taken from Cohen and Lewis 1978; Abdel Nour 1982; Guys 1862; Gerber 1979. The increase in the arable acreage mainly took place during the nineteenth century. The average village arable was between 10 to 20 faddans at the opening of the eighteenth century, and came to encompass over 25 faddans only during mid-nineteenth century. For eighteenth century, see Orhonlu 1988, 65–71; and Vakıflar Genel Müdürlüğü Arşivi, Ankara (hereafter VGM), (Volume) 1363 (1155/1742–1743); for nineteenth century, see Lewis 1988, 39; Başbakanlık Arşivi, İstanbul (hereafter BA), *Tapu Tahrir (TT)*, 963 (1291/1874–1875).

10. For export figures, see Murphey 1986, 249–50, fn. 10; and Panzac 1985a.

11. Archives Nationales (hereafter AN), Série affairs étrangères B^i, Consulat de France à Tripoly, Registre n° 15, le 10 mars 1812; AE, Correspondance consulaire, Consulat de France à Seyde, Registre n° 26, le 12 dècembre 1812; Braudel 1979, I: 121, 134; Ruppin 1918, 16.

12. The estimates are from Volney 1825, II: 211; Bowring 1840, 22; and *British Documents on Foreign Affairs* in Bourne and Watt 1978, Volume VII.

13. Venzke 1981, 220–37; VGM 1363 (1155/1742–1743): 1–6.

14. Makovsky 1984, 110–12; Abdel Nour 1982, 394–97; and Richard Wood in Cunningham 1966, 50–51.

15. Pascual 1984, 363.

16. For a compilation of the guesstimates on yield ratios, see Delbet 1877, 381–82; Refik and Behçet 1916/1335, 53, 58; Parmentier 1919, 9–10; and Issawi 1980, 214–15.

17. Delbet 1877, 393; Nagata 1976b; Parmentier 1919, 9; Dalman 1932, V: 182; Burckhardt 1812, 300; Cuinet 1896, 337; and *Accounts & Papers,* Commercial Report from Diyarbekir for the year 1863.

18. Braudel 1979, I: 121.

19. Hayatizade n.d., I: 315, and Stoianovich 1966.

20. AN, Série affairs étrangères, Consulat de France à Tripoly, Registre n⁰ 15, le 21 mars 1812; le 11 novembre 1812; AE, CC, Beirut (Volume) 1, le 31 décembre 1826; and CC, Beirut 5, le 16 septembre 1846; Carne 1842, III: 15; and Cuinet 1890, II, 135, 166, 209, 213.

21. Burckhardt 1812, 22; Whittman 1803, 214; Paxton 1839: 244, Public Record Office (PRO), Foreign Office (FO) 78/1418; Hayatizade n.d., I: 112, 227, 356; Russell 1794, 90; *Accounts & Papers,* Commercial Report from Alexandretta for the year 1858 (XXX), 1859, 447; *Accounts & Papers,* Commercial Report from Diyarbekir, 1863; Wetzstein 1857, 476, Sefercioğlu 1985; *Melce'ü't-Tabbahin* 1844/1260; and Abdurrahman bin Abdullah 1871–1872/1288, 37; Latron 1936, 107.

22. Russell 1794, I: 74, 92; and Post 1880, I.

23. Volney 1825, I: 283; Bowring 1840, 17.

24. French consular reports, dispatches from southern Syria during the mid-eighteenth century, eloquently attest to these changes.

25. The *Ahkam* series at the Vakıflar Genel Müdürlüğü contain numerous entries attesting to this observation. For example, VGM 343, 161 (1173/1759–60).

26. For changing production patterns, see Turkowski 1969; Morana 1799. *Fatwa*s issued at the end of the eighteenth century, when compared with those of the early 1700s, register fully these empire-wide changes, see Meşrebzade 1837/1252. Moreover, the circulation of labor was furthered by differing agrarian calendars. The main crops were first sown in the warmer climates of the valleys and maritime plains, and were harvested from the end of April through the whole month of May. In the north and on the mountains, however, the harvest did not begin until June or July. These timetables enabled people in the region to circulate freely. See Burckhardt, 1812, 221–22.

27. Wallerstein 1989, 303–31.

28. For a brief sketch of the mechanisms around which these holdings were structured, see Schilcher's article in this volume, especially 185–89.

29. Meriwether 1981, 164.

30. Thieck 1985, 129; See also Peri 1983; Abdel Nour 1982; Schilcher 1984, 104–05, Yediyıldız 1975; Pascual 1983.

31. Abdel Nour 1982, 237–38, 387. See also Khoury's article in this volume, especially fn. 30.

32. Owen 1981, 256–59.

33. See Wallerstein 1989, 129–31; Skinner 1979.

34. Abdel Nour 1982,74–80; also VGM, 328: 29 (1140/1727–28); 328: 53–54 (1141/1728–29); 328: 56 (1141/1728–29); 328: 106 (1142/1729–1730); 328: 414 (1145/1732–33); 351: 285 (1171/1757–58) 335: 124–25 (1172/1758–59); 349: 157 (1190/1776–77).

35. Meriwether 1981, 180–87.

36. Meriwether 1981, 190–93; al-Hamud 1981, 185–211. Bruce Masters' (1981, 153–64) calculations point in the same direction: the average amount of loan which increased from 318 guruş to 524 guruş between 1630 and 1690 soared thereafter, reaching 3,328 guruş during the 1730s. See also BA, *Halep Ahkam*, 1: 33 (1156/1743); 3: 26 (1176/1762); *Şam Ahkam*, I: 76 (1157/1744); I: 273 (1166/1753); I: 275 (1166/1753); II: 236 (1175/1762); II: 265 (1176/1762); III: 134 (1197/1783); IV: 9 (1197/1784); IV: 73 (1200/1786); IV: 81(1200/1786); IV: 87 (1200/1786); V: 43 (1210/1795); V: 75 (1212/1797).

37. Rafeq 1981, 674.

38. Slim 1988, 93–96.

39. An ayan, whose holdings were on the Black Sea coast, left a sum of 18,000 guruş when he died in 1802/1217, whereas another ayan from Central Anatolia left 82,000 guruş at the time of his death in 1808/1223. See Sakaoğlu 1984, 109–13; Cezar 1977. See also Chevallier 1960, for an inventory of the holdings of the al-Khazin family of Mount Lebanon in the 1850s which reveals a fortune of 28,000 guruş.

40. For notable exception, see, among others, Cuno 1984; Gerber 1987, 43–66; Khoury (in this volume).

41. This is the conclusion reached by Gerber 1987. For similar reservations, see Veinstein's article in this volume as well as McGowan 1981.

Chapter 9

1. See, for instance, Owen 1981; Issawi 1966, 1980. For Egypt, see Baer 1969. There are other studies for Syria and Palestine as well as Iraq. For Iraq,

the most comprehensive analysis of this view was given by Haider 1966. There have been studies on the introduction of commercial agriculture in eighteenth-century Arab lands, but these have concentrated on an analysis of port cities where the main impetus for cash cropping has been the European demand. See Cohen 1973; and for Lebanon, see Polk 1963.

2. See, for instance, Niewenhuis 1982, who concludes that the rural population lived in isolation of urban economic life. Peasants lived in their villages, accepting passively the increased exploitation of city notables. There existed little differentiation in the village community, and when it did exist, it was primarily the result of the peasants alliance with city notables, see also Hassan 1968.

3. By "commercial agricultural production," I mean the production of cash crops for the market accompanied by a change in the relations, if not the factors, of production.

4. İnalcık 1978a; Barkan 1975; Stoianovich 1953; McGowan 1981.

5. This increased the degree of exploitation to which the peasantry was subjected. It also transformed tax into rent to private individuals, thus changing the relation between state and reaya and between landlord and reaya. This development, even when it involved no change in factors and methods of production, had deep repercussions on the status of the peasantry especially in the late nineteenth century when their enserfment in the north of Iraq was made official.

6. al-'Umari. "al-Durr al-Maknun fi Ma'athir al-Madiya min al-Qurun." MS, al-Majma'al al-'Ilmi al-'Iraqi (Iraqi Scientific Council), 622; also by same author n.d, 138.

7. Ra'uf 1976, 266–67. *Has* villages were usually granted to governors and provincial officials to finance the provinces' administrative and military expenditures. The village of Qara Qush, registered as has in the sixteenth-century *defter* was turned into *malikane* in the seventeenth century and became *mülk* in the eighteenth at the special request of Husayn Pasha al-Jalili after the latter defeated Nadir Shah. The village of Karamlis also became a malikane of the Jalili family, while Bartilla was given to another prominent family, that of the 'Umaris.

8. See Mahkama Shari'a, Mosul (hereafter MSM). *Sicil (1242–1249)* (1826/27–1833/34), Sales document dated 1249 (1833/34). The village in question is that of Sayyid Kund.

9. The Jalilis, for instance, owned shares in the miri tax of the villages of Ba'shiqa, Bajarbu', 'Urta Kharab, and Drawish. They had bought some of these shares from another family. See MSM, *Sicil (1242–1249)* (1826/27–1833/34), document about the division of *miri* taxes dated 1247 (1831/32).

10. The same development took place in Damascus. See Schilcher 1985, 29–79.

11. McGowan 1981, 58.

12. The Jalilis were a large family. A section owned, for instance, the villages Karamlis and Shah Qulu, while others owned Tahrawa, Qara Qush and other hamlets. See al-'Umari. "al-Durr al-Maknun fi Ma'athir al-Madiya min al-Qurun." MS, 622; also the *temlik* document of the village of Qara Qush, translated and appended in Ra'uf 1976, 518–22.

13. On Mosul's strategic position see Buckingham 1827; Saleh 1966, 49–88, 145–60.

14. For an analysis of these hostilities and the struggle over the control of the silk trade routes, see Olson 1976, 117–35.

15. al-'Umari often mentions the great inflation in the price of coffee as a result of the disruption of the trade from Basra. He also shows awareness of the importance of trade with the areas around Mosul: 1955, 192–93; see also his "Ghayat al-Muram fi Ta'rikh Baghdad Dar al-Salam," MS 6295, Iraqi Museum, 103.

16. Gallnuts remained an important export item from Mosul throughout the eighteenth century, even though dyeing procedures in Britain had rendered it obsolete. The French still imported it from the Mosul-Diyarbakır region. Between the years 1785 and 1789, the French imported 1,711,000 livres worth of gallnuts: Masson 1911, 523.

17. Bowring 1973, 44–45.

18. al-'Azzawi 1935; al-Fa'iq 1961.

19. al-'Umari. "al-Durr al-Maknun fi Ma'athir al-Madiya min al-Qurun." MS, 624–26; see also Khan 1969, 354.

20. MSM, *Sicil (1242–1249)*(1826/27–1833/34).

21. Fattah presents an excellent analysis of the mechanisms of regional trade, 1986, 76.

22. Lanza 1953, 63.

23. Bowring 1973, 41–51.

24. See various *waqfiyyes* documenting Jalili holdings. These holdings comprised a substantial proportion of this urban real estate. The waqfiyya documents are kept at Da'irat al-Awqaf al-Amah, Mosul (hereafter DAA), Iraq.

25. al-'Umari. "al-Durr al-Maknun fi Ma'athir al-Madiya min al-Qurun." MS, 579, 600; also by the same author n.d., 131.

26. For a discussion of this development see Stoianovich 1953; and Sugar 1978.

27. McGowan 1981, 73–75.

28. McGowan 1981, 79.

29. See, for example, DAA, *Waqfiyya Jami' al-Nu'maniya* [1204 (1789/90)]; *Waqfiyya Ahmad Pasha al-Jalili* [1233 (1817/18)].

30. The examples are numerous, especially in waqfiyyas. What is noticeable in these documents is the increase in the number of mills made into waqf by the end of the eighteenth century.

31. See DAA, *Waqfiyya of Hajj Husayn bin al-Hajj 'Ali* [1275 (1858/59)]. This same individual bought with 11,240 guruş, 2 percent of another mill, six shops, 30 percent of a mill in disrepair, and two thirds of another mill.

32. The Jalilis owned mills near Ba'shiqa and Bahzani, also near Tall 'Uskuf and in various other strategic locations. The 'Umari and 'Ufuf families (both ulama) owned mills in the village owned by al-'Umari. See DAA, *Waqfiyya al-Hajj Husayn bin 'Ali Bey* [1260 (1785–86)]; also *Waqfiyya Hajj bin al-Hajj 'Ali* [1275 (1858/59)].

33. See DAA, *Waqfiyya Fathia 'Ubayd Agha Abd al-Jalilzade* [1204 (1789/90)]. The family of 'Ubayd Agha were descendants of Abd al-Jalil but are still known as 'Ubayd Agha rather than Jalilis.

34. See the waqfiyyas of the seventeenth and early eighteenth centuries, particularly those of merchants and Jalilis as well as ulama of that period.

35. MSM, *Qassamat (1268–1270)*(1851/52–1853/54).

36. Rich 1836, II: 70–73.

37. See DAA, *Waqfiyya, Jami' al-Nu'maniya* [1204 (1789/90)].

38. See DAA, *Waqfiyya, Jami' al-'Umariya* [979 (1571/72)].

39. See MSM, *Sicil (1242–1249)*(1826/27–1833/34), document dated 1242 (1826/27).

40. DAA, *Waqfiyya, Muhammad Amin Bey bin İbrahim Bey* [1214 (1799/1800)].

41. Haidar 1966, 178.

42. See MSM, *Sicil (1242–1249)*(1826/27–1833/34), document about Nu'man Pasha dated 1242 (1826–27).

43. MSM, *Qassamat (1268–1270)*(1851/52–1853/54), document dated 1269 (1852/53).

44. Ra'uf 1976, 272.

45. DAA, *Waqfiyya, Jami' al-Nabi Shit* [1231 (1815/16)].

46. Wolf 1966, 53.

47. Asad 1973.

48. Shanin 1971, 249–50.

49. Rich 1836, I: 96.

50. All following discussions of inheritance records were derived from reviewing 63 cases of court records covering the period 1268–70 (1851/52–1853/54). The sicils used are not numbered but are found in Mosul's Mahkama Shari'a. The three sicils used are *Qassamat (1268–1269)* (1851/52–1852/53); *Qassamat (1269–1270)*(1852/53–1853/54); *Qassamat (1270–1275)*(1853/54–1858/59).

51. Of these twenty-seven cases, five recorded the belongings of soldiers who left behind swords, money, firearms, a horse, or another animal. They seem to have been the poorest of the rural population. The middle peasantry were those who left behind 1,500–4,500 guruş, and they numbered twenty-two. The rich left more than 4,500 guruş, and numbered fourteen.

52. MSM, *Sicil (1242–1249)*(1826/27–1833/34), *Buyuruldu* issued on Ramadan 1242 (1826/27). I am indebted to Dr. Chris Murphy of the Library of Congress for his help in translating this document.

53. Ra'uf 1982.

54. The term "mugharasa" was also used in connection with similar arrangements in eighteenth-century Tunisia. See Valensi 1985, 105.

55. See MSM, *Sicil (1242–1249)*(1826/27–1833/34), which states the amount of grains accruing to a Jalili as part of the miri tax, and tevzi documents dated 1246–1251 (1830/31–1835/36) in the same *Sicil.*

56. See MSM, *Qassamat (1269)*(1852/53). One peasant left a grove worth 1,500 guruş, while another cultivated a small garden worth 150 guruş. In both cases the peasants not only owned trees but also the land. This was a new development since peasants usually owned and were taxed for trees and not land.

57. MS. 1275, Iraqi Museum. Also see al-'Umari 1967, 62, who states that there was a continuous fluctuation in the number of villages cultivated.

58. See MSM, *Sicil (1242–1249)*(1826/27–1833/34). Apparently part of the cizye of Mosul was allocated in the mosque by the Sultan in 1113 (1701/02).

59. See MSM, *Sicil (1242–1249)*(1826/27–1833/34), *Cizye ferman* issued in 1251 (1835/36).

60. See MSM, *Sicil (1242–1249)*(1826/27–1833/34), Tevzi documents for the years 1246–1251 (1830/31–1835/36).

61. MS 65/9. The Waqf Library of Mosul, Iraq. Manuscript I, dated 1726. "Three Manuscripts." Qara Qush was the stop for the Ottoman post. The *ocaklık* was located in it.

62. MS 65/9. The Waqf Library of Mosul, Iraq. Manuscript II, dated 1726.

63. Bartilla was owned by 'Umaris with annual income of 20,000 dinars. See MS. 11275, Iraq Museum. Qara Qush was mülk of the Jalilis, and Karamlis also belonged to another branch of the Jalili family.

64. MSM, *Qassamat (1270)*(1853/54). The peasant was from the village of Qara Qush.

65. An ox was valued at 100 to 250 guruş, a draft horse from 200 to 500 guruş.

66. al-'Umari n.d, 154-156; also "al-Durr al-Maknun fi Ma'athir al-Madiya min al-Qurun." MS, 635–36.

67. It is interesting to note that peasants who migrated into the city from villages owned by city notables carried their allegiances to these notables with them. When fighting broke out between the house of Husayn Pasha al-Jalili, owners of the village of Qara Qush, and the house of Fattah Pasha al-Jalili, owners of the village of Karamlis, migrants from these villages in the city allied themselves with the faction supporting the owners of their village.

68. Ra'uf 1976, Appendix 11: 545–47.

69. Ra'uf 1976, 167–72, 423–25. There was a brief period of hostility when Muhammad Pasha tried to curtail Catholic conversion in reaction to the French invasion of Egypt and Acre.

70. MS 65/9. The Waqf Library of Mosul, Iraq. Manuscript II dated 1756 (Manuscripts found in the village of Qara Qush).

71. Rich 1836, II: 74.

72. One of the complaints of the Patriarch was that not only were the peasants of the two villages not paying him his dues, they were also not paying cizye and were threatening the fabric of orthodoxy.

73. al-'Umari n.d., 137; and "al-Durr al-Maknun." MS, 621.

74. al-'Umari. "al-Durr al-Maknun." MS, 626.

75. al-'Umari n.d., 52–53; and "al-Durr al-Maknun." MS, 654–58.

76. al-'Umari. "al-Durr al-Maknun." MS, 609.

77. al-'Umari n.d., 74.

78. al-'Umari n.d., 70.

79. al-'Umari. "al-Durr al-Maknun." MS, 579.

Chapter 10

1. Careful production estimates were made by Bowring 1840, 9–10; von Südenhorst 1873; Cuinet 1896–1901; and Grobba 1923: 1440–46.

2. von Südenhorst 1873; Cuinet 1896–1901; Lewis 1966, 1987; Kalla 1969; Wirth 1971, 188–273; Schilcher 1975, 1981; Owen, 1981, 153–79, 244–72; Schölch 1986, 74–109.

3. Grobba 1923, 9.

4. Pascual 1979, 9; Warriner 1948, 87; Pellet and Jamalian 1969, 645–56; Hamdan 1979, 110–13.

5. Grobba 1923.

6. Dalman 1928–41; Rizqallah and Rizqallah 1978.

7. al-Qasimi 1960; Rafeq 1984.

8. Grobba 1923; Naff 1972; Schilcher 1981; Havemann 1983, 43–89.

9. Schilcher 1982.

10. Tresse 1937.

11. The most notable exception being Grobba (1923), which covers the period 1913–1923.

12. The lack of primary sources for the countryside is particularly limiting. The protocols of the provincial councils are not extant and/or not available for research. Another essential sources of information ought to be the Damascene Shari'a court records. These are now open to researchers and have been used in the writing of a number of papers dealing with rural areas around Damascus (e.g. Rafeq 1984, 1988; Vatter, 1979). Research on rural problems in these records is presently being pursued by James Reilly (University of Toronto) and Gerd Winkelhane (Free University of Berlin). In the published studies mentioned, very little material on the grain farming areas of Syria has emerged, and, to my knowledge, only the last of those researchers named has worked on the period after 1860, and he has not used the records dealing with grain lands. It remains to be seen, therefore, if the Damascene court records will reveal much about the grain farming areas in the late Ottoman period beyond 1860.

13. Landsberger 1973.

14. Abu-Husayn 1985.

15. Sluglett and Sluglett 1984.

16. Schilcher 1985, 136–55.

17. Schilcher 1985; Rafeq 1966, 24–42; Barbir 1980, 89–97.

18. Steppat 1979; Schölch 1981.

19. Hourani 1969; Barbir 1980, 69, 71, 93; Schilcher, 36, 52, 136.

20. Schilcher 1985, 162–80.

21. Schilcher 1985, 201.

22. Schilcher 1985, 136–44.

23. Owen 1981, 84; Schilcher 1985.

24. Schilcher 1985.

25. Schilcher 1985: 46.

26. Schilcher 1985.

27. Lewis 1987, 58–67.

28. Schilcher 1985, 215.

29. Wirth 1963; Lewis 1987, 96–123.

30. Schilcher 1981, 170–76.

31. The protégés' claims to these villages were locally contested and eventually lost. See Schilcher 1975, 497–501.

32. For example, see the Sursaq and Khuri acquisitions: Schölch 1986, 106–09.

33. For example, the Mardam acquisitions: Schilcher 1985, 211–13.

34. Owen 1981, 287.

35. Rafeq 1966, 108.

36. Schilcher 1985, 43, 98; Grobba 1923, 113.

37. Schilcher 1989.

38. Grobba 1923, 6; Ruppin 1917, 16–19.

39. Lewis 1966, 1987; Wirth 1971, 162–67; Schilcher 1981.

40. Wirth 1971, 68–107.

41. al-Qasimi 1960.

42. McDowall 1972; Schilcher 1981; Lewis 1987.

43. Wirth 1971, 163, 356 ff; Ochsenwald 1980.

44. Klima and Macurek 1960, 87 quoted in Wallerstein 1974, 324.

45. Bobek 1959, 1962.

46. Wirth 1971.

47. Bakhit 1982, 19.

48. Rafeq 1984, 376–77.

49. Rafeq 1984.

50. Rafeq 1984.

51. Rafeq 1984, 383.

52. Rafeq 1984, 377–78.

53. Rafeq 1984.

54. Rafeq translates mashadd maska as "basically . . . the ploughing of the land and its exploitation" and shaddad as "cultivator" 1984, 377, 381.

55. Rafeq 1984, 376.

56. Rafeq 1984, 376–77.

57. Rafeq 1984, 376.

58. al-Qasimi 1960, 255–56, 430–33, 438, 497.

59. This term is translated in a twentieth-century dictionary as "usurer" (Wehr 1966, 324). Rafeq has found ample evidence of this function and its indirect approval in the religious law courts of the earlier period (1984, 388–90).

60. al-Qasimi 1960, 95–96, 98, 128–29, 143, 155–56, 168, 216–17, 255–56, 309–10, 342–43, 354, 372, 415, 424–425, 427–28, 430–433, 438, 477, 497, 497–98, 500.

61. These kind of contractural relationships have been analysed in the case of Palestine by Firestone 1975.

62. al-Qasimi found this a "noble" profession which usually yields considerable profits, sometimes fortunes for those "who had not owned a thing" (1960, 256).

63. al-Qasimi finds those occupied in these two profession as rich but reprehensible (1960, 55–56, 290–92).

64. Public Record Office, Foreign Office, London. 195/806, Rogers, 11 August 1863.

65. al-Qasimi 1960, 55–56, 290–92.

66. Schilcher 1985, 190.

67. The case of the millers is interesting. al-Qasimi divides people who mill grain into two groups: commercial millers (*tahhan al-suqi*) and domestic millers (*tahhan al-bayti*). Whereas the former are reprehensible, the latter are noble and "trustworthy" (*ashab amana*). First of all, both were business people, practicing their trade outside the home for profit. Secondly, the former were concentrated in the city's peripheral quarters and especially in the Maydan. Thirdly, the terminology is indicative of the kind of word play often indulged in by ulama when describing the profane: the word *amana* has both religious connotations—coming from *amuna,* meaning "to be faithful"—and moral

economy connotations—referring to the institution of amana, a proto-banking system practiced in Muslim cities: Schilcher 1985, 65.

68. See, for example, the sketches on the fortunes of a number of Damascene families in Schilcher 1985, 136–218.

69. Schilcher 1981.

70. cf. Pamuk 1984.

71. *Accounts & Papers,* Vol. LXXVIII (1885), 961–64; Vol. LXXXVI (1887) 729–31, 487–90.

72. *Salname,* 1310/1892–93, 1314/1896–97, 1319/1901–02, 1322/1904–05, 1323/1905–06, 1324/1906–07, 1325/1907–08, "Statistics on the Hawran."

Glossary

agha	chief, master, a title borne by higher Ottoman officers; also a title of respect given to important persons not officially connected with the Ottoman administration, such as wealthy merchants
akçe	small silver coin, the asper
arpalık	appanage; land, stipend or allowance, given as a pension, usually in the form of a "fief", to high military and religious figures
ashraf	term used for those who claimed to be descended from the Prophet Muhammad; belonged to the *ayan* class in the eighteenth century
askeri	the Ottoman military ruling class in contradistinction to subjects
ayan	"notable persons"; provincial wealthy urban notables of the Ottoman Empire who were given official status by the government and acquired considerable power in the eighteenth century
avarız	tax collected by the central government, originally to meet emergencies
bağ	vineyard
bahçe	garden
başmaklık	revenues allotted to the Sultans and princesses
bey	Turkish title originally given to a noble, or high-ranking Ottoman officials and to sons of *pasha*s, lesser prince; later applied to any person of authority
beylerbeyi	governor of a province; the highest ranking official in Ottoman provincial goverment
buyuruldu	an Ottoman decree or command issued by a senior officer of the central government or more particularly by a provincial governer; a certificate or appoinment
Celali	rebels against the Ottoman government in sixteenth and early seventeenth century Anatolia

cizye	a poll tax paid by non-Muslim subjects in Islamic states
çift	unit of land that can be worked using a pair of oxen, usually between 6 to 15 hectares
defterdar	Ottoman head of the Treasury; also, head of a finance department, bookkeeper of a department, province, or state
derebey	rebel; often a local notable not unlike an *ayan* except that he was not accorded official status and operated outside the law
faddan	a standard measure of area; one faddan equals 1.038 acres
fatwa	legal opinion given by a *mufti*, juriconsult who issued opinions on points of Islamic law
guruş	larger silver coin, Ottoman or non-Ottoman, the piaster
gospodar	*agha* (in the Balkan provinces)
han	an inn or hostel for travellers and their wares
has	a domain of the sultan, a "special fief", usually given to a prince of the blood, a *beylerbeyi* or *sancakbeyi* which yielded an annual revenue above 100,000 *akçes;* a higher order of fief; a fief often attached to an office
ihya	land reclamation or improvement
ilmiye	the religious or learned class or profession
iltizam	tax farms granted to individuals
iqta	in Islamic practice, the act of bestowing state land in return for the collection of taxes or tithes
Janissary	the Ottoman infantry corps, same as *yeniçeri*
kadı	a judge in a court administering religious law; under the Ottomans the *kadı* administered both the shari'a and the Sultan's law
kanun	canon, custom, law
kaza	an Ottoman administrative unit roughly equivalent to a county; a subunit of *sancak*
kethüda	a steward, agent, or deputy of a *beylerbeyi* or other provincial governor; the representative of an urban quarter before the government; a senior officer of a craft guild representing the guild before the government
levend	a mercenary of *reaya* origin, usually a vagrant peasant youth who sometimes became a brigand; also a landless employed person
malikane	tax farm granted for life. A system developed by the Ottomans in the late seventeenth and eighteenth centuries intended to improve the condition of the peasantry; sometimes became hereditary

malikane-divani	a system of dual possessorship of the revenue generated from land by the state and its agents, and the holders of *waqf* and *mülk*
mevat	uncultivated land; unclaimed land; land without trace of cultivation or an owner
mazra'a	uninhabited cultivated land, distant from the village
miri	the possessions and revenue due to the government; something belonging to the government; state lands whose possession was granted to individuals
muaccele	preliminary down-payment made to the treasury
mugharasa	rental agreement
muhassil	an Ottoman revenue official responsible for the collection of provincial taxes; acquired wide-ranging authority in provincial administration and was often at the top of a hierarchy of provincial tax-farmers
muqata'a	a grant for the farming of revenues of a particular area, given by the governor or chief tax-farmer, or local tax-farmer; the lease of a tax farm
murabi	moneylender
musha'	land held in common and subject to redistribution among villagers (in Palestine and parts of Syria)
mühimme defterleri	register of important (i.e., public) affairs
mülk	land in freehold ownership
mültezim	tax-farmer, the holder of an *iltizam* who levied taxes on the peasants and paid a fixed tax to the government
müsadere	confiscation by the state
mütesellim	a deputy or a liuetenant-governor appointed by a provincial governor to collect revenues of a district; usually an *ayan*
nüzul	tax collected by the central government, originally an occasional tax
ortakçı	sharecropper
örf	unwritten custom as opposed to established law, *shari'a*
öşür	the tenth or tithe
qaysariyya	a building in the form of a compound, the rooms serving as workshops, warehouses, or dwellings
reaya	tax-paying subjects of the Ottoman Empire, particularly the peasantry as distinct from the ruling military class

sancak	subdivision of a province, a district; the chief administrative unit within an Ottoman province
shari'a	the religious law of Islam
shaykh	an elder; chief of a village, tribe, guild, or religious order
sicil	a register, record, or roll
sınırname	delimitation act
sipahi	Ottoman cavalryman, timariot
suq	market
sürsat	forced government purchases
şenlendirme	land reclamation
tahrir	survey register (of the sixteenth-century type)
Tanzimat	a general term applied to the Ottoman administrative and governmental reforms of the period 1839–80
tapu	deed-like land transfer document
tarikat	*sufi* orders or brotherhoods, often associated with craft guilds
temlik	property-like landholding
tımar	"fief", prebend, the revenue of which was granted to the holder in return for military service; fief of a smaller category yielding a revenue of up to 20,000 *akçes* a year
ulama	one learned in the Islamic religious sciences; the term ulama is loosely used to describe the whole Muslim religious class
ümera	chiefs, commanders, or senior officers; in the Ottoman provincial hierarchy, the *sancakbeyi*s
vali	the governor of an Ottoman province
vilayet	an Ottoman province
voyvoda	an agent or deputy of a governor whose duties resembled those of a *mütesellim;* in the eighteenth century the post was increasingly filled by *ayan*
waqf	endowment created by the dedication of property in the form of land and other revenue-yielding source for a charitable public cause, or for the support of the donor's family
waqf dhurri	*waqf* whose income is designated for the donor's family
waqfiyye	the charter or deed of trust of a religious or charitable endowment

zaim	a holder of a *zeamet;* also a term used for a town *subaşı*
zeamet	Ottoman military "fief", of a larger category yielding a revenue of between 20,000 and 100,000 *akçes* a year

General Bibliography

Unpublished Sources

France. Archives Nationales de France (AN), Paris.
Séries Affaires Etrangères.
    Sub-series B^i : Correspondance consulaire, Smyrne, Seyde, Tripoly, Beirut (AE B^i).
    Sub-series B^{iii}: Statistiques et mémoires (AE B^{iii}).
    Marine, B/7 Séries (Marine B/7).
Séries Administration générale.
    Sub-series F/12: Commerce et industrie (F/12).

France. Archives du Ministère des Affaires étrangères (AE).
Séries Correspondance consulaire et commerciale (CCC):
    Smyrne, Alep, Beirut.

France. Archives de la Chambre de Commerce de Marseille (ACCM).
Séries I : Statistiques (I).
Séries MQ, 5.1 : Administration et commerce, Smyrne (MQ, 5.1).

Great Britain. Public Record Office (PRO). London.
Foreign Office (FO).
    Series 78: General Correspondance (PRO, FO/78).
    Series 195: Consular Archives, Smyrna (PRO, FO/195).
State Papers (SP).
    Series 105: Levant Company Archives (SP/105).

Iraq. Da'irat al-Awqaf. Mosul.
    Waqfiyya Series.

Iraq. The Law-Court of Mosul, Mosul.
    Mahkama Shari'a Series.
    Qassamat Series.

Turkey. Osmanlı Arşivi (formerly Başbakanlık Arşivi), İstanbul.
    Maliyeden Müdevver (MM), 19759.

General Bibliography

Mühimme Defterleri (MD), 74.
Tapu Tahrir (TT), 54, 963.
Şam Ahkam, 1–5.
Halep Ahkam, 1.

Turkey. Tapu ve Kadastro Genel Müdürlüğü Arşivi, Ankara.
Kuyudu Kadime (KK), 14, 38, 152.

Turkey. Vakıflar Genel Müdürlüğü Arşivi, Ankara.
Ahkam Series, 328, 335, 349, 351.

Manuscripts

Three Manuscripts, MS 65/9. The Waqf Library of Mosul, Mosul, Iraq.
Unknown Manuscript, MS 1275. Iraqi Museum, Baghdad, Iraq.
Yasin bin Khayrullah al-'Umari. "al-Durr al-Maknun fi Ma'athir al-Madiya min al-Qurun." MS, al-Majma'al al-Ilmi al-'Iraqi (Iraqi Scientific Council), Baghdad, Iraq.
Yasin bin Khayrullah al-'Umari. "Ghayat al-Muram fi Ta'rikh Baghdad Dar al-Salam." MS 6295, Iraq Museum, Baghdad, Iraq.

Official Publications

Great Britain, Parliament, House of Commons, Accounts & Papers. (various volumes).
Turkey, Land Code. 1858/1257.
Turkey, Salname. (various years)

Secondary Sources

Abdel Nour, Antoine 1982. Introduction à l'histoire urbaine de la Syrie ottomane (XVIe-XVIIe siècles). Beirut: Publications de l'Université libanaise.
Abdulfattah, Kemal, and Wolf-Dieter Hütteroth 1977. Historical Geography of Palestine, Transjordan, and Southern Syria in the Late 16th Century. Erlangen: Erlangen Geographische Arbeiten.
Abdul Rahman, A., and Y. Nagata 1977. "The Iltizam System in Egypt and Turkey," Journal of Asian and African Studies, XIV, 169–194.
Abdurrahman bin Abdullah 1871/1288. Seyahatname-i Birazilya. İstanbul: Matbaa-i amire.
Abu-Husayn, Abdul-Rahim 1985. Provincial Leadership in Syria, 1575–1650. Beirut: American University of Beirut.
Adanır, Fikret 1979. "Die Makedonische Frage," Frankfurter Historische Abhandlungen, 20, 35–41.

Akarlı, Engin D., forthcoming. "Provincial Power Magnates in Ottoman Bilad al-Sham and Egypt" in *The Social Life of the Arab Provinces and their Documentary Sources during the Ottoman Period (The Second International Symposium of CERPAO-ACOS)*. Tunis.

Akarlı, Engin 1976. "The Problems of External Pressures, Power Struggles, and Budgetary Deficits in Ottoman Politics under Abdulhamid II (1876–1909): Origins and Solutions," unpubl. Ph.D. diss., Princeton University.

Akdağ, Mustafa 1963. *Celali İsyanları, 1550–1603*. Ankara: Ankara Üniversitesi Dil ve Tarih-Coğrafya Fakültesi Yayınları, no. 144.

Ali (Gelibolulu Mustafa) 1956. *Mevaid ün-nefais fi kava'id ül-mecalis*. İstanbul.

Ancel, J. 1930. *La Macédoine*. Paris.

Anderson, Perry 1974. *Lineages of the Absolutist State*. London: New Left Books.

Arıcanlı, Tosun 1986. "Agrarian Relations in Turkey: A Historical Sketch" in Alan Richards, ed., *Food, States and Peasants: Analyses of the Agrarian Question in the Middle East*. Boulder: Westview, 23–67.

Arıcanlı, Tosun, Raci Bademli, and İlhan Uğurel 1974. "The Abolition of Aşar," unpubl. ms.

Arık, Rüçhan 1976. *Batılılaşma Dönemi Anadolu Tasvir Sanatı*. Ankara: Türkiye İş Bankası.

Asad, Talal 1973. "The Beduin as Military Force" in Cynthia Nelson, ed., *The Desert and the Sown: Nomads in a Wider Society*. Berkeley: University of California Press, 61–75.

Aston, T. H. and C. H. E. Philpin (1985). *The Brenner Debate*. Cambridge: Cambridge University Press.

Athar Ali, M. 1975. "The Passing of Empire: The Mughal Case," *Modern Asian Studies*, IX, 3, 385–96.

Aymard, Maurice 1966. *Venise, Raguse et le commerce de blé pendant la seconde moitié du XVIᵉ siècle*. Paris: SEVPEN.

Ayn-i Ali 1872–73/1289. *Kavanin-i Al-i Osman*. İstanbul.

al-'Azzawi, 'Abbas 1935. *Ta'rikh al-'Iraq Bayn Ihtilalayn*. Vols. 5 and 6. Baghdad: Matba'at al-Tijara.

Babinger, Franz 1927. *Die Geschichtesschreiber der Osmanen und ihre Werke*. Leipzig: Otto Harrassowitz.

Baer, Gabriel 1969. *Studies in the Social History of Modern Egypt*. Chicago: University of Chicago Press.

Baer, Gabriel 1962. *A History of Landownership in Modern Egypt, 1800–1950*. London: Frank Cass.

Bakhit, Muhammad Adnan 1982. *The Ottoman Province of Damascus in the Sixteenth Century*. Beirut: Librarie du Liban.

Banaji, Jairus 1976. "Peasantry in the Feudal Mode of Production: Towards an Economic Model," *Journal of Peasant Studies*, III, 3, April, 299–320.

Barbir, Karl 1980. *Ottoman Rule in Damascus, 1708–1758*. Princeton: Princeton University Press.

Barkan, Ömer Lütfi 1983. "Caractère religieux et caractère séculier des institutions ottomanes" in Jean-Louis Bacqué-Grammont and Paul Dumont, eds., *Contri-*

238 General Bibliography

butions à l'histoire économique et sociale de l'Empire ottoman. Louvain: Peeters.
Barkan, Ömer Lütfi 1975. "The Price Revolution of the Sixteenth Century: A Turning Point in the Economic History of the Near East," International Journal of Middle East Studies, VI, 1, January, 3–28.
Barkan, Ömer Lütfi 1966. "Edirne Askeri Kassamına Ait Tereke Defterleri," Belgeler, III, 5–6, 1–479.
Barkan, Ömer Lütfi 1943. XV. ve XVI. Asırlarda Osmanlı İmparatorluğunda Zirai Ekonominin Hukuki ve Mali Esasları. I: Kanunlar. İstanbul: İstanbul Üniversitesi Edebiyat Fakültesi Yayınları, no. 256.
Barkan, Ömer Lütfi 1942. " Osmanlı İmparatorluğunda bir İskan ve Kolonizasyon Metodu Olarak Vakıflar ve Temlikler. I: İstila Devrinin Türk Dervişleri ve Zaviyeler. II: Vakıfların bir İskan ve Kolonizasyon Metodu Olarak Kullanılmasının Diğer Şekilleri," Vakıflar Dergisi, II, 279–304, 354–65.
Barkan, Ömer Lütfi 1940. "Türk Toprak Hukuku Tarihinde Tanzimat ve 1247 (1858) Arazi Kanunnamesi," Tanzimat, I, 321–421.
Barkan, Ömer Lütfi 1939. "Türk-İslam Hukuku Tatbikatının Osmanlı İmparatorluğunda Aldığı Şekiller I: Malikane-Divani Sistemi," Türk Hukuk ve İktisat Tarihi Mecmuası, I, 119–85.
Barkan, Ömer Lütfi 1937–1938. "Osmanlı İmparatorluğunda Çiftçi Sınıflarının Hukuki Statüsü," Ülkü, IX–XI.
Barkan, Ömer Lütfi. s.v. "Tımar," İslam Ansiklopedisi. İstanbul: M.E.B.
Barkan, Ömer Lütfi. s.v. "Çiftlik," İslam Ansiklopedisi. İstanbul: M.E.B.
Baykara, Tuncer 1980. "XIX. Yüzyılda Urla Yarımadasında Nüfus Hareketleri" in O. Okyar and H. İnalcık, eds., Social and Economic History of Turkey, 1071–1920. Ankara: Meteksan, 280–86.
Berkes, Niyazi 1964. The Development of Secularism in Turkey. Montreal: McGill University Press.
Berry, Sara 1987. "Concentration without Privatization? Some Agrarian Consequences of Changing Patterns of Rural Land Control in Africa," unpubl. ms.
Bloch, Marc 1966. French Rural History. London: Routledge & Kegan Paul.
Bobek, Hans 1962. Iran. Probleme eines unterentwickelten Landes alter Kulture. Frankfurt a.M.: Diesterweg.
Bobek, Hans 1959. "Die Hauptstufen der Gesellschafts- und Wirtschaftsentfaltung in geographischer Sicht," Erde, 90, 259–98.
Bodman Jr., H. L. 1963. Political Factions in Aleppo, 1760–1826. Chapel Hill: The University of North Carolina Press.
Bois, Guy 1978. "Symposium: Agrarian Class Structures and Economic Development in Pre-Industrial Europe—Against the Neo-Malthusian Orthodoxy," Past and Present, 79, May, 60–69.
Boserup, Ester 1965. The Conditions of Agricultural Growth: The Economics of Agrarian Change and Population Pressure. Chicago: Aldine Publications.
Bourne, Kenneth, and D. Cameron Watt 1985. British Documents on Foreign Affairs, Series B. The Near and the Middle East, 1856–1914. Frederick, Md.: University Publications of America.
Bowring, J. 1840. Report on the Commercial Statistics of Syria. New York: Arno Press.

Braudel, Fernand 1979. *Civilization and Capitalism, 15th–18th Centuries.* I, *Structures of Everyday Life.* New York: Harper & Row.

Braudel, Fernand 1972–73. *The Mediterranean and the Mediterranean World in the Age of Philip II.* 2 vols. New York: Harper & Row.

Brenner, Robert 1976. "Agrarian Class Structures and Economic Development in Pre-Industrial Europe," *Past and Present,* 70, February, 30–75.

Buckingham, J. S. 1827. *Travels in Mesopotamia.* London: Henry Colburn.

al-Budayri, Ahmad al-Hallaq 1959. *Hawadith Dimashq al-yawmiyya 1154–1175 A.H./1741–1762.* Edited by Ahmad 'Izzat 'abd al-Karim. Cairo: Matba'at al-Jam'iyyat al-misriyya li-l dirasat al-ta'rikhiyya.

Burckhardt, J. L. 1812. *Travels in Syria and the Holy Land.* London: John Murray.

Busch-Zantner, Richard 1938. *Agrarverfassung und Siedlung im Südost Europa unter besonders Berücksichtigung der Türken Zeit.* Leipzig: Otto Harrassowitz.

Carne, J. 1842. *Syria, the Holy Land and Asia Minor,* III. London: Peter Jackson, Late Fisher, Son & Co.

Cezar, Yavuz 1986. *Osmanlı Maliyesinde Bunalım ve Değişim Dönemi (XVIII. Yüzyıldandan Tanzimat'a Mali Tarih).* İstanbul: Alan Yayıncılık.

Cezar, Yavuz 1977. "Bir Ayanın Muhallefatı: Havza ve Köprü Kazaları Ayanı Kör İsmail-Oğlu Hüseyin (Müsadere Olayı ve Terekenin İncelenmesi)," *Belleten,* XLI, 161, December, 41–78.

Chapman, Murray, and R. Mansell Prothero 1983–1984. "Themes on Circulation in the Third World," *International Migration Review,* XVII, 4, Winter, 597–632.

Chater, Khelifa 1984. *Dépendance et mutations précoloniales, la Régence de Tunis de 1815 à 1857.* Tunis: Universitè de Tunis.

Chayanov, A. V. 1956. *Theory of Peasant Economy.* Illinois: Irwin Press.

Chevallier, Dominique 1960. "Que possédait un cheikh maronite en 1859? Un document de la famille al-Khazen," *Arabica,* VII, 72–84.

Cohen, Amnon 1973. *Palestine in the Eighteenth Century.* Jerusalem: Magnes Press.

Cohen, Amnon, and Bernard Lewis 1978. *Population and Revenue in the Towns of Palestine in the Sixteenth Century.* Jerusalem: Magnes Press.

Cook, M. A. 1972. *Population Pressure in Rural Anatolia, 1450–1600.* London: Oxford University Press.

Cook, M. A. 1970. *Studies in the Economic History of the Middle East.* London: Oxford University Press.

Cuinet, Vital 1890. *La Turquie d'Asie.* II. Paris: Leroux.

Cuinet, Vital 1896–1901. *Syrie, Liban et Palestine. Géographie administrative, statistique, descriptive et raisonnée.* Paris: Leroux.

Cunningham, A. B. 1983. "The Journal of Christophe Aubin: A Report on the Levant Trade in 1812," *Archivum Ottomanicum,* VIII, 5–131.

Cunningham, A. B., ed. 1966. *The Early Correspondance of Richard Wood, 1831–1841.* London: Royal Historical Society.

Cuno, Kenneth 1984. "Egypt's Wealthy Peasantry, 1740–1820" in Tarif Khalidi, ed., *Land Tenure and Social Transformation in the Middle East.* Beirut:

American University of Beirut Press, 303–331.

Cuno, Kenneth 1980. "The Origins of Private Ownership of Land in Egypt: A Reappraisal," *International Journal of Middle East Studies*, XII, 3, November, 274–75.

Cvetkova, Bistra 1960. "L'évolution du régime féodal turc de la fin du XVIe jusqu'au milieu du XVIIIe siècle," *Etudes historiques*, I, 171–203.

Cvijić, J. 1918. *La Péninsule balkanique*. Paris.

Dalman, Gustaf 1928–1941. *Arbeit und Sitte in Palästina*. 7 vols. Gütersloh: Bertelsmann/Hildesheim: G. Olms.

Darkot, Besim. s.v. "Niksar," *İslam Ansiklopedisi*. İstanbul: M.E.B.

Davison, Roderic 1963. *Reform in the Ottoman Empire 1856–1876*. Princeton: Princeton University Press.

Delbet, Maurice 1877. "Paysans en communauté et en polygamie de Bousrah dans les pays de Hauran" in F. Le Play, ed., *Les ouvriers de l'Orient*. 2nd ed., Tours.

DeVries, Jan 1972. "Labour/Leisure Tradeoff," *Peasant Studies Newsletter*, I.

al-Dimashqi, Mikha'il 1912. *Ta'rikh al-hawadith al-Sham wa Lubnan 1197–1257 A.H./1782–1841*. Edited by Luwis Ma'luf. Beirut: Imprimerie Catholique.

Domar, Evsey 1970. "The Causes of Slavery or Serfdom: A Hypothesis," *Journal of Economic History*, XXX, 1, March, 18–32.

Echinard, Pierre 1973. *Grecs et Philhellènes à Marseille (de la révolution française à l'indépendence de la Grèce)*. Marseilles: Institut Historiques de Provence.

Eldem, Edhem 1986. "La circulation de la lettre de change entre la France et Constantinople au XVIIIe siècle" in H. Batu and J.-L. Bacqué-Grammont, eds., *L'Empire ottomane, la Republique de Turquie et la France*. İstanbul-Paris: ISIS, 87–98.

Erder, Leila 1976. "The Making of Industrial Bursa: Economic Activity and Population in a Turkish City, 1835–1975," unpubl. Ph.D. diss., Princeton University.

al-Fa'iq, Sulayman 1961. *Ta'rikh al-mamalik "al-Kolamind" fi Baghdad*. Translated from Turkish by Muhammad Armnazi. Baghdad: Matba'at al-Ma'arif.

Farley, Lewis 1862. *The Resources of Turkey Considered with Especial Reference to the Profitable Investment of Capital in the Ottoman Empire*. London: Longman, Green, Longman & Roberts.

Faroqhi, Suraiya 1987a. *Men of Modest Substance: House Owners and House Property in Seventeenth–Century Ankara and Kayseri*. Cambridge: Cambridge University Press.

Faroqhi, Suraiya 1987b. "Political Tensions in the Anatolian Countryside around 1600: An Attempt at Interpretation" in Jean-Louis Bacqué-Grammont et al., eds., *Türkische Miszellen, Robert Anhegger Festschrift-Armağanı-Mélanges*. İstanbul: Divit Press, 117–30.

Faroqhi, Suraiya 1986a. "Town Officials, *Timar*-holders and Taxation: The Late Sixteenth-Century Crisis as seen from Çorum," *Turcica*, XVIII, 53–82.

Faroqhi, Suraiya 1986b. "Political Initiatives 'From the Bottom Up' in the Sixteenth and Seventeenth-Century Ottoman Empire" in Hans Georg Majer, ed., *Osmanische Studien zur Wirtschafts- und Sozialgeschichte.* Wiesbaden: Otto Harrassowitz.

Faroqhi, Suraiya 1984. *Towns and Townsmen of Ottoman Anatolia. Trade, Crafts and Food Production in an Urban Setting, 1520–1650.* Cambridge: Cambridge University Press.

Faroqhi, Suraiya 1981. *Der Bektaschi-Orden in Anatolien.* Vienna: Institut für Orientalistik der Universität Wien.

Faroqhi, Suraiya 1980. "Land Transfer, and Askeri Holdings in Ankara, 1592–1600" in Robert Mantran, ed., *Memorial Ömer Lütfi Barkan.* Paris: Adrien Maisonneuve, 87–99.

Fattah, Hala 1985. "The Development of a Regional Market in Iraq and the Gulf circa 1800–1900," unpubl. Ph.D. diss., University of California, Los Angeles.

Firestone, Ya'akov 1975. "Production and Trade in an Islamic Context: *Sharika* Contracts in the Transitional Economy of Northern Samaria," *International Journal of Middle East Studies,* VI, 2 and 3, 185–209, 308–324.

Fleisher, Cornell 1986. *Bureaucrat and Intellectual.* Princeton: Princeton University Press.

Frangakis, Elena 1985a. "The Ottoman Port of İzmir in the Eighteenth and Early Nineteenth Centuries, 1695–1820," *Revue de l'Occident Musulman et de la Méditerranée,* 39, 149–62.

Frangakis, Elena 1985b. "The *Raya* Communities of Smyrna in the Eighteenth Century, 1690–1820: Demography and Economic Activities," *Actes du Colloque International d'Histoire. La Ville néohellénique. Héritages ottomans et états grec.* Athens, I, 27–42.

Frangakis, Elena 1985c. "The Commerce of İzmir in the Eighteenth Century (1695–1820)," Unpubl. Ph.D. diss., King's College, London University.

Friedmann, Harriet 1978. "World Market and Family Forms: Social Basis of Household Production," *Comparative Studies in Society and History,* XX, 4, October, 545–86.

Gandev, C. 1960. "L'apparition des rapports capitalistes dans l'économie rurale de la Bulgarie du nord-ouest au cours du XVIIIᵉ siècle," *Etudes historiques,* I, 207–220.

Genç, Mehmet 1979. "A Comparative Study of the Life Term Tax Farming and the Volume of Commercial and Industrial Activities in the Ottoman Empire during the Second Half of the 18th Century" in N. Todorov, ed., *La révolution industrielle dans le sud-est européen. XIXᵉ siècle.* Sofia: Institut d'Etudes Balkaniques—Musée nationale polytechnique, 243–79.

Genç, Mehmet 1975. "Osmanlı Maliyesinde Malikane Sistemi" in Osman Okyar and Ünal Nalbantoğlu, eds., *İktisat Tarihi Semineri.* Ankara: Hacettepe Üniversitesi Yayınları, 231–96.

Georgiades, Demetrios 1885. *Smyrne et l'Asie Mineure au point de vue économique et commercial.* Paris: Imprimerie Chaix.

242   *General Bibliography*

Gerber, Haim 1987. *The Social Origins of the Modern Middle East.* Boulder: Lynne Rienner.

Gerber, Haim 1979. "The Population of Syria and Palestine in the Nineteenth Century," *Asian and African Studies,* XIII, 1, March, 58–80.

Glavanis, Kathy, and Pandelis Glavanis 1983. "The Sociology of Agrarian Relations in the Middle East: the Persistence of Household Structure," *Current Sociology,* XXXI, 2, Summer, 1–109.

Goffman, Daniel 1985. "İzmir as a Commercial Center. The Impact of Western Trade on an Ottoman Port, 1570–1650," unpubl. Ph.D. diss., University of Chicago.

Gökalp, Altan 1980. *Têtes rouges et bouches noires: Une confrérie tribale de l'ouest anatolien.* Paris: Société d'Ethnographie, 157–168.

Gökbilgin, Tayyib. s.v. "Tokat," *İslam Ansiklopedisi.* İstanbul: M.E.B.

Gökçen, İbrahim 1950. *Manisa Tarihinde Vakıflar ve Hayırlar.* II. Manisa.

Göknil, Nedim 1943. "Edremit Bölgesi," *Sosyoloji Dergisi,* II, 2, 338–57.

Gould, Andrew G. 1976. "Lords or Bandits? The Derebeys of Cilicia," *International Journal of Middle Eastern Studies,* VII, 4, October, 485–506.

Gramsci, Antonio 1980. *Selections from the Prison Notebooks.* Translated and edited by Quintin Hoare and Geoffrey N. Smith. New York: International Publishers.

Gran, Peter 1979. *Islamic Roots of Capitalism, 1760–1840.* Austin: The University of Texas Press.

Grobba, Fritz 1923. *Die Getreidewirtschaft Syriens und Palästinas seit Beginn des Weltkrieges.* Hannover: H. Lafaire.

Güçer, L. 1964. *XVI. ve XVII. Asırlarda Osmanlı İmparatorluğunda Hububat Meselesi ve Hububattan Alınan Vergiler.* İstanbul: Sermet Matbaası.

Guys, Henry 1862. *Esquisse de l'Etat politique et commerciale de la Syrie.* Paris: Chez France.

Habesci, Elias 1792. *Etat actuel de l'Empire ottoman.* 2 vols. Paris.

Haider, Salah 1966. "Land Problems of Iraq" in Charles Issawi, ed. *The Economic History of the Middle East, 1800–1914.* Chicago: University of Chicago Press, 164–78.

Hamdan, Muhammed Rafiq 1979. "Die Versorgung der Bevolkerung in Jordanien mit Grundahrungsmitteln: Energie und Energie liefernden Nahrstoffen," unpubl. Ph.D. diss., Landwirtschaftliche Fakultät, Bonn Universität.

al-Hamud, Nafwan Raca 1981. *Al-'askar fi bilad al-Sham fi al-qarnayn al-sadis 'ashar wa al-sabi 'ashar al-miladiyyayn.* Beirut: Dar al-afaq al-Jadida.

Hasan, Muhammad Salman 1970. "The Role of Foreign Trade in the Economic Development of Iraq" in Micheal A. Cook, ed., *Studies in the Economic History of the Middle East: 1800–1914.* London: Oxford University Press,

Hasselquist, Frederick 1766. *Voyages and Travels in the Levant in the years 1749, 1750, 1751 and Containing Observations in Natural History, Physick, Agriculture and Commerce.* London.

Havemann, Axel 1983. *Rurale Bewegungen im Libanongebirge des 19. Jahrhunderts.* Berlin: Klaus Schwarz Verlag.

Hayatizade, n.d. *Risale-i feyziye fi lügat-ı müfredat-ı tıbbiye*. Edited by Hadiye Tuncer 1978. I, Ankara: Tarım Bakanlığı Yayınları.

Hecksher, Eli 1922. *The Continental System*. Oxford: Clarendon Press.

Hintz, Walter 1955. *Islamische Masse und Gewichte*. Leiden: E. J. Brill.

Hope, Thomas 1820. *Anastasius or, Memoirs of a Greek*. London: John Murry.

Hourani, Albert 1969. "Ottoman Reform and the Politics of Notables" in William R. Polk and L. Chambers, eds., *Beginnings of Modernization in the Middle East*. Chicago: University of Chicago Press, 41–68.

Hüsameddin, Hüseyin 1927–1935. *Amasya Tarihi*. 5 vols., İstanbul: Hikmet Matbaası.

Hütteroth, Wolf-Dieter 1974. "The Influence of Social Structure on Land Division and Settlement in Inner Anatolia" in P. Benedict, E. Tümertekin, and F. Mansur, eds., *Turkey: Geographic and Social Perspectives*. Leiden: E. J. Brill, 19–47.

Hymer, S., and S. Resnick 1969. "Model of an Agrarian Economy with Non-Agricultural Activities," *American Economic Review*, LIX, 4, Part 1, September, 493–506.

İnalcık, Halil 1983. "The Emergence of Big Farms, *Çiftliks:* State, Landlords and Tenants" in Jean-Louis Bacqué-Grammont and Paul Dumont, eds., *Contributions à l'histoire économique et sociale de l'Empire ottoman*. Louvain: Editions Peeters, 105–26.

İnalcık, Halil 1982. "Rice Cultivation and the *Çeltükci-Re'aya* System in the Ottoman Empire," *Turcica*, XIV, 69–141.

İnalcık, Halil 1980–1981. "Osmanlı İdare, Sosyal ve Ekonomik Tarihiyle İlgili Belgeler: Kadı Sicillerinden Seçmeler," *Belgeler*, X, 14.

İnalcık, Halil 1980. "Military and Fiscal Transformation in the Ottoman Empire, 1600–1700," *Archivum Ottomanicum*, VI, 283–337.

İnalcık, Halil 1979–80. "Osmanlı Pamuklu Pazarı, Hindistan ve İngiltere: Pazar Rekabetinde Emek Maliyetinin Rolü," *METU Studies in Development*, Special Issue II, 1–65.

İnalcık, Halil 1979. "Servile Labor in the Ottoman Empire" in Abraham Ascher, Tibor Halasi-Kun and Béla K. Kiraly, eds., *The Mutual Effects of the Islamic and Judeo-Christian Worlds*. New York: Brooklyn College, 25–52.

İnalcık, Halil 1978a. *The Ottoman Empire: Conquest, Organization, and Economy*. London: Varorium Prints.

İnalcık, Halil 1978b. "Impact of *Annales* School on Ottoman Studies and New Findings," *Review*, I, 3/4, Winter–Spring, 69–96.

İnalcık, Halil 1977. "Centralization and Decentralization in Ottoman Administration" in T. Naff and R. Owen, eds., *Studies in Eighteenth Century Islamic History*. Carbondale: University of Southern Illinois Press, 27–52.

İnalcık, Halil 1973a. *The Ottoman Empire: The Classical Age, 1300–1600*. New York: Praeger Publishers.

İnalcık, Halil 1973b. "Application of Tanzimat and its Social Effects," *Archivum Ottomanicum*, V, 97–128.

İnalcık, Halil 1969. "Suleiman the Law-Giver and Ottoman Law," *Archivum Ottomanicum*, I, 105–138.

İnalcık, Halil 1969. "Capital Formation in the Ottoman Empire," *The Journal of Economic History,* XXIX, 92, October, 97–140.

İnalcık, Halil 1967. "Adaletnameler," *Belgeler,* II, 3/4.

İnalcık, Halil 1959. "Osmanlılarda Raiyyet Rüsumu," *Belleten,* 23, 575–610.

İnalcık, Halil 1954. *Fatih Devri Üzerine Tetkikler ve Vesikalar.* Ankara: Türk Tarih Kurumu.

İnalcık, Halil 1943. *Tanzimat ve Bulgar Meselesi.* Ankara.

İnalcık, Halil. "'Urf" in *El (2).* Leiden: E. J. Brill.

İnalcık, Halil. "Eshkindji" in *El (2).* Leiden: E. J. Brill.

İnalcık, Halil, "Çiftlik" in *El (2).* Leiden: E. J. Brill.

İnalcık, Halil, "Imtiyāzāt" in *El (2).* Leiden: E. J. Brill.

İnalcık, Halil. "Mā'" in *El (2).* Leiden: E. J. Brill.

İslamoğlu, Huri and Çağlar Keyder 1977. "Agenda for Ottoman History," *Review,* I, 1, Summer, 31–56.

İslamoğlu-İnan, Huri 1987. "State and Peasants in the Ottoman Empire: A Study of Peasant Economy in North-Central Anatolia during the Sixteenth Century" in Huri İslamoğlu-İnan, ed., *Ottoman Empire and the World-Economy.* Cambridge: Cambridge University Press, 101–59.

Issawi, Charles 1984. *An Economic History of the Middle East and North Africa.* New York: Columbia University Press.

Issawi, Charles 1980. *The Economic History of Turkey, 1800–1914.* Chicago: The University of Chicago Press.

Issawi, Charles 1977. "Population and Resources in the Ottoman Empire and Iran" in T. Naff and R. Owen, eds., *Studies in Eighteenth Century Islamic History.* Carbondale: Southern Illinois University Press, 152–64.

Issawi, Charles 1966. *The Economic History of the Middle East: 1800–1914.* Chicago: University of Chicago Press.

Kalla, Muhammad Sa'id 1969. "The Role of Foreign Trade in the Economic Development of Syria 1831–1914," unpubl. Ph.D. diss., American University, Washington, D.C.

Karpat, Kemal 1985. *Ottoman Population, 1800–1914.* Madison: University of Wisconsin Press.

Kasaba, Reşat 1988. *Ottoman Empire and the World Economy: The Nineteenth Century.* Albany: SUNY Press.

Keyder, Çağlar 1983a. "Cycle of Sharecropping and the Consolidation of Small Peasant Ownership in Turkey," *Journal of Peasant Studies,* X, 2–3, January–April, 131–45.

Keyder, Çağlar 1983b. "Small Peasant Ownership in Turkey: Historical Formation and Present Structure," *Review,* VII, 1, Summer, 52–108.

Keyder, Çağlar 1976. "The Dissolution of the Asiatic Mode of Production," *Economy and Society,* V, 2, May, 178–196.

Khan, Abu Taleb 1969. *Rihlat Abu Taleb Khan ila al-'Iraq wa Oropa, 1799.* Translated from Persian by Mustafa Jawad. Baghdad: Matba'at al-Iman.

Kiroski, P. 1973. "Čiftligarstvoto ve Polog" in *Kiril Pejčinovik i Negovoto Vreme.* Tetevo, 115–20.

Kitab-ı Müstetab 1974. Edited by Yaşar Yücel. Ankara: Ankara Üniversitesi Basımevi.

Klima, A., and J. Macurek 1960. "La question de la transition du féodalisme au capitalisme en Europe centrale (16ᵉ–18ᵉ siècles)" in *International Congress of Historical Sciences*. Stockholm.

Koçi Bey 1939. *Koçi Bey Risalesi*. Edited by A. K. Aksüt. İstanbul.

Kotschy, T. 1958. *Reise in den cilicischen Taurus über Tarsus*. Gotha.

Kula, Witold 1976. *An Economic Theory of the Feudal System*. London: New Left Books.

Kunt, Metin 1983. *The Sultan's Servants: The Transformation of Ottoman Provincial Government, 1550–1650*. New York: Columbia University Press.

Kurmuş, Orhan 1974. *Emperyalizmin Türkiye'ye Girişi*. İstanbul: Bilim Yayınları.

Landesberger, Henry A. 1973. "Peasant Unrest: Themes and Variations" in Henry A. Landesberger, ed., *Rural Protest: Peasant Movements and Social Change*. London: Barnes and Noble, 1–64.

Lanza, Dominico 1953. *al-Musul fi al-Qarn al-Thamin 'Ashar*. Translated from Italian by Raphael Didawed. Mosul: al-Matba'at al-Sharqiya .

Laoust, Henri 1952. *Les gouverneurs de Damas sous les Mamlouks et les premièrs ottomans 658–1156 A.H./1260–1744*. Damascus: Institut français de Damas.

Latron, André 1936. *La vie rurale en Syrie et au Liban*. Beirut: Imprimerie Catholique.

Le Roy Ladurie, Emmanuel, and Joseph Goy 1982. *Agricultural Fluctuations*. Cambridge: Cambridge University Press.

Le Roy Ladurie, Emmanuel 1977. *The Peasants of Languedoc*. Urbana: University of Illinois Press.

Levi, Giovanni 1985. *Das immaterielle Erbe. Eine bäuerliche Welt an der Schwelle zur Moderne*. Translated by Karl Flauber and Ulrich Haussmann, Berlin: Klaus Wagenbach Verlag.

Lewis, Bernard 1968. *The Emergence of Modern Turkey*. 2nd ed., New York: Oxford University Press.

Lewis, Bernard 1962. "Ottoman Observers of Ottoman Decline," *Islamic Studies*, I, 1, March, 71–87.

Lewis, Norman N. 1987. *Nomads and Settlers in Syria and Jordan, 1800–1980*. London: Cambridge University Press.

Lewis, Norman N. 1966. "The Frontier Settlement in Syria" in Charles Issawi, ed., *The Economic History of the Middle East 1800–1914*. Chicago: University of Chicago Press, 259–68.

Makovsky, R. 1984. "Sixteenth Century Agricultural Production in the Liwa of Jerusalem," *Archivum Ottomanicum*, IX, 91–127.

Mardin, Şerif 1962. *The Genesis of Young Ottoman Thought*. Princeton: Princeton University Press.

Masson, Paul 1911. *Histoire du commerce français dans le Levant*. Paris: Librairie Hachette.

Masters, Bruce 1988. *Origins of Western Economic Dominance in the Middle East: Mercantilism and the Islamic Economy in Aleppo 1600–1750.* New York: New York University Press.

McDowall, David 1972. "The Druze Revolt, 1925–27, and its Background in the Late Ottoman Period," unpubl. B. Litt. diss., St. Antony's College.

McGowan, Bruce 1981. *Economic Life in Ottoman Europe. Taxation, Trade and the Struggle for Land, 1600–1800.* Cambridge: Cambridge University Press.

McGowan, Bruce 1981. "The Study of Land and Agriculture in the Ottoman Provinces within the Context of an Expanding World Economy in the 17th and 18th Centuries," *International Journal of Turkish Studies,* II, 1, Spring–Summer, 57–63.

Melce'ü't-Tabbahin. 1884/1260. İstanbul.

Meriwether, Margaret 1981. "The Notable Families of Aleppo, 1770–1830, Networks and Social Structure," unpubl. Ph.D. diss., University of Pennsylvania.

Meşrebzade, Mehmed Arif 1837/1252. *Cami ül-icareteyn.* İstanbul.

Mironov, Boris 1986. "Le mouvement des prix des céréales en Russie du XVIIIᵉ siècle au début du XXᵉ siècle," *Annales E.S.C.,* XLI, 1, 217–51.

Morana, Antonio Maria 1799. *Relazione del Commerzio d'Aleppo.* Venice: Francesco Andreola.

Mouffe, Chantal 1979. "Hegemony and Ideology in Gramsci" in Chantal Mouffe, ed., *Gramsci and Marxist Theory.* London: Routledge and Kegan Paul, 168–209.

Murphey, Rhoades 1988. "Provisioning Istanbul: The State and Subsistence in the Early Modern East," *Food and Foodways,* II, 1, 217–63.

Murphey, Rhoades 1979. "The Veliyyuddin Telhis: Notes on the Sources and Interrelations Between Koçi Bey and Contemporary Writers of Advice to Kings," *Belleten,* XLIII, July, 547–72.

Moutafchieva, Vera P. 1962. *Agrarian Relations in the Ottoman Empire, XV–XVI. Centuries* (in Bulgarian). Sofia. English translation 1982. Boulder: East European Monographs.

Naff, Alixa 1972. "A Social History of Zahle, the Principal Market Town in 19th Century Lebanon," unpubl. Ph.D. diss., University of California, Los Angeles.

Nagata, Yuzo 1987. "Notes on the Managerial System of a Big Farm (Çiftlik) in the mid-18th Century Turkey," *Annals of the Japan Association for Middle East Studies,* 2, 319–41.

Nagata, Yuzo 1979. *Materials on Bosnian Notables.* Tokyo: Institute for the Study of Languages and Cultures of Asia and Africa.

Nagata, Yuzo 1976a. *Muhsin-zade Mehmed Paşa ve Ayanlık Müessesesi.* Tokyo: Institute for the Study of Languages and Cultures of Asia and Africa, Monograph Series, no. 6.

Nagata, Yuzo 1976b. *Some Documents on the Big Farms (Çiftliks) of the Notables in Western Anatolia.* Tokyo: Institute for the Study of Languages and Cultures of Asia and Africa, Studia Culturae Islamicae, no. 4.

Nanninga, J. G., ed. 1966. *Bronnen tot de Geschiedenis van den Levantschen Handel. Vierde deel: 1765–1826.* The Hague: M. Nijhoff.

Niewenhuis, Tom 1982. *Politics and Society in Early Modern Iraq: Mamluk Pashas, Tribal Shaykhs and Local Rule Between 1802–1831.* The Hague: Martinus Nijihoff.

Ochsenwald, William L. 1980. *The Hijaz Railroad.* Charlottesville: University Press of Virginia.

Olivier, G. A. 1801. *Voyage dans l'Empire ottoman, l'Egypte et le Perse.* II, Paris.

Olson, Robert 1976. *The Siege of Mosul and Ottoman–Persian Relations.* Bloomington: Indiana University Press.

Orhonlu, Cengiz 1988. *Osmanlı İmparatorluğu'nda İskan.* 2nd ed., Ankara: Eren Yayınları.

Owen, Roger 1981. *The Middle East and the World Economy, 1800–1914.* London: Methuen.

Özkaya, Yücel 1977. *Osmanlı İmparatorluğunda Ayanlık.* Ankara: A. Ü. Dil ve Tarih-Coğrafya Fakültesi.

Pamuk, Şevket 1987a. *The Ottoman Empire and European Capitalism, 1820–1913.* Cambridge: Cambridge University Press.

Pamuk, Şevket 1987b. "Commodity Production for Export and Changing Relations of Production in Ottoman Agriculture in the 19th Century" in Huri İslamoğlu-İnan, ed., *The Ottoman Empire and the World-Economy.* Cambridge: Cambridge University Press, 178–202.

Pamuk, Şevket 1984. "The Ottoman Empire in the Great Depression of 1873–1896," *Journal of Economic History,* XLIV, 1, March, 107–18.

Panzac, Daniel 1985a. "Les échanges maritimes dans l'Empire ottoman au XVIIIᵉ siècle," *Revue de l'Occident musulman et de la Mediterranée,* 39, 177–88.

Panzac, Daniel 1985b. *La Peste dans l'Empire Ottoman, 1700–1850.* Louvain: Peeters.

Panzac, Daniel 1973. "La Peste à Smyrna au XVIII siècle," *Annales E.S.C.,* XXVIII, 4, juillet-août, 1071–91.

Paris, Robert 1957. *Histoire du commerce de Marseille, V, de 1660 à 1789.* Paris: Librairie Plon.

Parmentier, P. 1919. *L'Agriculture en Syrie et en Palestine.* Marseille: Chambre de Commerce de Marseille.

Pascual, Jean-Paul 1984. "The Janissaries and the Damascus Countryside at the Beginning of the Seventeenth Century According to the Archives of the City's Military Tribunal" in Tarif Khalidi, ed., *Land Tenure and Social Transformation in the Middle East.* Beirut: American University of Beirut. 357–70.

Pascual, Jean-Paul 1983. *Damas à la fin du XVIe siècle après trois actes de waqf ottoman.* Damascus: Institut français de Damas.

Pascual, Jean-Paul 1979. "Environnement et alimentation dans le Hawran au XIXᵉ siècle" in *Proceedings of the Second International Conference on the History of Bilad al-Sham.* Damascus.

248 General Bibliography

Paxton, J. D. 1839. *Letters on Egypt and Palestine*. Lexington, Ky.: A. T. Skillman.

Pellet, P. L., and J. Jamalaian 1969. "Observations on the Protein-Calorie Value of Middle Eastern Foods and Diets" in Thomas Stickley *et al.*, eds., *Man, Food and Agriculture in the Middle East*. Beirut: American University of Beirut Press, 621–48.

Peri, Oded 1983. "The Waqf as an Instrument to Increase and Consolidate Political Power," *Asian and African Studies*, XVII, 1–3, November, 47–62.

de Planhol, Xavier 1958. *De la plaine pamphylienne au lacs pisidiens, nomadisme et vie paysanne*. Paris: Adrien Maisonneuve.

Polk, William 1963. *The Opening of South Lebanon, 1788–1840*. Cambridge: Harvard University Press.

Portes, Alejandro, and Robert L. Bach 1985. *Latin Journey*. Berkeley: University of California Press.

Post, George E. 1880. *Flora of Syria, Palestine and Sinai*, I. Beirut: American University of Beirut.

Posthumus, N. W. 1946. *Inquiry into the History of Prices in Holland*. Leiden.

al-Qasimi, Muhammad Sa'id 1960. *Qamus al-sina'at al-shamiyya (Dictionnaire des mètiers damascains)*. Edited by Zafir al-Qasimi, 2 vols., Paris: Mouton.

Quataert, Donald 1987. "A Provisional Report Concerning the Impact of European Capital on Ottoman Port Workers, 1889–1909" in Huri İslamoğlu-İnan, ed., *The Ottoman Empire and the World-Economy*. Cambridge: Cambridge University Press, 300–08.

Quataert, Donald 1973. "Ottoman Reform and Agriculture in Anatolia, 1876–1908," unpubl. Ph.D. diss., University of California, Los Angeles.

Rabbath, Antoine 1905. *Documents inédits pour servir à l'histoire du christianisme en Orient*. I. Paris: A. Picard et fils.

Rafeq, Abdul Karim, forthcoming. "Gesellschaft, Wirtschaft und politische Macht in Syrien, 1918–1925" in Linda S. Schilcher and Claus Scharf, eds., *Der Nahe Osten in der Zwischenkriegszeit*. Wiesbaden: Institut für Europäische Geschichte Mainz/Steiner Verlag.

Rafeq, Abdul Karim 1984. "Land Tenure Problems and their Social Impact in Syria around the Middle of the Nineteenth Century" in Tarif Khalidi, ed., *Land Tenure and Social Transformation in the Middle East*. Beirut: American University of Beirut Press, 371–396.

Rafeq, Abdul Karim 1981. "Economic Relations between Damascus and the Dependent Countryside, 1743–71" in Abraham Udovitch, ed. *The Islamic Middle East, 700–1900*. Princeton, N.J.: The Darwin Press, 653–85.

Rafeq, Abdul Karim 1966. *The Province of Damascus, 1723–1783*. Beirut: Khayats.

Ra'uf, 'Imad abd al-Salam 1982. "Sowar min al-'Ilaqat al-Zira'iyya fi Iban al-Qarn al-Thamin 'Ashar: Dirasa fi Wathaiq Ta'rikhiyya Jadida," *al-Mawrid*, XI, 29–38.

Ra'uf, 'Imad abd-al Salam 1976. *al-Musul fi al-'Ahd al-'Uthmani: Fatrat al-Hukm al-Mahali*. al-Najaf.

Refik, Mehmed, and Mehmed Behçet 1916/1335. *Beyrut Vilayeti.* İstanbul: Vilayet Matbaası.

Rich, Claudius James 1836. *Narrative of a Residence in Koordistan.* London: James Duncan, Peternoster, and Row.

Richards, Alan 1979. "The Political Economy of *Gutswirtschaft:* A Comparative Analysis of East Elbian Germany, Egypt, and Chile," *Comparative Studies in Society and History,* XXI, 4, 483–518.

Richards, Alan 1977. "Primitive Accumulation in Egypt, 1798–1882," *Review,* I, 2, Fall, 3–49.

Rizqallah, Kamel, and Fawzeya Rizqallah 1978. *La preparation du pain dans un village du delta égyptien.* Paris: FAO.

Röhrborn, Karl 1978. "Konfiskation und Intermediäre Gewalten im Osmanischen Reich," *Der Islam,* LV, 2, 345–51.

Röhrborn, Karl 1973. *Untersuchungen zur Osmanischen Verwaltungs geschichte.* Berlin: Walter de Gruyer.

Romano, Ruggerio 1956. *Commerce et prix du blé à Marseille au XVIIIᵉ siècle.* Paris: Armand Colin.

Ruppin, A. 1918. *Syria. An Economic Survey.* New York

Ruppin, A. 1917. *Syrien als Wirtschaftsgebeit.* Berlin: B. Harz.

Russell, Alexander 1794. *A Natural History of Aleppo.* London: G. G. and Robinson.

Sadat, Deena 1972. "Rumeli Ayanlari: The Eighteenth Century," *Journal of Modern History,* XLIV, 3, September, 346–63.

Sadat, Deena 1969. "Urban Notables in the Ottoman Empire: The Ayan," unpubl. Ph.D. diss., Rutgers University.

Sakaoğlu, Necdet 1984. *Anadolu Derebeyi Ocaklarından Köse Paşa Hanedanı.* Ankara: Yurt Yayınları.

Saleh, Zaki 1966. *Britain and Mesopotamia: 1600–1914.* Baghdad: Ma'arif Press.

Schilcher, Linda Schatkowski, forthcoming. "The Famine in Syria of 1915–1918" in D. Hopwood, M. Maoz, and J. Spagnola, eds., *Festschrift in Honor of Albert Hourani.* London.

Schilcher, Linda Schatkowski 1985. *Families in Politics. Damascene Factions and Estates of the 18th and 19th Centuries.* Stuttgart: Steiner Verlag, Berliner Islamstudien no. 2.

Schilcher, Linda Schatkowski 1975. "Ein Modelfall indirekter wirtschaftlicher Durchingung: Das Beispiel Syrien," *Geschichte und Geselschaft,* I, 4, 483–505.

Schölch, Alexander 1986. *Palästina um Umbruch 1856–1882, Untersuchungen zur wirtschaftlichen und sozio-politischen Entwicklung.* Stuttgart: Steiner Verlag, Berliner Islamstudien n°. 4.

Schölch, Alexander 1981. "Zum Problem eines aussereuropäischen Feudalismus: Bauern und Händler im Libanon und in Palästina osmanischer Zeit," *Peripherie. Zeitschrift für Politik und Ökonomie in der Dritten Welt,* V, 6, 107–121.

Scott, James 1977. "Hegemony and the Peasantry," Politics and Society, VII, 3, 267–96.

Sefercioğlu, Nejat 1985. XVIII. Yüzyıla Ait Yazma Bir Yemek Risalesi. Ankara: Feryal Basımevi.

Seddon, David 1986. "A New Paradigm for the Analysis of Agrarian Relations in the Middle East," Current Sociology, XXXIV, 2, Summer, 151–72.

Shanin, Theodore, ed., 1971. Peasants and Peasant Societies. Middlesex: Penguin Books.

Skinner, W. G. 1985. "The Structure of Chinese History," Journal of Asian Studies, XLIV, 2, 271–92.

Slim, Souad Abou el-Rousse 1987. Le métayage et l'impôt au Mont-Liban (XVIIᵉ et XVIIIᵉ siècles). Beirut: Dar el–Machreq Sarl.

Sluglett, Peter, and Marion Farouk-Sluglett 1984. "The Application of the 1858 Land Code in Greater Syria: Some Preliminary Observations" in Tarif Khalidi, ed., Land Tenure and Social Transformation in the Middle East. Beirut: American University of Beirut Press, 409–421.

Soysal, Mustafa 1976. Die Siedlungs- und Landschaftsenwicklung der Çukurova. Erlangen: Vorstad der Fränkischen Geographischen Gesellschaft.

Stahl, Henri 1980. Traditional Romanian Village Communities. Cambridge: Cambridge University Press.

Steppat, Fritz 1979. "Die Entwicklungskraft der ländlischen Gesellschaft. Ein Versuch vergleichender Geschichtsbetrachtung" in Ulrich Haarman and Peter Bachmann, eds., Die Islamische Welt zwischen Mittelalter und Neuzeit. Wiesbaden: Steiner Verlag, 642–56.

Stoianovich, Traian 1979. "Balkan Peasants and Landlords and the Ottoman State: Familial Economy, Market Economy and Modernization" in N. Todorov, ed., La révolution industrielle dans la sud-est européen. XIXᵉ siècle. Sofia: Institut d'Etudes Balkaniques—Musée national polytechnique, 164–204.

Stoianovich, Traian 1966."Le maïs dans les Balkans," Annales E.S.C., XXI, 5, 1026–40.

Stoianovich, Traian 1960. "The Conquering Balkan Orthodox Merchant," The Journal of Economic History, XX, 2, June, 234–313.

Stoianovich, Traian 1953. "Land Tenure and Related Sectors of the Balkan Economy, 1600–1800," Journal of Economic History, XIII, 4, Fall, 398–411.

Südenhorst, Julius Zweidinek von 1873. Syrien und seine Bedeutung für den Welthandel. Vienna: A. Hölder.

Sugar, Peter 1978. "Major Changes in the Life of the Slav Peasantry under Ottoman Rule," International Journal of Middle East Studies, IX, 2, 297–305.

Sunar, İlkay 1980. "Economie et politique dans l'Empire ottoman," Annales E.S.C., XXXV, 3/4, 551–79.

Svoronos, Nicolas 1956. Le commerce de Salonique au XVIIIᵉ siècle. Paris: Presses Universitaires de France.

Syrett, David 1985. *Neutral Rights and the War in the Narrow Seas, 1778–1782*. Fort Leavenworth, Kansas: Combat Studies Institute, US Army Command and the General Staff College.

Taeschner, Franz. s.v. "Çorum" in *EI (2)*. Leiden: E.J. Brill.

Tahir, Mehmed 1911–12/1330. *Siyasete muteallik asar-i islamiyye*. İstanbul.

Tahir, Mehmed 1907–08/1325. *Ahlak Kitablarımız*. İstanbul.

Tezel, Y. Sezai 1982. *Cumhuriyet Döneminin İktisadi Tarihi (1923–1950)*. Ankara: Yurt Yayınları.

Thieck, Jean-Pierre 1985. "Décentralisation ottomane et affirmation urbaine à Alep à la fin du XVIIIème siècle" in *Mouvements communautaires et éspaces urbains au Machreq*. Beirut: CERMOC, 117–68.

Thompson, E. P. 1971. "The Moral Economy of the English Crowd in the Eighteenth Century," *Past and Present*, 50, 76–136.

Tresse, R. 1937. "Usages saisonniers et dictons sur le temps dans la région de Damas," *Revue des études islamiques*, X, 1, 1–40.

Türkiye'de Vakıf Abideler ve Eski Eserler 1977. II, Ankara: Vakıflar İdaresi.

Turkowski, Lucien 1969. "Peasant Agriculture in the Judean Hills," *Palestine Exploration Fund Quarterly*, January–June and July–December, 21–33, 101–12.

Uluçay, Çağatay 1955. *18. ve 19. Yüzyıllarda Saruhan'da Eşkiyalık ve Halk Hareketleri*. İstanbul: Berksoy Basımevi.

Uluçay, Çağatay 1946. *Manisa Ünlüleri*. Manisa.

Uluçay, Çağatay 1944. "Karaosmanoğullarına Ait Bazı Vesikalar," *Tarih Vesikaları*, II, 193–207, 300–308, 434–440; III, 13, 117–26.

Uluçay, Çağatay and Gökçen, İbrahim 1939. *Manisa Tarihi*. İstanbul: Resimli Ay Matbaası.

al-'Umari, Muhammad Amin 1967. *Manhal al-'Awliyya wa Mashrab al-'Asfiya min Sadat al-Musil al-Hadba*. Edited by Sa'id Diwache. Mosul: Matba'at al-Jumhuriyya.

al-'Umari, Yasin bin Khayrullah 1955. *Munyat al-'Udaba fi Ta'rikh al-Musil al-Hadba*. Edited by Sa'id Diwache. Mosul.

al-'Umari, Yasin bin Khayrullah, n.d. *Zubdat al-Athar al-Jalia fi al-Hawadith al-Ardiyya*. Edited by 'Imad Abd al-Salam Ra'uf. al-Najaf: Matba'at al-Adab.

Valensi, Lucette 1985. *Tunisian Peasants in the 18th and 19th Centuries*. Cambridge: Cambridge University Press.

Van Bath, Slicher 1963. *The Agrarian History of Europe, A.D. 500–1850*. London: Edward Arnold.

Vatter, Sherry 1979. "Sales Documents in Shari'a Court Records of the 19th Century" in *Proceedings of the Second International Conference on the History of Bilad al-Sham*. Damascus, 101–22.

Veinstein, Gilles 1987a. "Une communauté ottomane: les Juifs d'Avlonya (Valona) dans la deuxième moitié du XVIᵉ siècle" in Gaetano Cozzi, ed., *Gli ebrei e Venezia. Secoli XIV-XVIII*. Milan: Comunità, 781–828.

Veinstein, Gilles 1987b. "Le patrimoine foncier de Panaybte Bénakis, *kocabaşı* de Kalamata," *Journal of Turkish Studies (Raiyyet Rüsûmu. Essays Presented to Halil İnalcık)*, II, 211–33.

Veinstein, Gilles 1986. "Un achat français de blé dans l'Empire ottoman au milieu du XVIᵉ siècle" in Hamit Batu and Jean-Louis Bacqué-Grammont, eds., *L'Empire ottoman, la République de Turquie et la France*. İstanbul/ Paris: Isis, 15–36.

Veinstein, Gilles 1984. "Les 'çiftlik' de colonisation dans les steppes du nord de la mer Noire au XVIᵉ siècle," *İstanbul Üniversitesi İktisat Fakültesi Mecmuası (Ömer Lütfü Barkan'a Armağan)*, XLI, 1–4, 177–210.

Veinstein, Gilles 1981. "Trésor public et fortunes privées dans l'Empire ottoman (milieu XVIᵉ-début XIXᵉ siècle)" in *L'argent et la circulation des capitaux dans les pays méditerranéens (XVIᵉ-XXᵉ siècles), Cahiers de la Méditeranée*. Nice, 121–134.

Veinstein, Gilles 1979. "Review of Nagata's 'Some Documents on the Big Farms'," *Turcica*, XI, 296–97.

Veinstein, Gilles 1976. "'Ayan' de la région d'Izmir et commerce du Levant (deuxième moitié du XVIIIᵉ siècle)," *Etudes balkaniques*, XII, 3, 71–83; also in *Revue de l'Occident musulman et de la Méditerranée* 1975, 20, 131– 47.

Veinstein, Gilles and Yolande Triantafyllidou-Baladié 1980. "Les inventaires après décès ottomans de Crète" in Ad van der Woude and Anton Schuurman, eds., *Probate Inventories. A New Source for the Historical Study of Wealth, Material Culture and Agricultural Development. A.A.G. Bijdragen*, nᵒ 23. Wageningen: Afdeling Agrarische Geschiedenis Landbouwhogeschool, 191– 204.

Venzke, Margaret 1981. "The Sixteenth-Century Ottoman *Sanjak* of Aleppo: A Study of Provincial Taxation," Unpub. Ph.D. diss., Columbia University.

Vergopoulos, Kostas 1978. *Le capitalisme difforme*. Paris: Maspero.

Volney, C. F. 1825. *Voyage en Syrie et en Egypte pendant les années 1783, 1784 et 1785*. 2 volumes, Paris: Parmentier.

Wallerstein, Immanuel 1989. *The Modern World-System. III: The Second Era of Great Expansion of the Capitalist World-Economy, 1730–1840s*. New York: Academic Press.

Wallerstein, Immanuel 1980. "The Ottoman Empire and the Capitalist World-Economy: Some Questions for Research" in Halil İnalcık and Osman Okyar, eds., *Social and Economic History of Turkey, 1071–1920*. Ankara: Meteksan, 117–22.

Wallerstein, Immanuel 1974. *The Modern World-System. I: Capitalist Agriculture and the Origins of the European World-Economy in the Sixteenth Century*. New York: Academic Press.

Warriner, Doreen 1948. *Land and Poverty in the Middle East*. London: Royal Institute of International Affairs.

Weber, Max 1906. "Capitalism and Rural Society in Germany" in H. Gerth and C. W. Mills, eds. 1958. *From Max Weber*. New York: Oxford University Press.

Wehr, Hans 1966. *Dictionary of Modern Written Arabic.* Ithaca: Spoken Language Service.

Wetzstein, J. G. 1857. "Der Markt in Damascus," *Zeitschrift der Deutchen morgenländischer Gesellschaft,* XI, 475–525.

Williams, Blow J. 1972. *British Commercial Policy and Trade Expansion, 1750–1850.* Oxford.

Wirth, Eugen 1971. *Syrien, eine geographische Landeskunde.* Darmstadt: Wissenschaftliche Buchgesellschaft.

Wirth, Eugen 1963. "Die Rolle tscherkessischer 'Wehrbauern' bei der Wiederbesiedlung von Steppen und Odland im Osmanischen Reich," *Bustan,* IV, 16–19.

Wittman, William 1971. *Travels in Turkey, Asia Minor, Syria, and Across the Desert into Egypt during the Years 1799, 1800, and 1801.* New York: Arno Press.

Wolf, Eric 1982. *Europe and the People Without History.* Berkeley: University of California Press.

Wolf, Eric 1966. *Peasants.* New Jersey: Prentice Hall.

Wright, W. L. 1935. *Ottoman Statecraft. The Book of Counsel for Vezirs and Governers (Nasa'ih ül-vüzera ve'l-ümera) of Sarı Mehmed Pasha, the Defterdar.* Princeton: Princeton University Press.

Yannoulopoulos, Yannis 1981. "Greek Society on the Eve of Independence" in R. Clogg, ed., *Balkan Society in the Age of Greek Independence.* London: Macmillan, 18–39.

Yediyıldız, Bahaeddin 1975. *Institution du vaqf au XVIIIᵉ siècle en Turquie: étude socio-historiques.* Paris.

Contributors

Tosun Arıcanlı teaches economics at Harvard University and is an affiliate of Harvard's Center for Middle Eastern Studies. He is co-editor (with Dani Rodrik), *The Political Economy of Turkey: Debt, Adjustment and Sustainability.*

Elena Frangakis-Syrett teaches history at Queens College, the City University of New York. She is the author of *The Commerce of Smyrna in the Eighteenth Century, 1700–1820* (forthcoming).

Suraiya Faroqhi teaches at the University of Münich, is an affiliate of Institut für Geschichte und Kultur des Nahen Orients and is the author, *Men of Modest Substance.*

Halil İnalcık teaches history, University of Chicago. He is the author of *The Ottoman Empire: The Classical Age, 1300–1600.*

Huri İslamoğlu-İnan teaches at the Middle East Technical University, Ankara and is the editor of *The Ottoman Empire and the World-Economy.*

Reşat Kasaba teaches at the University of Washington and is the author of *The Ottoman Empire and the World Economy: The Nineteenth Century.*

Çağlar Keyder teaches sociology at SUNY-Binghamton and is the author of *State and Class in Turkey.*

Dina Khoury is a Professorial Lecturer at Georgetown University. She is currently working on "Trade in Iraq during the First Three Centuries of Ottoman Rule."

Linda Schilcher teaches history at Villanova University and an affiliate of the Center for Contemporary Arab and Islamic Studies, she is the author of *Families in Politics. Damascene Factions and Estates of the 18th and 19th Century.*

Faruk Tabak is a Research Associate at Fernand Braudel Center, SUNY-Binghamton.

Gilles Veinstein is Professor of Ottoman History at the Ecole des Hautes Études en Sciences Sociales of Paris, and the Director of the Centre d'Études sur l'U.R.S.S, l'Europe Orientale et le Domaine Turc. He is co-author with M. Berendli of *L'Empire ottoman et les pays roumains, 1544–45.*

Index

advance purchasing, 111
Aegean, the (littoral and islands):
   *çiftlik*s located in, 50; immigrants
   from, 103, 116
agha(s), 29, 30, 31, 33, 94; in Edremit,
   81, 83, 89, 90, 94; in Salonica, 51;
   in Syria, 176, 177, 179; in the Vidin
   region, 29–30, 31, 60; in Western
   Anatolia, 101, 102, 103
agricultural equipment and implements,
   26, 27, 32, 104, 163, 184
agricultural techniques and methods,
   67, 132, 145–146
Albania, 25, 40, 50
Aleppo, 145, 148; concentration of
   *waqf*s in, 149; indebtedness in, 151;
   taxes levied in, 142; trade of, 157,
   158
appanage(s) (*arpalık, başmaklık*), 19,
   23, 24, 44, 46
appropriation act(s) (*temlikname*), 20,
   38
Araboğlu family, 32, 102
ashraf: in Syria, 179
*askeri: çiftlik*s in the hands of, 208
   n. 30; usurpation of *reaya* lands by,
   22, 41–42
assart(s), 68; forest (*balta yeri*), 67, 68,
   205 n.39
avarız-ı divaniye, 205 n.47
ayan(s), 9–10, 12, 59, 78; of central
   Anatolia, 219; of Rumeli, 33; of the
   Black Sea coast, 93, 219; of western

Anatolia, 34, 80, 101, 103, 114–117;
   the rise of, 23–24; the fall of, 12
Aydın, 12, 81; cotton production in, 98;
   landholding in, 102; migratory labor
   in, 103; olive-oil production in, 87
'Azm family, 51, 148, 151, 177, 178,
   179

Baghdad, 158, 160; trade of, 157, 166
bakkal, 160, 163, 168
barley, 27, 92; in Edremit, 90; in
   Mosul, 164, 174; in north-central
   Anatolia, 67, 69, 72; in Syria, 139,
   144, 148; production on *çiftlik*s, 28,
   48
Basra, 157, 159
Beirut, 144, 145, 181
bey(s), 45, 176, 177
Bursa, 107, 118

cash crops, 117, 142, 160, 163, 168
Celali rebellions, 22, 43, 51, 75
cizye, 167, 169
cloth, 73; trade in, 105–111
confiscation of estates (*müsadere*), 11,
   12, 52, 53, 91, 94–95
corvée labor, 2; the abolition of, 30,
   31, 70, 104
cotton, 21, 25, 29, 33, 51, 69, 73, 88,
   140, 148; cultivation on *çiftlik*s, 26,
   28, 48, 49; trade, 25, 51, 97–104,
   166
credit, 85–86, 88, 103, 109, 151